BANQUET OF CONSEQUENCES:

A Juror's Plight
The Carnation Murders Trial of Michele Anderson

By

Paul Sanders

The 13th Juror MD.com

Photo Credits:
Pamela Mantle Photo Archives
KIRO-TV (Seattle)
KOMO-TV (Seattle)
King County Prosecutor's Office
The Seattle Times
Paul Sanders

Book formatting and cover design:
www.bookclaw.com

Library of Congress Control Number: 2017904629
CreateSpace Independent Publishing Platform North Charleston, SC

Available as eBook, Paperback and AudioBook

Awards:

- *2018 eLit Awards Gold Medal Winner "True Crime" – Copyright by Jenkins Group and Independent Publisher.com (Cover front and back).*

- *2018 International Book Awards Silver Medal Winner "Non-Fiction: Historical" – Copyright Readers' Favorite Reviews and Awards Contest (Cover front).*

- *2018 Best Book Awards - Finalist "True Crime" – Copyright 15th Annual Awards Sponsored by American Book Fest. (Cover front)*

- *2018 Readers' Favorite Five Stars – Copyright Readers' Favorite Book Reviews and Award Contest (Cover front).*

- *2018 Florida Book Festivals Award – Winner "General Non-Fiction" – Copyright JM Northern Book Festivals. Orlando, FL*

- *2018 London Book Festivals Award – Runner-Up "General Non-Fiction" – Copyright JM Northern Book Festivals. London, England*

- *2018 New England Book Festivals Award – Honorable Mention "General Non-Fiction" – Copyright JM Northern Book Festivals. Boston, MA*

- *2017 The Halloween Book Festivals Award – Winner "General Non-Fiction" – Copyright JM Northern Book Festivals. Los Angeles, CA*

- *2017 Southern California Book Festivals Award – Runner-Up "General Non-Fiction" – Copyright JM Northern Book Festivals. Los Angeles, CA*

- *2017 Great Midwest Book Festivals Award – Honorable Mention "General Non-Fiction" – Copyright JM Northern Book Festivals. Chicago. IL*

Dedicated to the memory of Wayne, Judy, Scott, Erica, Olivia and Nathan Anderson; their families and all the people they touched in their lives.

With special acknowledgements to:

- ❖ Pamela and Tony Mantle
- ❖ Judge Jeffrey Ramsdell
- ❖ Scott O'Toole
- ❖ Detective Scott Tompkins
- ❖ Michelle Morales
- ❖ David Sorenson
- ❖ Colleen O'Connor
- ❖ Donna Gilligan-Miller
- ❖ Katie Van Buren
- ❖ Angela De Nunzio
- ❖ Tiffany St. Claire
- ❖ The Jury (2015 – 2016)
- ❖ Alison Grande (KIRO7 - Seattle)
- ❖ Michelle Esteban (KOMO – Seattle)
- ❖ Sara Jean Greene (The Seattle Times)
- ❖ KC Wuraftic
- ❖ Ed and Debbie McClintock
- ❖ Matt Schild

FURTHER ACKNOWLEDGEMENTS

Thank you to the fans and administrators of:

- ❖ The Trial Diaries
- ❖ Trial Talk Live
- ❖ Justice For Six
- ❖ Current News, Trials, Etc.
- ❖ Trial Addictions
- ❖ We Want Justice Trial Forum
- ❖ Court Chatter Live
- ❖ Trials
- ❖ Wild About Trials
- ❖ Trials And Things
- ❖ The Seattle Times
- ❖ KIRO TV Seattle
- ❖ KOMO TV Seattle
- ❖ Jarrett Seltzer
- ❖ Cathy Russon
- ❖ Jennifer Wood
- ❖ Buca Di Beppo - Seattle

CONTENTS

AUTHOR'S NOTE:

It was an honor to be seated in Judge Jeffrey Ramsdell's courtroom and I thank him for his graciousness. I would also like to thank Scott O'Toole, Senior Deputy Prosecutor, for his support and attention to detail. His advice was immeasurable. Further, I have special appreciation for the Court Reporter, Kim Girgus. I appreciate your help and have great respect for the task you do.

As I thank all the jurors for their service and sacrifice, I would especially like to recognize jurors Angela, Donna, Tiffany and Katie for their additional sacrifice. Thank you for the many additional hours we spent getting this correct. My empathy for you and your difficult task was unfathomable.

Not only would I like to thank the employees of King County Courthouse for their professionalism from the first floor to the ninth floor, I would like to thank those who keep our community safe as employees of the Washington State Department of Corrections. I appreciate your allowing me to spend time with Joseph McEnroe in a safe and controlled environment.

I want to thank all those who have followed on Facebook and Twitter. Your comments and support have helped me strive to a higher level.

To my editor, Kathryn, I thank you from the far reaches of my soul. I could not have done this without you!

Finally, and most importantly, I would like to thank Pamela and Tony Mantle for their support. I hope I have done honor to the victims.

Paul Sanders

There is never, ever, an excuse for murder.

Kimberly Moody

(Victim Impact Statement)

March 15, 2015

STEALTH JUROR

The murders took place on Christmas Eve of 2007. Judy and Wayne Anderson welcomed their daughter and her boyfriend into their home. The smell of a roast filled the air as the front door opened. Within the hour, Wayne and Judy would be dead. It was a lengthy two and a half hours later that the daughter and her boyfriend welcomed Scott, Erica, Olivia and Nathan into Wayne and Judy's home. The next four victims would be dead within the hour. Since the murders occurred in Carnation, Washington, the incident would become known as the Carnation murders.

Although some might think the killing of six was a mass murder, it was not because there was a pause between the killings and the killers had time to reflect before the killings had continued.

There would be two trials. It was decided by the State of Washington that Joseph McEnroe would be tried first. As with all trials, a jury was selected. The McEnroe trial would envelop their lives for five months.

Leah was selected as one of the final twelve deliberating jurors.

Leah entered the jury room on what she knew would be one of their last days of deliberation. There was a part of her that hoped they could surpass the hurdles in front of them. Another part told her they would be hopelessly deadlocked, a situation she never expected.

The deliberations the day prior had ended early because two jurors had almost begun physically fighting. The tension could still be felt as she walked over and poured a cup of coffee. As each of the jurors came in, greetings were shared more out of politeness than of warmth.

The jury room was a small room with a deliberation table taking up most of the space. Office chairs loosely lined the circumference of it. Off to the side, there was a doorway to a restroom. A small counter was in one corner with a small refrigerator tucked under it. There was a pile of coloring books on one of the shelves that held their jury notebooks. A button was on the wall should the jurors need to contact the court.

"Does anyone have anything they would like to cover before we get started?" Leah asked after the bailiff had chained the sign on the deliberation door. It was her job as the presiding juror, often known

12

as the jury foreman, to facilitate the commencement of deliberations.

"The way I see it," one juror said, "is that this should be a really simple question to answer. Did the State show that there were not enough mitigating circumstances as to merit leniency? In other words, should McEnroe get death for what he did?"

"Are we going to be like Saudi Arabia or China?" one juror asked. "There should not be a death penalty at all. Are we really that primitive to believe in an eye for an eye?"

Leah listened patiently. The past four days had been full of periodic speeches about the merits of having or not having the death penalty. She waited until he was done before she spoke. "I understand your position except that it's not a position you should have in here. We're here to answer the question as it was put forth. Whether you believe in the death penalty or not is something that should be brought to your legislators. We're not here to change the law. We're here to assign the law from the evidence and to make our decision based on that."

A juror flipped through his juror notebook. He stopped when he found a page. "From our jury instructions, the judge told us it was our duty to decide the facts based upon the evidence presented during the trial. Look here," he directed the others, "It is also our duty to accept the law from the judge's instructions, regardless of what we personally believe the law is or what it should be."

"In other words, we should not talk about the death penalty," a female juror volunteered. "We should be talking about whether Joseph McEnroe gets the death penalty, not whether the death penalty should exist."

Leah looked toward the anti-death penalty juror.

The juror shook her head and went back to her iPhone.

Another juror spoke up.

"She's right. Look at everything we have up on the walls," she said as she pointed toward the plethora of lists taped throughout the jury room. "We're supposed to be looking at mitigating factors. Those of you who think he shouldn't get death, help us see what factors should influence us. I don't see any. I can't excuse him for shooting two little kids!"

Although there were twelve jurors seated around the table, one juror had her chair faced the opposite way. Leah asked her to turn around and face the group. It had not been the first time that she had seen a marked lack of participation from a number of jurors. It was frustrating.

One of the holdout jurors was asked by another juror, "Why do you believe we should spare his life? What did he do to deserve leniency? Please. Show us. Please!"

"I don't have to say anything and I don't have to give an answer," she responded. She went back to her iPhone and refused to discuss the topic any further.

"In my opinion, Scott O'Toole is a 'boot strap Nazi'. Did you hear what he did to another defendant he tried?" another dissenting juror commented.

"How do you know about the prosecutor?' Leah asked him. "Are you looking up information on this case?"

The juror did not respond.

"Let's look at the mitigating factors again," a juror offered. He

14

walked over to the list on the wall. "Please show us how these factors are reason to give leniency. Is it because Joseph never knew his father? Should we give leniency because Joseph's mother worked a lot? What about the C.P.S. (Child Protective Services) report that suggested abuse? Does this mean we should be lenient? Tell us one mitigating factor that we should consider. We're open."

"Joseph McEnroe wasn't crazy and he was not on drugs," a juror volunteered. "I don't think he was under the spell of his girlfriend Michele Anderson, either. Those two walked up the steps with two loaded guns on Christmas Eve for the sole purpose of killing the family if they did not get their money. They knew what they were doing when they walked in. Imagine your family being lost to such violence. I have two children and I hug them a little tighter every night when I think about what these two people did. He did not show leniency when he fired the gun. He had time to change his mind and he didn't!"

The jurors had done a number of polls throughout the process. In the guilt phase, the jurors had raised their hands when they made their collective decision. The penalty phase, however, was handled by anonymous polls, each submitting their votes on a piece of paper and placing them in a pile at the center of the table. This step was taken to prevent jurors from getting beaten up for whatever decision they made. In spite of the anonymous polls, it was clear that four jurors were holding out and all the other eight knew who they were.

She listened to the jurors as they argued aggressively with a majority who spoke vehemently for the victims while four argued the validity of whether there should be a death penalty.

Jury duty had been nothing like what had been expected. She remembered being floored that she was selected to be a juror.

Three thousand people had been summoned for jury duty for this trial the prior September. Six hundred jurors had been asked to complete a sixty-page questionnaire. From those six hundred, four hundred had been asked to return for individual questioning by the attorneys. On the final day of jury selection, almost two hundred people arrived and the day was completed after the selection of a mere sixteen.

Throughout that process, she would never forget the question that caused her to look deep into her soul. She was asked if she, given that the State proved its case, could vote for the death penalty for a defendant. The question had initially caught her off guard. It also caused her to question her religious beliefs. Having been raised Catholic in an Italian family, she was not positive that the death penalty was in line with the religious precepts. In her heart, she felt she could be fair and impartial and only do what the law told her to do. The main goal for her in being a juror was to do the right thing.

The arguments were heated and the commentary returned was vehement. The jury had split into two factions.

"You can't change my mind," a female juror commented steadfastly. "I'm holding my position for the betterment of the world. I'm saving Joseph McEnroe's life."

"What about the kids?" a juror asked. "How can you say that after what he did to the two little children? You're sending a message that says we don't punish those who kill!"

Deliberations fell into an exchange of inflammatory remarks and passionate rebuttals. It had, once again, degenerated into polarization. Those who were once on the fence had chosen their sides. Eight were on one side while four were on the other.

In a final bid for justice, Leah asked the jurors to refer to the jury instructions and the words of Judge Ramsdell. She read it aloud:

"As jurors, you are officers of the court. You must not let your emotions overcome your rational thought process. You must reach your decision based on the facts proved to you and on the law given to you, not on sympathy, prejudice or personal preference. To assure that all parties receive a fair trial, you must act impartially with an earnest desire to reach a proper verdict."

Leah looked around the room. "Would anyone here like to revisit their positions? This is our last chance to do what the law tells us to do."

The four dissenting jurors avoided Leah's eyes. Two other jurors had broken out in tears.

The Foreperson completed the paperwork and affixed her signature. She wanted to cry but held her composure.

The jurors waited silently in the jury room while the court let its personnel know a verdict was going to be announced. She could picture the media scrambling to fill the rows in the gallery. She could also imagine the devastation the family was going to feel upon the rendering of their words. It was a horrible feeling and she felt powerless.

The mood was quiet, awkward and somber as many of the jurors focused their attention on their iPhones. Leah thought of all the jurors who had put their heart forward in telling their personal stories. She felt great empathy for those on the jury who had been touched by murder. She understood the jurors who cried when they thought of the horrible thing done to Olivia and Nathan and how it made them think of their own kids and the horrible end that can come to people.

When the jury was finally called out to the jury box, Leah kept her head down as she accompanied the other jurors to their seats. She could not look at the defendant and she certainly could not look at the family seated in the front row. The file in her hand was a disservice to justice.

The proceedings started with Kenya as she took the file from the Foreperson's hands and brought it to the judge.

Judge Ramsdell took the file, opened it and read aloud.

"Question: Having in mind the crimes of which Joseph McEnroe has been found guilty, are you convinced beyond a reasonable doubt that there are not sufficient mitigating circumstances as to merit leniency?"

The judge glanced at the jury before he continued.

"The answer that is checked says, 'No unanimous agreement' in which case Joseph McEnroe will be sentenced to life in prison without the possibility of early release and parole," the judge stated.

"I would like to poll the jury and I will ask two questions. Whether this is your own individual verdict that the jury is unable to reach a decision and, number two, whether you believe that this is a verdict of the jury as a whole, that you could not reach a unanimous verdict."

The judge looked at Juror #1, and proceeded to ask her the first question.

"Ah, no," the female juror responded.

The judge cocked his head as if he did not hear her right.

"That wasn't my verdict," she answered.

"Then I am going to ask that you all go back to the jury room," he ordered.

Leah knew, as they made their way back to the jury room, that Juror #1 had misunderstood the question.

"It isn't my verdict," the juror explained once the door was closed in the deliberation room. "I felt the mitigating circumstances did not merit leniency. I voted that he get death."

"That was not what he asked you. He asked if you agreed with your own verdict."

"Oh, so I was supposed to agree to saying that we agree to disagree?" she asked.

"That's exactly what you are doing," Leah told her.

"Alright then," she said. "I still think he should have gotten death though."

Ten minutes later, the McEnroe jury assembled in the jury box for the final time. The polling of the jury went flawlessly. Each juror agreed that they were in disagreement with each other.

It was the hardest day of each of the juror's lives despite what position they had held in the determination of the sentence for Joseph McEnroe.

Joseph McEnroe would eventually be sentenced to life in prison without the possibility of parole in the deaths of Wayne, Judy, Scott, Erica, Olivia and Nathan Anderson.

Leah would always believe that he should have gotten the death penalty. He had manipulated members of the jury. He was the ultimate predator.

When Leah heard that Michele Anderson's trial was scheduled, she felt great empathy for the jurors. She hoped that in the end, they each might feel a sense of closure, something that she and the family of the victims were denied.

THE CALLING OF THE FLOCK

I have been unlucky enough to see the face of evil not once, but twice.

The first time was when Marissa DeVault pleaded for her life in front of me as I was seated in the jury box with fourteen others. It was a face we spoke of in the jury room and the words were not kind. Dale Harrell, the victim, would always be a part of me.

The second time I saw the face of evil was when Jodi Arias smiled toward three of us seated in the gallery as Kirk Nurmi argued to have us banned from the courtroom. Travis Alexander, the victim, had become a part of me.

It was lessons learned from those two trials that I carried with me as I went to the King County Courthouse in Seattle, Washington for the first time. Jury selection for the trial of Michele Anderson was scheduled to start in about a week's time. This would be the first trial I was to attend without the benefit of knowing Jen Wood, Beth Karas, Troy Hayden and the many others I was used to seeing from the previous trial. I was a long way from Phoenix, Arizona and there would be no one to ask for guidance.

The closest and least expensive parking I found was on top of Yesler Way near Broadway. Even though it cost $15, the three-block walk down the hill saved me $20 for more convenient parking. One of the first things I learned about jury duty in King County was that parking was not provided for jurors.

The King County Courthouse was a large granite and imposing building that took up the entirety of the block between Jefferson and Third. A park where the homeless slept was adjacent to the building while the hum of buses could be heard as they made multiple stops in front of the courthouse. The shadow of the 72-story Columbia Tower could be seen just to the north.

I entered the brass doors and went through security, a process I knew very well from previous trials. I quickly learned that Judge Jeffrey Ramsdell had presided over the Joseph McEnroe trial and would be the same to handle Michele Anderson's. I found his courtroom on the eighth floor. It was closed.

I searched for a Public information Officer and found myself with the head of security for the courthouse. I inquired whether I would need a media pass. I remembered the final day of the Arias trial when I was not selected in Janet's "lottery". I did not want a reoccurrence. I also thought it a smart idea to be entirely transparent. I expected to write and post to social media daily updates on the trial.

The head of security recorded my information on a notepad and assured me that open seating would be available daily in the gallery.

I graciously thanked him for his help and, with my reconnaissance completed, I left the courthouse. The Carnation murders trial would be high profile case but it would not have the crazy components that the Arias trial had.

Or, so I thought.

It was a week later when fifteen hundred potential jurors were summoned to the Superior Courthouse of King County, Washington on a cold, dreary and blustery day that was typical for December. Each clutched a 3 x 5 jury summons in hand to do their civic duty. Although the day was gloomy outside, the court personnel were friendly but studious in their duties. Many wore Seahawks football jerseys, as was the custom allowed by many employers on certain days of the week throughout the city.

The jurors were directed to a large jury assembly room on the first floor and the gleaning of the flock would only begin after each one was accounted for and numbered. Court assistants and the bailiff would be kept busy for the next few hours ensuring that each juror was properly accounted for and given their two placards that were to be carried with them throughout the day.

It would have been expected that there would be many who wanted to ask questions and most were told to follow the direction of the court staff and all would be revealed in due time. Time was spent on certain jurors who had explained that jury service would cause them great financial hardship. Most jurors would be patient and some would be content that they were at least being given something to do to occupy their day of civic duty.

I waited upstairs on the ninth floor outside the courtroom where the second two hundred jurors were expected to come through in the next hour. I had missed the first round of jurors because I had waited in the hallway where Judge Ramsdell's courtroom was located. It took me until the lunch hour to realize that the potential jurors would gather in a separate, expanded courtroom in order to accommodate the large number. The first parcel of two hundred jurors from the morning session had already been dismissed for the day when I had rebounded from my mistake and found myself in the right spot.

I was seated on a hardwood oak bench and felt as if I were a stranger in a foreign land. On the same bench, toward the other end, a cameraman named Greg tinkered on his cell phone. His camera gear bag was perched on the floor between his legs while his TV camera leaned against the bench. Off to my right, adjacent to me, a female reporter, Alison Grande, from KIRO-7 (Seattle) chatted in hushed tones with a gentleman seated next to her. He wore a dark brown subtly patterned suit with a beige shirt and gold and black tie. Had I been asked, I would have thought him to be a news anchor.

In actuality, it was Scott O'Toole, the prosecutor for the State of Washington in both the Joseph McEnroe and Michele Anderson case.

Twenty minutes later, two ladies could be heard as they walked down the hallway toward us, their high-heeled shoes clicked in almost perfect unison on the marble tiled floors. The four of us who were waiting immediately perked up. Kenya, the bailiff, and Suza, the court clerk, walked up to the courtroom doors and taped some papers on the door

"Are you ready?" Alison asked Scott, casually, off the record.

"I am," he answered. He took a deep breath. "There are challenges that the death penalty trial brings. This trial should be a little less complicated."

"We hope," Allison quipped.

"Carnation Two-Point-Oh, I'm ready," Scott said.

It was not long before we heard sounds from an army of feet as they approached us, having exited from the eight elevators that released the jurors in a rotunda style lobby. My heart jumped, knowing that this was the beginning of a long journey for a select few. For one, some or all, the experience would affect them for the rest of their lives and in ways that most could never have foreseen.

Kenya and Suza beckoned the potential jurors our way.

I watched the jurors without making any eye contact with them as they were split into two separate queues prior to their entry into the courtroom. For the most part, it was organized and went almost flawlessly as attendance records were matched to the papers clutched in the jurors' hands. Here and there, one or more of the flock would be confused and learn he or she was in the wrong line.

One man, who wore an orange shirt and blue jeans, raised both his arms in unison and looked toward the ceiling. He framed his hands in such a manner as if he were a great director, setting a picture for his next great shot. One of his thumbs twitched involuntarily as he peered deeply into something on the ceiling. Eventually, he lowered his hands, was checked in by the court assistant, and walked into the courtroom.

"Are we going in?" Greg, the photographer, asked Alison after the all the potential jurors were in the courtroom.

"No, I don't think so," she answered. "We saw it this morning and there's nothing else to be learned. You've seen one round; you've seen them all. Instead, let's get a shot of the defendant as she's brought into the courtroom."

The cameraman busied himself as I got up and approached the court assistants. I briefly introduced myself and, before I knew it, I was led to the jury box, past two hundred potential jurors seated in the courtroom. I felt like I was walking on hallowed ground as I took my seat.

I looked to the left of me and saw the potential jurors as they waited. They were exceptionally quiet without even a cough to break the silence. The jury box was perpendicular to the vacant judge's bench. Slightly to the right of me, Suza worked on a computer. Below me, to the left, two long tables with six vacant chairs faced the potential jurors. If one did not know any better, it could have been an auditorium filled for those ready to take a college examination.

The irony and serendipity of my being seated singularly in the jury box did not elude me.

The doors opened off to the left of the courtroom and eyes watched silently as the defendant was led in, directed to a table and faced the jury pool. She wore all black, loosely fitted, clothes. Her hair was tied back as two armed officers stood behind her chair. A female officer had previously removed her handcuffs outside the view of the potential jurors. As the officer stepped away, the defendant raised a hand to the jurors as if she were saying hello and then took her seat.

Two lawyers sat down on either side next to her, with David Sorenson to her left and Colleen O'Connor to her right. Colleen rubbed the defendant's back consolingly as they sat down.

Michele Anderson looked down at the table. She was an overweight girl, downtrodden in her countenance. Her skin had pasty-white jailbird pallor, the color lost after having not been warmed by the sun for almost eight years. Most of the jurors would hardly give her a second look, the presumption being that they would probably not end up on the jury.

Some potential jurors, however, would know much about this defendant and the brutal slaying of six members of her family. Some jurors may have witnessed the trial of her accomplice and boyfriend, Joseph McEnroe, whose trial ended in a hung jury. Those jurors would have a more than difficult time starting with a presumption of innocence and would likely not be selected in the long run.

Scott O'Toole and Michelle Morales made their way to the table adjacent to the defense table. Michelle wore a black, tapered business suit. The prosecutors smiled at Scott Tompkins, the lead detective, when he joined them. He wore a gray suit, white shirt and blue striped tie.

Moments later Judge Ramsdell confidently walked in and sat at his bench at the front of the courtroom. Kenya directed everyone to be seated.

"We are here in the matter of the State of Washington vs Michele Kristen Anderson. My name is Judge Jeffrey Ramsdell. You have been asked to come in as potential jurors in this matter. I have two goals today as we prepare to empanel a jury. The first is the completion of a questionnaire and the second is to explain your obligations as a juror. At this time, I need all of you to stand and be sworn in."

The jurors stood as the judge read the jury oath aloud. A confident "I do," resonated from the gallery as the jurors agreed.

Judge Ramsdell waited as the jurors sat.

"Given this is a criminal case, you will see the prosecution team to your right. Please, introduce yourselves to the jury," the judge instructed the team with a wave of his hand.

"I am Scott O'Toole and this is Michelle Morales, deputy prosecutors in this case," he said. He motioned toward the third person at the table. "This is Detective Scott Tompkins, Lead Detective."

The three of them stood briefly and then sat down.

"You will see the defense team at the second table," Judge Ramsdell said as he directed the jurors' attention toward the adjacent table.

"I am David Sorenson," the middle-aged attorney said as he stood.

The woman on the other side of the defendant stood. "I am Colleen O'Connor and we are honored to represent Michele Anderson in this matter."

The judge got right back to business. He began to read from a document aloud. On occasion, he would pause to adjust his glasses and then look over the sea of jurors in front of him as if he wanted to make sure they knew of the gravity of the situation.

"Michele Kristen Anderson is being charged by the State for six counts of aggravated murder in the first-degree in the deaths of Wayne Anderson, sixty-years old; Judith Anderson, sixty-one years old; Scott Anderson, thirty-two years old; Erica Anderson, thirty-two years old; Olivia Anderson, five-years old and Nathan Anderson, three-years old. The State of Washington alleges and accuses Michele Kristen Anderson of the crime of aggravated murder in the first-degree in the deaths of each of the victims, a crime of the same or similar character and based on a series of acts connected together with another crime charged herein, which crimes were part of a common scheme or plan, and which crimes were so closely connected in respect to time, place and occasion that it would be difficult to separate proof of one charge from proof of another, committed as follows," the judge read.

He took a sip of water.

The courtroom was silent while the defendant looked down. Colleen O'Connor continued to rub Michele Anderson's back in a little circle pattern.

"That the defendant," the judge continued, "Michele Kristen Anderson, in King County Washington, on or about December 24, 2007, with premeditated intent to cause the death of Wayne, Judith, Scott, Erica, Olivia and Nathan Anderson, human beings, who died on or about December 24, 2007; that further aggravating circumstances exist. The defendant committed the murder to conceal the commission of a crime or to protect or conceal the identity of any person committing a crime, and there was more than one victim and the murders were part of a common scheme or plan or the result of a single act."

"As charged in Counts One through Six, you will be asked to determine if the defendant was armed with a firearm during the commission of the crime," the judge finished.

He rearranged his documents and looked at the jurors.

"You are to presume the innocence of the defendant despite the writ of information submitted by the prosecution. The State must prove these charges beyond a shadow of a doubt. Shortly we will be handing questionnaires to each of you. You will be asked questions to determine your views on certain matters. These questions are not meant to embarrass you or to pry into your private life, they are meant to reveal any biases that you may have. We ask that you be honest and forthright. You should not withhold information. Your questionnaire will ask you what you have heard about this case and its influence on you. Again, please be honest," Judge Ramsdell, reiterated.

"The court is prepared to compensate you ten dollars per day. If you have made it to my courtroom, then claims of financial hardship have been heard and the court will give you one last opportunity today to state your case," the judge noted.

No one made mention of parking available for jurors.

The judge briefly explained the calendar of the court and informed the jurors that the trial would be held Monday through Thursday from 8:30 AM until 4:00 PM until the jury reached the deliberation stage. Once they were in deliberations, they would be required to deliberate on Fridays. The trial was expected to last six weeks beginning on January 19, 2016. Jurors were instructed to visit the court's website on December 22, 2015. If their juror number appeared on the list, then their jury service would be considered complete. On the other hand, should their number not appear on the secure website, those jurors were expected to be back on January 11, 2016 at 8:30 AM. Upon their return, those jurors would be subject to questioning by the court. The jury selection process would be completed by the day's end on January 14, 2016.

"It is important that you follow all court instructions," Judge Ramsdell stated firmly. "Your conduct during jury selection is critically important. When you are completing your questionnaire, you are not allowed to discuss any matter on the questionnaire nor are you to ask for help. Until you are dismissed, you are not to discuss this case, questionnaire or any matters involving this case with your family, friends, co-workers or church members. You are ordered to ignore the Internet, television and any media coverage. I assure you, there will be media coverage on this trial."

I really hoped each juror listened to his words carefully.

"You may not," the judge continued, "ask about, look up or research anything on this case. You may not seek out evidence. You are not allowed to research the law in any manner. I hope I have made everything clear and the State thanks you for your service."

The judge stood up, nodded his head toward Kenya and exited as quickly as he had appeared. Moments later, the defendant was led out of the courtroom followed by her attorneys. The prosecution team departed while Kenya and Suza got busy about their task.

The jurors were quiet as the court assistants handed out questionnaire packets, the most important tool in the voir dire process for each team of attorneys.

It took about forty-five minutes before the first of the jurors got up, gathered his things and brought his completed questionnaire to the back of the courtroom. One by one, they turned in their document along with their juror badge and informational papers. It was an orderly and quiet process done without interruption.

An hour and a half later, the last of the jurors got up from his seat and returned his information to the assistants. It was the juror in the orange shirt and blue jeans. He turned around and looked toward the front of the courtroom.

Once again, he raised his arms in the air and framed a picture with his hands toward the ceiling. He peered through the box he made of a picture frame with his hands. He scrutinized his view carefully, dropped his arms and left the courtroom. I could not help but wonder what the future looked like in the picture frame he had made.

I knew from my former experience as a juror that this trial was not only about justice and it was not only about evidence. This trial would be a journey into the horrific details that was the cause for the end of the lives of an innocent six. I gathered my things and thought about six victims I did not know. I knew, just as a future jury would know, that each of us would become intricately involved in the lives of these people and each of them, ultimately, would forever be a part of our lives.

I wondered if I would see the face of evil again.

The jurors who had not been eliminated on line during the Christmas holiday would return on January 11, 2016. It would be a day of jury interrogation and jurist elimination. The flock would be reduced significantly as the attorneys searched for their lambs to the law. It would not be long before a jury of sixteen would be seated, a simple one-percent of the sixteen hundred called. Four of the sixteen, should they make it through the trial without being dismissed, would become alternate jurors at the end of closing arguments.

The hoeing of the road to the path of justice had begun again.

I stepped onto the street in front of the courthouse as rain fell from the sky. I could not help thinking the raindrops were like the tears falling from those who knew the victims from Carnation, Washington: Wayne, Judy, Scott, Erica, Olivia and Nathan.

DAY 2
January 11, 2016

CHALLENGE FOR CAUSE

Three days before Christmas, 1500 jurors checked the court's website to learn if they were expected to return on January 11, 2016. 1352 potential jurors learned that they had completed their civic duty to the State of Washington and would not be on the jury panel to determine the fate of Michele Anderson.

However, one hundred and forty-eight souls were not on the elimination list and arrived at 8:30 AM, seated in the gallery of Judge Jeffrey Ramsdell's court. There was a sense of unease as well as anticipation in the air as we waited twenty or thirty minutes for the proceedings to start.

Again, I was afforded the opportunity to sit within the confines of the jury box, separated from the potential jurors.

"Good morning, everyone," Judge Ramsdell said. "I want to thank you again for your time today and the time you spent with us last December when you filled out your questionnaires. We thank you for your willingness to serve."

He paused and looked over the courtroom.

"Today, we are going to be asking you questions. Those questions are not meant to embarrass you, but rather they are there to reveal any bias you may have. We call this process 'voir dire'. The attorneys and myself are trying to determine your frame of mind in the presumption of innocence. Remember that you're still under oath from last December." The judge reminded them.

"Obviously, we are not going to need all of you for this jury. In that, we will be dismissing jurors for either a challenge for cause or for a pre-emptory challenge. I know a lot of you have no idea what this means so let me explain briefly."

"Let's say the litigant in this case was Boeing International. Now, let's say you work for Boeing. After being questioned by the attorneys, you reveal you work for Boeing. It is more than likely that you would be dismissed because you work for them and there may be an inherent bias. We call that dismissed for cause."

The judge looked up and straightened his glasses.

"In the second case, that of pre-emptory challenges, the attorneys on each side have a limited number of jurors they can excuse for their own reasons. This will occur at the end of voir dire. And, mind you, just because you are dismissed from this trial, it does not prevent you from being a juror in another trial," he explained, educational in his tone.

A few jurors laughed and a few jurors groaned.

Judge Ramsdell asked the attorneys to re-introduce themselves to the jurors. Scott O'Toole and Michelle Morales stood. Detective Scott Tompkins was not present.

David Sorenson stood up and briefly introduced himself while the defendant sat quietly. She wore a black, loose fitting outfit.

"My name is Colleen O'Connor and it is our pleasure to represent Miss Anderson in this matter," the defense attorney said.

The judge proceeded to read the charges filed against the defendant as he had done on the first day. The names of the six victims were read aloud again, one at a time.

"So, we will be asking questions today," Judge Ramsdell continued. "We want you to be honest and candid. Please do not answer any questions the way you think we might want them answered. There will be questions that we ask that are innocuous to us but may make you uncomfortable personally. In the event that it's an issue, that you are uncomfortable speaking about it in front of the people around you, we can consult with you in private. Just let us know. Is everyone comfortable with that?" he asked.

Many jurors nodded their heads affirmatively.

"Since we last saw you, have any of you had hardships that could prevent you from being a juror in that time? If so, please raise your juror number so that we can review each situation. When we call on you, please state your hardship in two or three sentences."

Thirty-one jurors raised their 8 ½ x 11 placards in the air. The judge and court reporter noted the numbers that each juror held. One by one, each spoke into the microphone as Judge Ramsdell queried them.

Occasionally, the court reporter would ask a juror to speak up or speak closer to the microphone.

"I just found out we are having an eightieth birthday party for my mother. It would conflict with the trial," one juror said.

"I live alone and have no one to take care of my dog. He's at the end of his life and he's stopped eating. I couldn't concentrate on being a juror," another juror said.

"Thank you for listening, Your Honor," a juror offered. "I have been diagnosed with cancer and I am taking a new medication. "

"Let me ask you this," Judge Ramsdell said. "What does the medication do? Does it make you tired?"

"It's really unpredictable," the juror answered.

A significant number of jurors argued that their employers compensated jury duty for either a short time or not all. The potential jurors could not bear the financial hardship that lengthy jury duty would cause. Mortgages and bills still had to be paid and six weeks was too long to go without a paycheck. Other jurors were self-employed or worked for small companies who could not afford their absence. Ten dollars a day would do nothing to help pay their rent.

The judge, court reporter and attorneys took notes studiously as each juror spoke their case.

"I'm a mother of two kids and I have no one to take care of them for that length of time and I surely can't afford a babysitter. It would be too much of a burden," one lady said. It was a concern shared by many jurors.

It crossed my mind that these jurors had a month to think about their situation since the last time they had been in the courtroom. I do not think any of the potential jurors wanted to tell the court that the sacrifice would be too great for them. I am sure they spent the prior thirty days agonizing over the situation that a long-term trial would do to their personal lives.

"Mr. O'Toole, why don't you go ahead and take over," he directed the prosecutor after he heard the arguments from each of the thirty-one jurors.

Scott O'Toole stood up and smiled at the room. He wore a navy blue suit, with a white and red tie. He moved the podium so it faced the jurors; tap tested the microphone for sound and settled into his role quickly.

"As the judge said, we will be asking questions," he began. "When you do answer or comment, please raise your card so we know who you are. Most of what we ask you will refer to some of the questions asked on the questionnaire you completed the last time we were here. You had sixty-six questions to answer so there are some answers we may want clarification on. I hope it doesn't make you too uncomfortable."

The jurors looked at ease with the prosecutor.

"Years ago, the way we used to do this was to ask questions of each of you one at a time. It was hard on everyone," he told the prospective jurors.

He was right. I had referred to this stage in jury selection as 'jury interrogation'.

"Instead, we are going to do this the "Donahue" way," Scott offered warmly. He leaned forward and pulled the cordless microphone from its perch. He paced the aisle in amongst the jurors.

"Like Phil Donahue or Oprah might do, we want to elicit candid conversation. We want to get you talking. This isn't a Jerry Springer show, though."

A good number of the jurors chuckled.

"What we want as the State is to get the best jury possible that is fair to us as well as Miss Anderson. Give me a show of hands, who has negative feelings about lawyers?"

Ten or twelve jurors raised their numbers.

One juror responded, "I hate lawyers. My ex was one."

A lot of jurors laughed.

"Really," Scott responded. "What kind of lawyer?"

"A city attorney," the juror answered.

The prosecutor shook his head. "I hope it wasn't me," he retorted.

The room laughed again.

"I grew up in Texas and people get railroaded there all the time," another juror said. "I think it's the attorneys' fault."

Scott nodded.

"A lot of people think that. You know, twenty years ago, it was the O.J. trial that affected everyone's negative opinion of defense attorneys. Years later, Kenneth Starr went after President Clinton. It made a lot of people hate prosecutors. Now, you have TV, a new show about the making of a murderer. Do you think it contributes toward creating a negative image of attorneys and law enforcement? "

A couple jurors responded that it did.

"You bet it can," Scott agreed as he paced leisurely along the aisles. Sometimes he sauntered and other times, he paused to look at the juror he conversed with.

"How about the media? Do they always get it right?" he asked the room.

A few jurors raised their cards.

"Do they get it wrong a lot?"

Most of the room raised their hands.

"And why do they get it wrong? Is it because they don't get all sides of the story? How many of these TV shows that you see, like the 'Making of a Murderer', actually interview jurors?"

"I saw them interview one juror," someone replied.

"It doesn't happen often, does it?" the prosecutor reminded the juror. "You see, as a juror, if you are selected, you do have control in the system. You are the finder of facts. You will be able to make decisions, very important ones. You will have a perspective that will be different than everyone else, including the attorneys. You will have a say in right and wrong. We trust in the members of our community. You hold us, the State, to a standard that the Magna Carta established eight hundred years ago. It is a great responsibility to be a juror and you keep us in check."

"This is an extraordinarily serious case," he continued. "Anyone notice that there were six victims?"

Everyone raised his or her hands.

"Any comments?"

"I would be very emotional," a female juror commented.

"That's a good point. There were six victims and two of them were children. And, in feeling emotion, should that preclude you from being on a jury? Or, do we acknowledge the emotion and then set is aside to hear the evidence presented. Can you still keep an open mind despite the strong emotions that will arise?" the prosecutor asked.

"I think I could separate the emotion," a juror said. "I am

shocked that something like this could happen but I think it's vital that jurors take notes and not waiver on emotions. Aside from the defendant, there're a lot of lives that we could impact."

"Absolutely," Scott responded. "Any other comments?"

Another juror raised her hand. "I'm nervous about it. I'm not sure what we're going to get exposed to. Could we get PTSD over this? Does the Court provide counseling? I am willing to do my duty but it's a lot."

The prosecutor assured her counseling was available after jury service was completed.

An older juror raised his hand. "I have a lot of mistrust in the system. Last night, there was an episode on 60-Minutes that told the story of an innocent guy who got put away for thirty years. I don't trust the system."

"If you are selected, can you still be fair?" the prosecutor inquired.

"Seems to me that the little guy always gets trampled," he answered.

"But, as a juror," Scott reiterated, "you do have a say in the system. You're in the front row making sure we do things right. Are you still skeptical?"

The juror shook his head. "Yeah, yeah, I am…"

I saw Michelle Morales look up at the juror and then make a note on her legal pad.

"It's the two children that really bother me," a juror volunteered. "The person who did this has no conscience. Children are defenseless and I think it's inexcusable! How could someone do that?"

"Do you think it would affect your impartiality knowing children were involved when it came to making a decision?"

"I don't know," she answered slowly.

The prosecutor acknowledged the next raised hand.

"Jesus loves everyone. The Bible says we all have sin. I believe in the Bible and I don't believe in capital punishment. If the jury voted for death, and I was on the jury, I would vote against it because I don't believe in the death penalty," the juror stated firmly.

Scott stopped, looked at the jurors and then turned around toward the judge. It appeared he was about to ask for help and then thought better of it.

The room waited.

"Let me ask you this," he started. "Would knowing what the punishment could be, whether it be life or death, would that make a difference?"

Had I been asked, I would have said that it would make all the difference in the world.

The juror shrugged his shoulders. "Are we going to give someone the death penalty?"

The prosecutor turned around and looked at the judge again.

Ramsdell took a breath and looked toward the jurors. He took his glasses off and rubbed the lenses with a tissue. He put his glasses back on.

"I can tell you that the Governor in this state has placed a moratorium on the death penalty while he is in office. It means no one will be executed during his term. The Supreme Court has put limitations on what I can say. We cannot advise you whether the death penalty is involved."

"I thought something like that would be on our questionnaire," the juror remarked.

"I cannot tell you the potential punishment," the judge said.

The prosecutor stepped back in. "If you do not know the punishment, will if affect your ability to be fair and impartial?"

The juror shrugged again. "I don't know."

"Can I see a show of hands?" Scott asked the room. "Who thinks not knowing the punishment would affect their ability to be fair and impartial?"

Twenty-five jurors raised their placards in the air.

Both teams of attorneys noted who the jurors were.

The judge politely informed Scott his time was up and directed Colleen O'Connor from the defense team to begin her segment.

She stepped to the podium. She had long dark hair streaked with gray. She wore a maroon colored dress, gray patterned coat and white blouse.

"There are a lot of jurors we have not heard from so I am going to ask each of you the same question," she told the jurors. "Are there any distractions in your being on the jury and do you think you could start with a presumption of innocence for the defendant?"

One by one, she asked everyone the same question. Most of the responses were brief and short. There was a different energy than when Scott O'Toole had been in charge.

A juror responded when it was his turn. "I have followed this story since it happened in 2007. It was a horrendous murder. I do not think I can be unbiased at all. It was horrible."

The attorneys took notes while Colleen O'Connor moved to the next juror's comments.

"I have no distractions because I am retired," the juror responded. "I really think this is an awful crime. I've been thinking about why it took over eight years for the prosecutors to bring this case to trial. I was emotional when I thought about it. The more I think about it now, is what if she really is innocent? I am trying to be rational about this, but part of me wonders if I should not be on the jury. I am capable either way but, if you asked me today, I would rather not be on the jury."

"I appreciate your honesty," the defense attorney commented.

Colleen managed to get through half the room before Judge Ramsdell signified that her time was up.

The judge pulled out a sheet of paper and read a series of juror numbers as he looked at the jury pool. In one fell swoop, he summarily dismissed the thirty-one jurors who had claimed financial hardship at the beginning of the day.

The 'challenge for cause' gate had opened and the dismissed jurors were most likely relieved.

"Thank you for your service and please check out with Kenya, the Bailiff, before you depart," he said.

I could see that relief on a lot of juror's faces as they left.

Voir dire was not done, yet. The jurors who remained, about one hundred, were told to return the next day at 8:30 AM. The court still had a lot of work to do to trim the field to a simple sixteen.

The judge closed the day as he reminded the jury of the admonishment not to speak about or discuss the case with anyone. They were told not to research the case or to be on the Internet about the case. It was an order not unfamiliar to those who attended the first day of jury selection.

I put my notepad in my briefcase and prepared to step out of the jury box.

Then, the unthinkable happened.

"Do you work for a magazine?" one of the jurors asked me from the other side of the jury box.

I froze for a moment. He had just violated an admonishment given only moments before and it was now my problem.

Somehow, I found some words to respond.

"What magazine do you work for?" he asked.

"My apologies," I said as I glanced at my watch. "I'm running late."

Without another word, I left the courtroom as soon as I could.

It was a big, big problem.

DAY 3
January 12, 2016

QUERY OF THE LAMBS

The moment I left the courthouse, I called my old friend, Jen Wood, and told her what had happened with the juror.

"You have to tell the Court."

"I was afraid you would say that. I really do not want to end up like Beth Karas did in the Arias trial," I said.

A seated juror who wanted to know if Beth was Nancy Grace had approached the reporter during the trial. She had to testify about the experience on the witness stand.

Jen laughed. "I doubt it. You are in the early stages of jury selection. It would be a different story if the juror was already selected."

I was somewhat relieved.

"Just find a bailiff and take her aside before court proceedings," Jen advised.

The next day, I got to the courtroom thirty minutes early. It was not long before I saw Kenya bustling about as she prepared for the day. Fortunately, no one else was in the courtroom.

She listened carefully to my tale and thanked me.

As I went to my seat in the jury box, I felt as if a great weight had been lifted from my shoulders. It was not about being a rat or a tattletale. It was about integrity and my fiduciary responsibility to the rules of the Court while seated in the courtroom.

As I settled in the jury box, I noticed the casual and friendly conversations amongst jurors as they went to their seats. Some of these folks had known each other for a month now. Most were now familiar with their neighbors as they sat on the hard, oak benches assigned by jury number. Greetings were shared and tensions were light.

I did not see the juror who had approached me and breathed a sigh of relief. The problem had gone away.

Judge Ramsdell opened the proceedings in the same manner as the day prior and then called out to a particular juror. His eyes searched the sea of jurors.

A young man raised his hand.

"Sir, did you have a chance to speak with your employer? I know a concern was raised that this might be a hardship for you," the judge recalled.

The juror cleared his throat. "Uh, yes, Sir. I did. My employer will only cover the first two weeks of the trial. There's no way I can pay the rent without it."

"Very good," the judge responded. "Thank you for the follow up. I thank you for your service and you are excused."

The juror nodded his head gratefully, packed his things and exited the courtroom with a smile toward some of the jurors he had come to know.

"So, Mr. O'Toole, I think you're up," the judge said to the prosecutor.

Scott O'Toole smiled, stood up and carried his notepad to the podium. He looked at the jurors in front of him and greeted them warmly. "I used to say 'welcome back' until a juror hollered back, 'it's not like we had a choice'!

Most of the jurors chuckled in response. It was clear that Mr. O'Toole had everyone's attention from the start.

"I would like to spend a half hour or so talking about some elements of this case. We had talked about emotions but I would like to elevate that a little so you have an understanding of what we are about to go into," Scott began.

His hands held the sides of the podium.

"This case is about multiple victims. It is also about aggravating factors in the counts for numbers four, five and six. We allege that there was intentional concealment of the crime or to conceal the identities of those who committed the crime. For anyone, does this raise additional concerns?"

A male juror raised his hand.

The Court Reporter noted his number.

"A friend of mine was murdered in the Philippines over a pack of cigarettes. Personally, I don't think I could be impartial."

"Thank you for sharing that with us," Mr. O'Toole said. "I am assuming, but was it that the person who committed the crime was never found?"

"A little," the juror answered. "I'm still pretty angry about it."

"Yes?" the prosecutor said as he acknowledged the next raised placard.

"I don't understand what you mean by aggravating. Can you explain it?" she asked.

"An aggravating factor changes the nature of the crime. In this case, the aggravating factors affect nature of the murders," the prosecutor explained. "Was that precise enough to be vague?"

The room laughed but it looked like she understood.

"If I am one of the final twelve," a juror offered, "I could not help but search for the motivation in this crime. I would want to know why somebody could do something so horrific. I would have to hear an explanation."

"That's a good point," Scott O'Toole said. "The law does not see it quite that way. We have the burden of strictly proving that it happened. We do not have to prove why. You may never know the answer to that. You just need to know that a person or persons did the crime. This must be proven beyond a reasonable doubt. Make sense?"

Another juror raised his hand. "Is there a numeric percentage to that? Like, say, we're ninety-nine percent sure it happened that way?"

The prosecutor shook his head.

"No, there is not. You as a jury decide in the truth of the charge. That is not a quantifiable thing. In a civil case, a jury decides by a preponderance of evidence, which can be attributed to a percentage, for example, 51% as a majority. This does not apply in a criminal case. You will decide individually and collectively. Does that seem unfair to anyone?" he asked the room.

Nobody responded.

"If the State is going to take the liberty of someone," Scott continued, "then all of the burden of proof is on Miss Morales and myself. You decide what's reasonable and every case is different. Remember, it is what the defendant did, not whether she is a good or bad person. Anyone else have a comment?"

"What if I am on a jury and I am the only one who votes for innocence, exactly for the reasons you just gave? Will everyone know that I'm the one who didn't vote like everyone else?" a juror inquired.

"Good point," the prosecutor responded with a raised finger. "That is up to you. If you choose to keep it private, that is your right. Remember that a guilty verdict must be unanimous and it must be beyond a reasonable doubt. I hope that helps a little."

"It does," the juror said.

"Which leads me to my next thought," Scott said as he stepped away from the podium. "Raise your hand if it concerns you that we are accusing the defendant of six counts of murder and that she is a woman. Does it make a difference to you if it's a woman?"

"I don't think it matters," someone volunteered. "The law does not say anything about men or women."

"You're correct," Scott responded. He raised a finger in the air. "What if we told you someone else was involved and that it was her boyfriend? Would a girlfriend/boyfriend dynamic affect your decision-making process?" he asked, a reference to Joseph McEnroe.

"It depends upon the evidence," a juror replied

"Time," Mr. O'Toole," the judge stated.

The prosecutor thanked the jurors and sat down.

David Sorenson ran his hand through his brush cut, salt and pepper hair, straightened his glasses and made his way to the podium. He turned a page on his legal pad and inspected it for a moment. He wore a gray suit with a light gray shirt complimented with a gold and black diamond patterned tie. He straightened his notepad on the podium and looked across the room before he began.

"Some things I would like to follow up on, things we touched upon in the last couple days were regarding the words 'fair and impartial'. I want to explore whether this is the right jury for you to sit on. Everyone in this room comes from different backgrounds, both good and bad, as evidenced on your questionnaires. Is this the right jury for you?" he asked rhetorically. "These allegations are shocking but we must get past that to determine who can be fair and impartial. So, I am going to call on many individuals. There are almost fifty jurors we have not heard from and I want to hear from you. Juror #111?"

The juror raised her card, seated in the second row.

"What is shocking about this case to you?"

"That children were involved," she answered quickly.

"Do you think that fact would make it difficult for you to follow your legal instructions?"

"No," she answered. "It's just shocking with the age of the children."

David made a note on his legal pad.

"Juror #208, we haven't heard from you. What are your feelings?"

"I've thought about this a lot. It doesn't leave your mind," the juror said pensively. "I have friends in law enforcement. It's hard to put the idea of six people being murdered aside. I would try to be impartial, though."

The defense attorney made a note and then called on another juror. "What are your concerns if you were selected as a juror?"

She appeared to have been caught off guard. The room waited patiently while she thought about her response.

"What if we have zero experience in matters like this?" the juror finally asked emphatically. "What can I offer? I have never been a juror before. I wish I were better prepared. How could I do a good job if I don't know what I'm doing?"

The attorney did not seem particularly comfortable with the question. "That is a valid concern," he said.

A juror from the back of the room spoke up. "I thought this was going to be easy when we first started this process. Now I don't know how I feel. It's a lot more than I anticipated."

"Thank you," Sorenson acknowledged. "It is not an easy process. The events that happened are going to weigh on you. I will not lie to you and tell you any different. This is a painful case. The fact remains that everyone deserves a fair trial and we are looking for the right people to ensure that happens."

Many of the jurors nodded their heads.

"What about graphic evidence?" Sorenson asked. "Who might have an issue with that?"

"It depends," an elderly female juror said. "What are we talking about here? How bad are the pictures? Is this something we are going to see every second of the trial? Can we look and then look away? What if I cry? Are we allowed to show emotion?"

"It's okay to show emotion," he reassured her. "Your job is to be impartial. You must be able to put it aside at some point. It is a difficult task."

"I would have a problem with graphic pictures of the children," another juror said.

"How about body language?" the attorney queried. "How many in here were off put by Michele?"

Twenty jurors raised their hands. One juror said he saw her wave at them on the first day when she sat down. He did not feel it acknowledged the situation she was in and the charges against her. It was inappropriate in his mind. Another juror commented that it was hard to determine anything just on the short time they had seen her. Still another juror empathized with the defendant; saying she would not know how she herself would react had the same charges been placed against her.

Michele Anderson stared down at the table in front of her. It occurred to me that I had not seen her speak with either attorney.

After the morning break, Scott O'Toole took over the podium again.

"So, if I may, let's review some of the things we have covered. We talked about emotion and being able to separate it from our interpretation of evidence. We discussed graphic evidence, and I promise you that any that is shown will only be when necessary and immediately removed from your sight. We will not leave it to linger on the screens for you."

A lot of jurors seemed relieved.

"We also spoke of a boyfriend, Joseph McEnroe," Scott reminded them, "and that we would wait to see what the evidence tells us about their relationship. Further, we discussed the body language of Michele Anderson; and as some of you noticed, she waved at you. You will see her for four to six weeks throughout the trial. But, you won't see the body language of Wayne, Judy, Scott…"

"Objection!" David Sorenson said as he quickly stood. "We have already covered the victim's names."

Judge Ramsdell sustained the objection.

Scott looked toward the family and relinquished the podium to Mr. Sorenson

David fielded thoughts from particular jurors after he referenced his notepad. For a time, he discussed witnesses in general and how particular jurors might judge the validity of their character and truths. He spent a significant amount of discussion on reasonable doubt. One juror responded that she could tell if someone was a liar just by looking at them.

Both teams of attorneys made a lot of notations.

David Sorenson called on Juror #13, a professionally dressed young woman seated in the front row.

"In your questionnaire, you stated you were a juror on a murder trial. Is that correct?"

The potential juror straightened in her seat. A notepad was on her lap. "Yes, sir."

"Can you tell us what happened?" Sorenson asked. "I don't want specifics. Did you reach a verdict?"

"We really tried," she responded. "In the end, we could not reach an agreement."

"Do you feel like justice was served?"

"I wish we had reached a decision and it bothers me," she answered. "It was a difficult trial."

"Did it impact your beliefs in the judicial system?"

"Not really," she said. "I think we have a good system."

David made a note and then called on another juror. "You said in your voir dire that you were on a murder trial, as well?"

"I was," he answered as he cleared his throat.

Sorenson adjusted his glasses.

"What happened?" he asked.

"We did what we had to do," the juror answered confidently. "We listened at the trial, deliberated, followed the law and then reached a verdict. He was guilty."

"How did it make you feel?"

The juror shrugged his shoulders. "We just did our job."

I would have expected that both jurors would not be back the next day. Lawyers do not typically like experienced jurors especially those who have served on a murder trial.

It was late into the afternoon session when Scott took the podium. He glanced at his notepad and began to speak.

"We start with a presumption of innocence and that cannot change until you go into deliberations. We talked about probabilities and percentages and we know it cannot boil down to a shadow of a doubt but instead, making a decision based on evidence that is beyond a reasonable doubt. We want reasonable men and women who can stick to the standard that the law has set for you. We must prove she is guilty but you must presume her innocence all the way throughout and that will be difficult," he said with a wave of his hand toward the defendant.

"The elements of the crime have to be proved by us and we are obligated to meet that standard. This is not about probabilities. Big case or small, the burden of proof is the same. It is only after you completely review the evidence, all of it, that you make a determination. You are the ones that will tell us if we have proved our case. If we have not, you will tell us that, too," he finished.

The jurors were dismissed for the day, except for a number who chose to have a private conference with the judge and attorneys regarding matters on their voir dire questionnaire. It was an option given on the first day.

"Also," Judge Ramsdell had said before the jurors were dismissed, "As we have done since this process started, I want you to check the website tonight after 5:00 PM to see if you have been dismissed. If not, please return here tomorrow at 8:30 AM. If we are successful with both teams of the attorneys, we may be able to have our jury selected by the day's end. Although I cannot promise it, I am pretty sure that we are ahead of schedule."

It would seem an impossible task to select such few from the many who were qualified. The gleaning of the flock was in full swing while the search for the lambs to the law would continue behind the closed doors of the lawyers' offices. It had been the query of the lambs that would yield those who would, one day, be the purveyors of justice.

Hopefully, the players of the court had learned lessons from a jury picked in the Joseph McEnroe case. The stakes were different but the victims would always remain the same.

THE LAMBS TO THE LAW

Kenya, the Court Bailiff, took me aside before I entered the courtroom. She wore a long, black dress complimented with a beige sweater.

"You can sit in the jury box during the morning session but you will have to move to the gallery this afternoon. We'll be selecting a jury," she said apologetically.

"Thank you," I said. Neither of us made mention of our jury issue a couple of days ago.

I had been humbled and honored to have had the opportunity.

Judge Ramsdell opened the day by thanking the jurors for their patience and commitment throughout the process. He promised to be respectful of their time throughout the day and the upcoming trial. He formally dismissed two jurors at the outset, one for a medical note and the other for financial hardship.

"With that," Judge Ramsdell stated, "let's give the attorneys a chance to speak one more time."

Scott O'Toole, attired in brown slacks, blue suit coat, white shirt and a brown tie, stood up and confidently walked to the podium. He smiled at the jurors, reiterated his thanks and promised he would only talk to them a few minutes.

"Juror #200? I have seen your questionnaire but I do not think we have heard from you. Did you get a chance to talk?"

"No," the juror answered.

"Do you think there will be any work hardship for the next six weeks?"

"Not at all," he answered.

"Do you have any impressions on this case that you might want to share?" O'Toole prodded.

"Not really," Juror #200 responded. "I would be okay with it. I think it would be a good experience."

The prosecutor nodded and made a mark on his legal pad.

"How about Juror #210? Would this trial be a hardship for you?"

"Yes," she answered. "I made a note on my questionnaire, as well. There are only three people in my department and this would overload the other two. It would be extremely difficult for me."

"Thank you," Scott O'Toole said. "Uh, Juror #21?"

A lady with dark hair raised her number from the front row.

"On your questionnaire, you mentioned that you had a family member within the justice system," Scott said as he referenced his legal pad. "Is this a close relative?"

"It was a cousin," Juror #21 answered. "He was prosecuted in 2000."

"Would you say he was fairly or unfairly treated?"

She thought about it for a moment. "It's hard to say. I was not familiar with the trial and exactly what the crime was. I did, however, see the impact it had on the family. It was a difficult circumstance. I was not close to my cousin so I don't have that much of an opinion."

"Do you think he was fairly treated?" Scott asked again.

"I guess so. I don't think it will affect me on this trial at all. I could still be fair and impartial."

"Why do you say that?"

"If it was someone closer to me, maybe it would impact me. My job affects me more than this," she answered.

The prosecutor smiled and then referred back his legal pad.

"Juror #70? You haven't spoken. Can I pick on you for a moment?"

"Sure," she answered.

"You said that you were a novelist? Is that right?"

"I write romance books but I'm changing over to children's books."

"So, you don't write True Crime books?"

"Oh, no," she responded with a chuckle.

"You also said you were a crisis counselor for a time," O'Toole noted. "Did you have to work with victims of major crimes?"

"I worked in the area of suicide prevention. It was a lot of phone work," she explained. "I didn't really have any contact with major crimes or victims thereof."

"Okay," Scott said. "Do you have any impressions on what it might be like to be on a jury?"

"No," Juror #7 said. "It would be a new experience for me."

She had my vote to be on the jury had I been asked.

The Prosecutor walked over to Michelle Morales and had a quick, whispered discussion. He walked back to the podium and smiled at the jurors as he picked up his paperwork.

"No more questions."

David Sorenson quickly walked to the podium. He wore a light gray suit, blue shirt and a mauve tie. He adjusted his glasses, set his notepad down, glanced at it and then put his hands on either side of the podium.

"I have a few more questions than Mr. O'Toole had and I'm sorry about that. As you know, today is the last day and now is the time to speak or forever hold your peace. This is your opportunity for you to tell us that this is something you really don't want to do. Anyone?"

A number of jurors raised their placards in the back of the room. The attorney selected one.

"I would be impartial. I have no doubt about that," she said. "This would be a work hardship for me, though. I was just transferred to a new store and, to be honest, I thought I would have been dismissed by now."

Sorenson thanked her, made a note and recognized the next juror.

"Personally, it is not a big hardship on me. However, I am a special education preschool teacher and this would be hard on my students and on the other teachers. I am not against doing my duty but you asked," a juror proclaimed.

The attorney made a notation and moved quickly to the next juror.

"Yeah, glad you asked," the male juror, responded. "Look, I don't really want to do this. Six weeks is way too long and I don't look forward to six weeks of boredom. I don't have money problems but I really don't think I could sit that long."

"We appreciate your honesty," Sorenson said.

He wrote a note on his pad and stepped away from the podium. He put his hands in front of him and clasped them.

"Now, who wants to tell me that they're so excited to be on this jury that they can't stand it? It would be just awesomeness to be a juror! Raise your number if you feel that way," he encouraged them.

Four jurors raised their numbers while the attorney made notations. Each of them said it would be an interesting process and each could begin with the presumption of innocence.

"I think we are almost done," the attorney commented. "Like we said, there will be media coverage on this trial. Does that concern anyone?"

The room returned blank stares. No one raised his or her hand.

"No one? This is the final call. Does anyone feel uncomfortable being on this jury?"

A male juror stood up from the back row of the room, his card raised.

"Yes?" the attorney asked.

"I thought your term, awesomeness, in regards to being on the jury was offensive. There is nothing awesome about any of this. Six people are dead and someone killed them," he stated obstinately.

I saw the attorney's face flush.

"I'm sorry," David stammered, obviously caught off-guard. "I didn't mean it to come across that way. I was only asking if anyone thought this would be a good experience."

Despite the juror's stand for the victim, I suspected he would end up in the graveyard for jurors, those jurors who would be dismissed without explanation, the peremptory challenge. I knew by the end of the day that the cemetery of jurors would be full of civic servants who had almost made it to the final sixteen.

The silence that ensued was broken as Judge Ramsdell moved to the matter of the dismissal of two more jurors.

"Are there any other challenges for cause?" he asked after the jurors were released.

Scott O'Toole and David Sorenson shook their heads.

"Very good," Judge Ramsdell said perfunctorily. "We will go ahead and take the morning recess. Upon our return, we will seat sixteen jurors for challenge. Our goal is to have our final sixteen sat today."

I am sure it was the longest break these jurors had taken thus far even though it had only been fifteen minutes. Not one of them had any confidence that they would be seated in the jury box. Each one thought of all the reasons that they probably would not be picked for the jury.

For the first time since the start of the trial, I took my seat on a hard, oak bench in the gallery of the courtroom.

"All right, Ladies and Gentlemen," Judge Ramsdell began. "We are going to call each of you by number. I want you to take a seat in the jury box. Two jurors at a time will be dismissed."

In his hands, he held a sheet of paper. He called juror numbers numerically until the jury box was filled with sixteen.

Each juror looked on, their faces stoic. They watched as the judge took his sheet of paper and handed it to Kenya. She took the sheet to Scott O'Toole's desk. He and Michelle Morales scrutinized the document while Kenya stood behind them. Michelle, pen in hand, made a notation on the paper after a brief and whispered discussion. She handed the sheet over her shoulder to Kenya, who then walked it to the defense table.

David Sorenson centered the sheet in front of the defendant while Colleen O'Connor whispered quietly back.

The defendant wore all black and stared straight ahead. She did not volunteer any help and seemed to trust what was going on. After a few moments, David made a notation and handed the sheet to Kenya who took it back to the judge's bench.

The judge looked toward the jury and smiled.

"In the land of Microsoft, this is how we do it here," he said as he waved the sheet of paper.

The jurors in the gallery and the jury box laughed nervously.

Judge Ramsdell inspected the sheet and then looked to the jury box. "Juror #32 and Juror #61, you are dismissed. The court thanks you for your service. Please turn in your juror information at the back of the room."

The sequence repeated itself with different jurors for the next ninety minutes until both teams of attorneys finally agreed upon a jury of sixteen.

With the benefit of good notes on my part and details obtained from interviews held with jurors after the trial, I was able to create a broad paint-stroke of who the chosen were:

Juror #1 was a male juror who would come to be known by the other jurors as 'Quiet Bill'. On the first day of jury selection, Colleen O'Connor had asked if he was comfortable with the presumption of innocence for Michele Anderson. Further, would there be any distractions that might inhibit the juror's performance?

Bill had responded that the presumption of innocence would be the starting point and that there would be no distractions in performance. "It is inconvenient, though."

Although Juror #1 could be seen as reserved, it did not take away from his dedication. Oftentimes, when he did speak, the jurors would note that his statements were often profound and sensible.

Juror #2, Rio, was retired and the most senior person on the jury. All the jurors would find him to be a sweet man. If asked, most of the jurors would say they genuinely cared for him. For him, despite his prior experience on a murder trial before, this trial would be especially disconcerting as he considered the number of victims; when the crime allegedly happened and the fact that it was the decimation of a family by another family member. It was one of the most traumatizing tasks he would ever take on in his life.

"A few years ago, I sat on a murder case," he had told David Sorenson during voir dire, "we just hashed it out in the jury room. We concluded the defendant was guilty and the evidence proved it that way. Right now, I am comfortable in saying this defendant is innocent. Everything depends upon the prosecutor."

Juror #3, Tiffany, had never expected she would be a juror and had been shocked when she was selected. The trial would prove very difficult for her especially in consideration of the victim, Olivia. Tiffany had two daughters and one was almost the same age as Olivia. Once selected, she was focused on doing the right thing each day she was in the jury box. She did not anticipate the depth of emotion and impact of the murders on her life. She wore a flower in her hair every day.

There was a point in voir dire as she responded to Scott O'Toole, when asked how one might determine the credibility of a witness and what role body language might play.

"For me," she had said, "I'm very skeptical about judging somebody on just body language. Everyone's situation is unique. I am one to listen calmly before speaking. This comes from my dealing with lots of students daily. Demeanor is certainly important but one needs to take it in context," he had responded.

Later that same day, Scott O'Toole asked her to state her opinion as to whether the world felt safer today than it did twenty-five years ago, which, he noted, that some media polls had suggested.

"I don't believe it is a safer world. Most people said it is because of the media, but I say it's because of the improvements in technology and information being available to so many people. In a way, technology makes things worse because it lessens our ability to be aware of our surroundings," she answered calmly.

Juror #4, Crystal, had children so the trial would be especially impactful. She called her son every morning from the jury room. She worked for the State of Washington as a case manager and was used to people and the variety positions they found themselves in.

The experience had made her very resilient and also gave her an ability to see things as they were. She was not afraid to 'tell it as it was' if she were asked.

She spoke a number of times in the voir process. At a particular point, Scott O'Toole discussed whether it made a difference that Michele Anderson had a boyfriend accomplice and would the idea of a boyfriend in the case affect decision-making.

"No. Men, women and children do things," she had said.

"Do you think things are safer nowadays than a quarter of a century ago?" Scott asked.

"My kids' childhood is no safer than mine was."

Juror #5, Tiffany, was a middle-aged female and always professionally attired. She had been an internal auditor for seven years and was accustomed to the separation of emotion and facts. She felt she excelled at her job because she was naturally unbiased.

A discussion ensued between her and Scott O'Toole when he inquired upon her experience with the justice system, an answer he noticed on her voir dire questionnaire.

"Someone in your family was involved with the justice system?" Scott had asked.

"Yes."

"When?"

"It would have been in 2000," she answered. It had taken her a moment to recall the year. "A cousin of mine had committed a crime, a pretty serious crime, and he went through the system."

"Was the cousin fairly treated?" he asked.

"It's hard to say," she responded slowly. "I really only saw what kind of impact it had on the family. I was not close to him. Like I said, it was a serious case."

"In your opinion, was he fairly treated?"

"I couldn't tell you because I really knew very little about what happened. I suppose if it were someone closer to me, I would have an opinion. As far as this case goes, I think I could be fair and impartial. My job impacts me more than this as an internal auditor, partly because I know so many people. This case depends upon facts and evidence and I separate emotions very well."

Juror #6, Katie, was passionate about being a juror and took it seriously from the moment she had received her jury summons. She had no reservations about speaking her mind if called upon, yet maintained her ability to avoid making any decision until all the facts were in. She was excited to arrive in court every day but did not anticipate the depth of the emotions that would threaten to surge inside her.

Her varied shoe selection, a different pair worn every day, was always a good topic of conversation with the female jurors.

She was surprised that she had been selected because she had only been called upon once during jury questioning. Colleen O'Connor had asked her to discuss the ability to set aside pre-conceived notions. Additionally, she wanted the juror to discuss any financial concerns she might have on a long-term trial.

"I have the ability to be unbiased and avoid pre-conceived ideas," she explained. "I think there is going to be an emotional impact on this trial and I have to set those feelings aside, too. My work is allowing me to do this so I am not worried financially."

Juror #7, Kristine, was a young Hawaiian woman who came in with her hair tied back every day. She was mature, attentive and had been called upon by David Sorenson more than once. She had commented that details were important to worry about in a murder case. On the final day, David Sorenson pursued the subject of the difficulty in letting someone go even though there was a suspicion that person might have been guilty.

"The jury needs to talk it out," she had said resolutely.

"You said in your questionnaire that you were involved with victim's rights," Sorenson commented. "How so?"

"I was with an agency that dealt with domestic violence. We handled the youth primarily."

"Did you have a title there?"

"I was a youth coordinator."

Kristine was always reserved and quiet. She was focused every day and took many notes.

Juror #8, Andre worked for the Gates Foundation. He was unsure if his work was going to compensate him during the trial. He had both a five and seven year-old child. When asked if having two children gave him pause when he thought about the trial, he responded calmly,

"There's a threshold that has to be met regardless of the seriousness of the punishment and the crime. Having two kids does give me pause. There will be a natural sympathy. However, this depends upon the prosecution."

The trial would be difficult for Andre and it would be difficult to separate emotion. However, he had a good sense of humor, which would help many of the jurors during the dark times of testimony. He had many stories about his travels around the world to keep people entertained. The jurors adored him.

Juror #9, Abe, was a middle-aged man. During voir dire, when asked by David Sorenson if the trial presented any hardship for him, he responded that it was a matter of juggling things. He foresaw an emotional impact but thought he could set those feelings aside.

At another point, Sorenson had asked whether he had heard of the trial in the media. He had heard some things regarding the murders but did not have feelings either way as toward guilt or innocence.

When asked if he thought it would be tough to stay away from the news, he had stated,

"I'm a news junkie. I like to know what's going on in the world. So, yes, it will be tough but not impossible."

"Are you sure it wouldn't be too much temptation to look up something on this trial?"

"It's not that," the juror replied. "It's that the news is accessible everywhere and I wouldn't want to be exposed to it accidentally."

The jurors would never get to know him because, without reason given to the Court, he never showed. In that, he reduced the alternate pool by one. Maybe it was best not to have a news junkie on the trial after all.

Juror #10, Greg, was a mature man with gray hair. The only time he spoke during voir dire, in response to a question on how he might feel about being on a jury, he responded, "It would be fascinating."

Greg had a good head on his shoulders and was adept with helping other jurors with questions as well as being a devil's advocate. He was always actively engaged. He took the bus to Court every day and was an avid reader of The Seattle Times.

Juror #11, TC, was educated and she considered herself well

informed. She was an event coordinator and thought it gave her a good understanding of human nature. It was her idea to bring in additional coloring books for the other jurors to doodle with during the times they saw extended stays in the jury room. She always carried a countenance of seriousness to her work yet also had a dry sense of humor. She was good with words and semantics, which would prove helpful during deliberations.

When asked during voir dire, TC did not anticipate financial hardship and the trial wouldn't be too much of an inconvenience because it was the slow season at work. The juror expected the trial to be difficult with the emotion that was inherent but that it would have to be set aside.

"I don't know how I'll feel because I have never been through a trial."

Juror #12, Ken, had great empathy for the victims of the murders as well as the survivors of the tragedy since he was the father to a daughter and a son. There were times it was difficult to keep emotion at bay and his experience at Microsoft gave him the tools to think with a presumption of innocence while being coolly analytical.

When asked by Colleen O'Connor whether there might influential distractions and whether a presumption of innocence could be maintained throughout the trial, Ken had explained,

"I prioritize distractions. They will always be there. I think the emotions will be taxing throughout this process but I could maintain the presumption of innocence until we are given the case."

He would prove himself very capable. Many of the jurors would consider him a peaceful person and levelheaded, which would be valuable attributes for his eventual selection as the Presiding Juror.

Juror #13, the romance novelist, Lisa, came to be well liked by the other jurors and was known for always wearing a dress to jury duty. When other jurors would comment how nice she looked, she would laugh and say her outfits were just "onesies". She was passionate about her jury service and was a quiet juror for the most part. Some would say she was spiritual and metaphysical which made for a nice balance for those jurors who were a bit more black and white.

The first time we heard from her Lisa during voir dire was when she was asked whether the trial would be an inconvenience and whether she could be unbiased in a difficult trial. She said she was self-employed and was a flexible boss.

In another instance, David Sorenson asked if reasonable doubt would be difficult in letting someone free, she responded that it would not be pleasant if there were a suspicion of guilt. There was a standard that the prosecution had to reach.

Juror #14, Donna, was a middle school teacher who carried a handful of stress at home with an autistic son. She had heard nothing of the Carnation murders until the original call for jurors in December. She felt she could be unbiased. She was concerned about the length of the trial and the stress it would cause the other teachers at work.

The other jurors liked Donna because she was well educated and had a calm demeanor about her. She was very studious and always took notes. The emotion the trial brought forward was difficult to keep at bay for her and it was extremely difficult not to share her experience with anyone throughout the trial.

"I agree with the other juror who said that reasonable doubt has the same standard in a small case as in a big case," she told David Sorenson during voir dire. "The size of the crime doesn't matter. I teach middle schoolers. I hear lots of stories and there is always an element of doubt. I've learned that it's hard to figure out the truth sometimes because of doubt. But I believe in people and I believe in the justice system."

"Have you ever studied law?" Sorenson asked.

"I once thought about going to law school. I even helped my brother study throughout his going to law school. He's an Industrial Appeals Judge."

Sorenson nodded and made a note on his legal pad.

"One more thing," he asked, "will this trial create a work hardship for you?"

"Oh, no," she answered. "I have a substitute teacher who is trained very well. I will still be going in on Fridays so I don't lose touch with my students. They are already wondering what is going on. We have some students who have to wear ankle bracelets so they have seen the system a lot in their lives. One even asked me what crime I had committed to be going to court all the time."

David Sorenson tilted his head, apparently confused.

"Well, we talked and I used it as a teaching moment opportunity. Not all people who go to court are bad."

"Ah," he laughed.

Juror #15, Enrique, would be considered by the other jurors as one of their favorites to be around with his affable nature. He was a family man and had a great love for his family and friends in Peru as well as his family at home. He, also, had two children, which would take an emotional toll. He was adept at hiding the personal strain from his family and other jurors. He became good friends with Juror #2, Rio.

"Let's say you were on a jury," David Sorenson offered during voir dire, "would there be concerns that your reasonable doubt could let someone go?"

"I believe in doing our duty and doing what the law tells us to do. If we have to let someone go, then we did what the law told us. I believe that juries should base their decisions on facts and evidence. It is not personal."

Finally, Juror #16, Matt, a young man in his late twenties, was the final juror selected. The thing that many jurors noticed about Matt was that he was not afraid of hard work and was even known to do IT tasks for his employer during his lunch hour. He was an avid diver and loved to tell stories of the amazing creatures he had seen. He was considered very thoughtful by the rest of the jury and people liked his affable and friendly nature

When he was asked his thoughts concerning reasonable doubt, Matt responded,

"I agree with what the last juror said. Reasonable doubt doesn't change, no matter what case you're on. Even though this crime is more serious it does not change the bar and the law will tell us what to do. The prosecution has a job to prove the case and if they do not, then we have to return a verdict of not guilty."

"You work for Amazon, don't you?" Sorenson asked.

"I do."

"We just saw a documentary that it's a bad place to work. It told the story of a lot of unhappy employees. Is it like that?" the attorney asked.

"Not for me," the juror said. "My department is fine. I have a good manager. He is very understanding and our team works well together."

The jurors listened to the judge as he read their jury instructions. They would receive a written copy of the instructions as well. Although they did their best to pay attention to the judge, thoughts raced in their heads in a thousand different directions. It would have been difficult to focus.

The judge finished and instructed the jury of sixteen to return at 8:45 AM, on Tuesday, the day after Martin Luther King Day.

At the forefront of each juror's conscience, there would be chagrin. The souls of Wayne, Judy, Scott, Erica, Olivia and Nathan were the voices that once walked the earth and it was now the juror's task to hear their words. Had the Court chosen the right person to be a juror?

A thousand jurors had become sixteen. Each of the sixteen would have the weekend to feel the pride that came with being selected as a juror. On the other side of that weekend, they would enter the world of Michele Anderson and the events of Christmas Eve of 2007.

The one thing that all the jurors had in common was that each was surprised that they had been selected and, to that, the odds of there being a stealth juror on the panel had been greatly reduced.

Over the weekend, the defense team petitioned the court to be released from the case. The defendant had continued to be uncooperative with her attorneys and had not spoken to them in years.

The trial was delayed until a decision could be made.

CHRISTMAS EVE, 2007

It was apparent that the motion by the defense team to withdraw from the case had been denied when I saw Colleen and David take their seats in Judge Ramsdell's courtroom. The motion had caused the start of the trial to be delayed by one week.

I sat quietly in the gallery and watched as the family of the victims entered and took their seats. The first two rows had been reserved specifically for them yet they filled the first three rows. The people who sat in the courtroom were the same that had sat through the many months of the Joseph McEnroe trial that had ended six months prior.

There were six seats in the front row that remained empty.

"Good morning, Ladies and Gentlemen," Judge Ramsdell greeted the new jury. "You're about to hear opening statements. If you remember, a week ago, I told you that you would be afforded the opportunity to take notes. You will also note that I have not provided you with notebooks or pens. The reason for that is something that I want to reinforce."

A jury of fifteen watched him attentively, as butterflies fluttered in their stomachs. One of the sixteen jurors never showed.

"Opening statements are the opportunity for counsel to present statements," the judge continued. "Counsel statements, however, are not evidence itself. So, I am going to withhold notebooks until the conclusion of opening statements. Statements of counsel are not evidence themselves," he reiterated. "With that, Mr. O'Toole, are you willing to present opening statements for the State?"

Scott O'Toole stood up. He wore a charcoal gray suit, light blue shirt and red tie. He carried a packet to the podium and set it down. The packed courtroom watched as he moved the podium to his liking, directly in front of the jurors. He put a packet underneath the podium and proceeded to remove a paperclip from a thick stack of papers. He set the paper down and looked up briefly at the jurors.

"May it please the Court," he said as he rubbed his hands together and looked around the courtroom. "Counsel, Miss Anderson, members of the jury: good morning. "

"Those of us who live in King County know that, as big as Seattle is, whether it be along the I-5 corridor, over the Interstate 405, along the I-90 corridor and up the 520, if you go east just a few miles from this building, it's a very, very different place."

"It's a very different part of King County. It's rural, the terrain tends to be hilly, almost mountainous and it's heavily forested. Many of the roads out there are not really roads at all but almost gravel driveways. The houses are far apart. Sometimes the neighbors go days or weeks without seeing each other. There's nothing unusual about that."

The prosecutor straightened his notes.

"As you travel along one of these gravel roads, 346th Avenue Northeast, you pass a number of residences. Immediately on the left, as you go past the mailboxes, you'll see a small modest house. Up the road on the right is the Wilson home. As you pass their home, a little further up that driveway, the "S" begins to gain a little elevation, and you come to a gate. The gate is locked and secure. On the posts on either side of the chained gate is a sign that reads, 'Keep Out' and 'No Trespassing'."

For some jurors, the opening statement might have seemed similar to the innocuous opening of a Stephen King novel.

"When that gate swings open, the road continues upward. It curves up and to the right, and just as it turns to the right, there is another residence to your left, a singlewide trailer. There is a truck parked outside of it. If you continue up the driveway, you will get to the main residence, the home of Wayne and Judy Anderson."

The prosecutor's voice was easy to listen to. He seemed to speak with the jurors instead of speaking at them. They were entranced with each word. In their minds, they walked up the driveway with him as he weaved his argument.

"The Anderson house is a single story home, blue in color. It rests on about five and a half acres. It's very rural and very secluded. It's about a quarter mile up from the main road, 346th Avenue Northeast. You'll see a number of outbuildings surrounding the home. Inside the big garage, is the shop where Wayne used to work on his many hobbies. On the back side of the home, there's a storage shed."

He turned a page and looked back over at the jury.

"Members of the jury, on December 24, 2007, Christmas Eve, more than eight years ago, two people: this woman, Miss Anderson," he said as he waved toward the defendant, "and her boyfriend, Joseph McEnroe, walked out of that mobile home, got in their truck and they drove up to the main house. They parked the truck, walked up onto the porch and through the front door."

"Nobody lives in that house anymore. Michele Anderson and her boyfriend stayed but a few hours, a very short time indeed. When they were done, a family that had lived in that home for thirty years lay dead. Six people: Two grandparents, their son and daughter-in-law and their two grandchildren. When Michele Anderson and her boyfriend, Joe McEnroe walked into that house, they were well prepared and well armed. Michele Anderson carried a 9 MM semi-automatic pistol in her sweatshirt while he carried a .357 caliber revolver."

"But they were armed with something else," Scott pointed out with an upraised finger. "They were armed with the trust of the people inside that home and armed with hatred for the people in that home. When they were done inside the home at the top of the driveway, they walked out, got back into their truck and drove back down to their mobile home. They began to destroy evidence and they also began to plan their next move, which was to flee."

"Members of the jury, I'm going to take you back in time more than eight years, to Christmas Eve, 2007. When that Christmas Eve began, Wayne, Judy, Scott, Erica, Olivia and Nathan Anderson were six live human beings. Their only mistake was to be related to this woman, Michele Anderson. Their only mistake was to have befriended her boyfriend, Joseph McEnroe."

"Let me tell you about the victims. Wayne Anderson, in December of 2007, was sixty years old. He was retired and had worked for Boeing for many, many years. He was a husband who had been married to Judy for thirty-one years. This is a picture of Wayne and Judy at a work function," Scott said as he reached down and picked up a two-by-three foot poster-board of Wayne and Judy in happier times.

Slowly, in a semi-circle, Scott O'Toole showed it to the length of the jury box.

"Wayne was also a father. He adopted Judy's child, Mary Victoria Anderson. He also had a son named Scott who was born in 1975 and a daughter, Michele, born in 1978. It is Michele Anderson who sits in Court with us today."

The jurors knew who she was without looking at her.

"Wayne and Judy had bought the property in Carnation in the late 1970's which included the residence of Michele Anderson, the mobile home located just down the driveway."

"Judy Anderson was sixty-one years old in 2007. She was married to Wayne and worked for the post office for many years in Carnation. Judy knew everybody and everybody knew Judy. She was also mother to Mary Victoria, Scott and Michele. Of course, she was the grandmother to Olivia and Nathan."

The prosecutor reached down to the side of the podium and picked up another large placard with the picture of a smiling Scott Anderson.

"In December of 2007, Scott was thirty-two years old. The middle child between two sisters, he grew up in Carnation and graduated from Cedar Crest High School. He played football, was a very good student and graduated from the University of Washington. He worked construction, carpentry and married his high school sweetheart, Erica," he said as he panned the jury with his photograph.

The prosecutor set the picture down and lifted another.

"Erica Anderson, Scott's wife, was also thirty-two years old in December of 2007. She grew up in Carnation and graduated from Tolt High School a year before Scott. She was the young mother of Nathan and Olivia," he said.

Slowly, he displayed the picture of Erica, taken a number of years prior when she had been pregnant with her first child, Olivia. He set the picture down.

"Olivia was born in 2002. On December 24, 2007, Olivia was five years-old," he said as he reached down for another placard. "This is a photograph of Olivia Anderson."

The girl in the photograph was precious. She wore a red fuzzy sweater with small cartoon cat patches on the front of it. She had sandy brown hair and dancing brown eyes.

Judge Ramsdell looked down with his hands clasped and his lips slightly pursed.

"Nathan Anderson was born on December 10, 2004 and had just turned three years-old on Christmas Eve of 2007."

The jurors did not want to see the next picture. Some of the jurors worried it was going to break their hearts. Little did those jurors know how really close to the truth they were to become.

Nathan wore a light blue football jersey with a t-shirt underneath. His profile had a piano behind him. He had fine blonde and brown hair. His blue eyes and smile stung the jury in its countenance of innocence and happiness.

The prosecutor slowly set the picture down and grasped the sides of the podium with his hands. He took a breath and continued.

"Members of the jury, Christmas Eve of 2007 was like Christmas Eve in many homes all across America. That afternoon, there was a roast in the oven and a Christmas tree was up and decorated. Judy was wrapping presents back in the craft room. Wayne was watching television."

"He was in the family room, relaxing, because for Wayne, Christmas Eve was *his* holiday. That's when he liked having his children and grandchildren over. In fact, a big family get-together had been planned for that afternoon. There would be presents and they would celebrate the holiday. He knew that Michele and her boyfriend were coming as well as Scott, Erica and the two grandchildren. They would be there late in the afternoon," O'Toole told the jury. His voice was easy and calm.

Some of the jurors stole glances at the defendant.

"Perhaps," Scott O'Toole continued, "the oldest daughter, Mary Victoria Anderson, would be coming over on that holiday evening."

The prosecutor carefully reset a page. He looked at the jurors.

"At about four o'clock in the afternoon, on December 24, 2007, the defendant, Michele Anderson and Joe McEnroe got into that truck, drove up the driveway to the main residence and walked onto the porch. They walked through the front door and everything changed."

"At some point, Joseph McEnroe, by Michele's design, went back into the craft room to help Judy wrap Christmas presents while Michele confronted her father in the living room. His role was to distract Judy while she shot Wayne. A toy truck was on the floor in the craft room. It would never be wrapped."

"Michele Anderson fired her first shot at her father and, in all likelihood, missed. Then, her 9 MM jammed after it got caught in the fabric of the sweatshirt she was wearing. It jammed, she panicked and Joseph McEnroe rushed into the room, pulled out the .357 and held it up to Wayne's head. He fired a shot."

Not one juror moved in his or her seat.

"Judy ran into the living room area of the house from the craft room. She saw that Wayne had been shot in front of her and began to scream. Judy ran into the kitchen, trying to escape but she was trapped. She was pinned between the wall of her kitchen and the refrigerator in a corner."

"Joseph McEnroe then advanced on her and fired a bullet into her neck which lodged in her spine. She collapsed to the floor. And then he shot her in the head. Wayne and Judy were now both shot dead and the killers wondered what to do. Well, there was more," Scott continued.

"Because this was Christmas Eve and Scott, Erica and the children were on the way over."

"When Michele Anderson spoke to detectives and was asked why she had done it, she told investigators that she had done it because her brother owed her a lot of money. Further, her parents wanted rent from her after living in the mobile home down the driveway for a year rent-free. She was angry that her parents always seemed to side with Scott."

"Michele Anderson and Joe McEnroe described to detectives how they had dragged the bodies of her parents out of the house through the back door. Michele had dragged Judy's body to the shed in back. Wayne, however, required the two of them to drag Wayne's body outside since he stood six feet tall and weighed two hundred and seventy pounds. Since he was too heavy to put in the shed, they took a piece of old weather-worn carpet and threw it over his body to conceal it."

"The two of them spent the next hour or so wiping up all the blood in the house and there was a lot of it. They used towels and rugs to clean up and then they waited for the rest of the family to arrive around five o'clock in the evening," Scott explained.

He turned a page on his notes and then put his hands back on either side of the podium.

"Scott, Erica and the kids showed up and settled down, relaxing. Erica took off her shoes and sat on the loveseat. The kids began to play on the family room floor while Scott took his favorite seat at the end of the couch. At one point, Scott finally asked where their mother and father were. Michele Anderson had responded casually that they were in the bathroom."

The prosecutor paused and turned a page.

"And then she began to argue with her brother about the money she said he owed her. She wanted her money back and she wanted her car back. While she's talking to Scott, he's seated on the couch; she's standing behind a Lazy Boy chair, her father's favorite chair. She's shielded from Scott in standing behind the chair. Hidden inside her sweatshirt, she had the .357 revolver. She argued with her brother while Joseph McEnroe was standing next to her because, as she told detectives, 'I was just going to shoot everybody. Joe was just there in case the gun got jammed.' At some point, she pulled out the .357 revolver. As you can imagine, Scott would have become alarmed."

"Scott's wife and children were less than six feet away. He was aware that his parents were mysteriously not around. He began to rise off the couch and when he did that, Michele Anderson cocked back the .357, pointed it at him and shot him in the face."

The prosecutor paused a moment and framed his notes on the podium with his hands.

"The bullet entered just below his mouth and eventually was found lodged in his lung. He was grievously wounded. He went toward Michele Anderson to get the gun away from her and they struggled across the room over toward the curtains. All that time, he knew his wife and kids were only feet away and in danger. Eventually, though, that gunshot wound was too much. He collapsed on the floor, lying on his back. He was not dead but unable to move."

Scott paused a moment.

"There was more because Erica was next. She was by the couch holding her children when her husband had been shot in the face. Michele Anderson hated her sister-in-law. After Scott had fallen on the floor, Michele Anderson then took the .357 revolver and turned it on Erica. She fired one shot that, in all likelihood, missed. But the second shot did not nor did the third. Erica was shot multiple times, at least two times by the defendant, who used the .357."

The prosecutor took a breath and continued.

"Erica began to scream and scream and tried to get away, to crawl away. What she managed to do, despite having been shot multiple times, was to climb over the back of the loveseat, across an end table as she tried to get to the telephone table. She wanted to call 911. And," O'Toole enunciated, "she managed to call it."

"The call was connected and logged in at 5:13 PM on December 24, 2007. Just as the operator answered, though, the line went dead. Erica then crawled back toward where her children were, in front of the couch. She collapsed on the floor, seated partially against the couch with her legs in front of her. She was seated upright but barely alive."

"Olivia was next. In all likelihood," O'Toole explained, "she had already been shot once. Of the four shots Michele Anderson told detectives she had shot at her brother, we know that at least one or two of them missed. The line of fire would have been such that Olivia would have been standing right behind her father when she was errantly shot in the abdomen."

"The bullet that struck Olivia in the abdomen had passed completely through her body, came out her lower back and lodged itself into a pillow that was on the couch. Olivia then crawled on the floor to where her mother had collapsed in front of the loveseat, facedown. She then tried to hide underneath her mother."

Jurors would do their best to keep emotion at bay. Even though they did not know the victims, their significance became more important by the moment.

"Meanwhile, Joseph McEnroe got the 9 MM unjammed. He then stood directly over Olivia as she was trying to hide underneath her mother and fired a bullet into the back of her head. That bullet came out the front of her head and lodged itself into the floor underneath her. And, next, Joseph McEnroe turned his attention toward Nathan. He pointed the 9 MM and fired a bullet into the left side of Nathan's head," Scott said as he raised his left hand and touched the side of his head

"The bullet passed completely through Nathan's head. Nathan was three years-old."

The prosecutor allowed his words to marinate in the minds of the jurors.

"There is no doubt that the person who did this, is sitting in this room and her name is Michele Anderson. She murdered three generations of a family including two children. Nathan was still in his diapers on the autopsy table."

Scott paused again and turned a page in his notes.

"To give you an idea of the coldness of this crime, you will hear from Dr. Harruff, who performed the autopsy on Erica Anderson. There was a large wound in her chest. Some of the deputies had even commented that it looked strange, beyond the stippling of the skin, the tiny gunshot residue markings that are the earmarks of a close contact shot. It seemed that there was hair around the wound."

The jury's eyes were transfixed on the prosecutor.

"The Medical Examiner removed the bullet and found similar hairs as to those that surrounded the wound. He referred to the wounds as 'kissing wounds' with the similarities between Nathan's head wound and the wound on Erica's chest matching almost precisely. It showed extremely close contact at the time of the injury from one bullet."

"Nathan had crawled into his mother's arms for safety, holding his head close to her heart. The bullet that went through Nathan's head was the same that took his hair and skull fragments into her chest. That clump of hair and bone fragment inside of her was not Erica's but Nathan's. In the final, furious, last moments of her life, she had looked into the eyes of the man and the woman who were killing her family."

Somehow, the prosecutor had kept his tone free of empathy or anger.

"They then turned the gun on Erica and fired a shot between her eyes. She had been shot six times total with twelve bullet wounds."

"Ladies and Gentlemen," Scott said. "This is a serious case and I would ask you to examine all of the evidence presented to you. All of the evidence, in its totality, reaches far beyond a reasonable doubt that the defendant committed the crimes she is accused of. At the time of closing arguments, I will ask you again to find the defendant, Michele Anderson, guilty of six counts of aggravated murder in the first-degree. I will ask you to find her guilty of the murder of Wayne, Judy, Scott, Erica, Olivia and Nathan Anderson. Thank you."

The prosecutor picked his things up from the podium and solemnly walked back toward Michelle Morales and Detective Tompkins. The courtroom felt as if everyone had just run a lengthy marathon and people needed time to breathe. The room and its occupants welcomed the time to exhale.

"Mr. Sorenson?" the judge asked as he called attention to Anderson's defense attorney. "Do you have anything for the State?"

David Sorenson wore a light gray suit with a white shirt and gray and black striped tie.

"Good morning, Your Honor. We would like to reserve our opening argument. Thank you," he said. Just as quickly as he had stood up, he sat down.

"All right," Judge Ramsdell responded. "Thank you very much."

Very few of the jurors, if any, would have understood what had just taken place.

"Ladies and Gentlemen," the judge said, "what we're going to do at this time is take the morning recess. When you come back, then you will start to hear the State's evidence."

87

The jury was excused to the jury room located at the back of the courtroom. They silently walked while most of them looked at their shoes as they left the courtroom. It was not until they were in the jury room and the door was secured behind them, would they realize what an island each of them was stranded upon.

Those first fifteen minutes in the jury room represented the first test of their integrity as a unit of fifteen and it was probably the most difficult challenge they had to face so far.

Somehow, they had to remain silent and avoid any discussion of the horrors they had just shared.

DAY 5 Part 2
January 25, 2016

KISSING WOUNDS

While the jurors were in the deliberation on their first recess, I was seated in the gallery.

"Are you with the media?" somebody asked.

I turned around to see a lady seated with an iPad in her hands.

"Sort of," I answered. "I write books on trials and I'm a trial reporter for an Internet talk show called, Trial Talk Live."

"Never heard of it," she said.

I gave her a business card with my social media contact information on it.

"Are you with the family?" I asked.

"I'm here to make sure Michele's rights aren't violated. I've already seen what the system has done to her. I spent over four years being incarcerated with her," she said.

I was taken aback.

"They had her in the Psych Ward for two years. Can you imagine? I'm a Pro Se attorney and it's clear that the whole system is stacked against her. Even this O'Toole guy, he's a criminal. He should be locked up for what he's done to her," she said.

"Ah," I responded as I turned back around and pretended to be busy with my notes.

After what seemed an eternity, the jury returned. On each of their seats, a blank spiral notebook awaited their return. Each juror picked it up as they sat down while some opened the book and readied a pen.

Detective Scott Tompkins was called to the stand for the State. The detective stood at average height and was slightly stocky. He wore a black suit with a white shirt complimented with a red, gray and black striped tie. He was soft-spoken and easy to listen to. He was confident without being arrogant and even, some would say, amiable.

Scott O'Toole handled the introduction of the lead detective quickly and efficiently.

"In regards to our next exhibit, Exhibit #1, is it common to video tape crime scenes?"

Tompkins looked toward the jurors and then back at Scott. "Over the years it has become a valuable tool."

"Why is that?"

"Any crime scene is in a constant state of deterioration," Tompkins explained. "We do everything we can to protect a scene but as any investigation continues, it will deteriorate every time a new investigator arrives. Once a crime scene is secured, the video can help us out later."

Scott slid a CD out of a sleeve and handed it to Morales to insert in the device. He turned around and looked at Tompkins.

"Can you give the jury an idea as to how you were called to the scene?"

"A 911 call had come in at 8:10 AM regarding a possible multiple homicide or murder. It was an evolving situation with increasing reports of more bodies being discovered. I was given the case by Sergeant Gates and arrived on the property at 9:15 AM," Detective Tompkins recalled.

"Can you give us an idea what the scene looked like at 1806 346 Ave Northeast?"

"It was a cold and wet day. It was still pretty dark at that time. Multiple deputy vehicles had already arrived on the scene. Crime scene tape had gone up and the road was secured down by the gate," Tompkins said. "We had a discussion down on the road. We did not know if there was an active shooter still on the property. We also had someone on the line with an operator from 911. We needed to extricate her from a location inside the residence without getting harmed ourselves."

I noticed a good number of jurors utilized their notepads.

"Was there an active shooter on the property when this video was taken?"

"No, there wasn't. The video was taken after the property was contained. It's a sizable area," he said.

Scott looked toward Michelle as she pressed 'play' on Exhibit #1, a video.

The jurors watched in rapt attention as they set their pens aside.

The detective narrated the soundless recording as which began at the base of a driveway. A weatherworn wooden post held a collection of mismatched mailboxes in various stages of age. The rough, gravel driveway was under a tunnel of unkempt trees that extended into the forest. The dirt was black from the drizzling rains. The side of the road was lined with ferns while the trees reached into a cloud-filled dark sky.

The walk up the driveway detoured about halfway up and to the left as the camera came upon a stand-alone singlewide trailer. The yard had patchy and overgrown grass. Across from the single residence, a lean-to garage exposed two vehicles: an old truck and a powder blue 80's IROC Camaro faced outward.

The jurors watched as the camera came up the steps of the trailer and as it peered inside into darkness.

"What was it like inside?" Scott asked.

"It was kind of strange and eerie," Tompkins recalled. "It was cold, dark and damp. I remember the interior of the singlewide trailer being very messy and dirty. You could smell old food and mold from the dirty dishes in the kitchen. What I thought was really odd was that it seemed colder inside the residence than it was outside."

The camera then retreated down the steps and paused to pan over a fire-pit with ashes. Partially burned papers were scattered about. The fire-pit border was made of rocks of various sizes. It was primitive and blackened.

Detective Tompkins explained that, although the jurors could not hear it, the helicopter that buzzed overhead was of the Sheriff's Department.

At the top of the driveway, a modest brown house loomed

against a dark forested background. A front porch light was on. Police tape surrounded the perimeter of the house. The camera slowly moved up the porch steps to a screen door. Against the wall, a large old tin held an unstrapped umbrella, its handle exposed, ready for the next use.

Thankfully for the jurors, the video journey did not go inside but turned along the sidewall of the house. A large garage was on the left of the house. There were a lot of random vehicles on the property. One could not tell if some of the vehicles were in working condition.

The camera paused at a window on the side of the home. It focused on a hole in a window. The jurors did not have to be told it was a bullet hole,

In the backyard, its grass overgrown, a doghouse was seen along a far edge. In the center of the lawn, garden and patio items were centered under a canvas gazebo, which offered the items little protection from the regular Northwestern rains. A rusted swing set stood in the long grass, while, some distance away, an old shed begged a further look as the camera walked forward.

It was not the open door of the shed that drew the interest of the person who took the video but the white and wet bundle that was in front of the door. The camera peered closer and it became the first view of a victim. It was Wayne Anderson covered in a roll of carpet scrap.

The open doorway of the shed saw the feet of Judy Anderson.

Michelle Morales pressed 'stop' on the exhibit when the video went dark. The judge allowed the jurors a break.

Upon the resumption of court, Scott O'Toole and Detective Tompkins discussed Exhibit #2, an extensive collection of still photographs taken on the property via the same route of the video the jurors had just seen. In the sequence, they took their first journey into the house.

It was impossible for any juror to be mentally prepared for the impact of the first images.

The jury saw Scott Anderson, deceased, just inside the doorway; his body in a prostrate position and the blood was dark. At another point, they saw a picture of Erica and Nathan. They were both deceased and laid only feet from each other by a couch at the far end of the room.

Although they saw the rest of the house, which included the craft room, the computer room, kitchen, dining room, bathroom, laundry room and the two bedrooms, the only images they would truly remember were the first images of the deceased. Although Olivia was in the pictures, the jurors could not distinguish her from the clothing folds of the body of Erica.

A journey into the home of the Anderson's had begun the process of scarring the juror's hearts. The jurors would respect that the prosecutor had left the pictures of those murdered on the screen for only moments. He was doing as he had promised during jury selection, that the pictures of violence would not be gratuitous and they would only be shown when absolutely necessary.

Detective Tompkins completed his segment of testimony before the lunch recess.

Tiffany Alcorn testified after lunch. She had medium length reddish-brown hair and wore a black pantsuit. She had been a 911 dispatcher for nine years and was now a custodian of 911 call records. She spoke in a soft tone especially in comparison to Michelle Morale's distinct and strong voice.

Michelle Morales stood perpendicular to the jury behind a podium that faced the witness. She wore a black business suit with a conservative gray blouse. She had long black, slightly curly hair and walked with confidence.

Exhibit #5 was entered into evidence. It was the 911 log of calls made to and from Wayne Anderson's residence from the period of December 24, 2007 through December 26, 2007.

A recorded call made on December 26, 2007 at 7:58 AM was processed into evidence listed as Exhibit #6, while Exhibit #7 was a recorded series of calls made on Christmas Eve.

"According to the 911 log, the call made from Wayne Anderson's home was made at 5:13 PM on December 24, 2007," the witness explained. "It was dispatched to the King County Sheriff's Office at 5:19 PM with the suggestion that party noise or arguing could be heard. It was an open line hang up."

"Is there a term commonly used when you reference this type of call?"

"They are known as dropped calls," Tiffany responded.

Michelle Morales walked from the podium to the prosecution table and quietly directed Scott to play the CD recording. She turned down the lights.

The jurors listened intently as the seconds long 911-recorded call consumed the courtroom.

"9-1-1, please state your emergency," the operator asked.

In the background, faintly, two female voices were heard as they cried. Then, words could be heard but they were unintelligible. The recording stopped.

"9-1-1, please state your emergency," the operator asked again as the call was disconnected.

The chilling recording was only eleven seconds in length.

Nobody moved when the next audio began. It was the same dispatcher as she followed up with a return phone call to the residence, as was protocol in dropped calls.

The electronic ring of a phone could be heard. It rang five times before the call went to a voicemail.

"This is King County 911. We just received a call from this line. We have dispatched authorities to your residence. Please call us back if this call was made in error."

"When did the police arrive on that location according to the log?" Michelle asked.

"They would have arrived at 5:45 PM. The gate at the base of the driveway was locked and the police did not have cause to go beyond the gate," the former dispatcher responded.

"There was another call from that residence on December 26, 2007, wasn't there?"

"Yes," Tiffany said as she glanced at her notes. "The call was made from the landline of Wayne Anderson's residence at 7:58 AM by Linda Thiele. She stayed on the call a significant amount of time until the first authorities got on the premises."

"Thank you," Michelle said. "No more questions."

Judge Ramsdell looked up and toward the defense table where David Sorenson and Colleen O'Connor sat with the defendant between them. "Cross examination, Counsel?"

David Sorenson stood up. "No, Your Honor."

"Very good," the judge said. "State's next witness?"

Scott O'Toole stood up and pressed his tie lightly against his shirt. "The State would like to call Mary Victoria Anderson."

The jury watched her intently as she was sworn in and began her testimony. Her voice was tremulous and hard to hear at times. Scott O'Toole handled her respectfully as she revealed that Wayne had adopted her when she was five.

"You were familiar with the home at 1806?" Scott asked at one point.

"I grew up in that home," she answered. I lived there since 1980 and lived there with Scott and Michele."

"How did you know Erica?" the prosecutor inquired.

Mary put a tissue to her eye and took a deep, controlled breath.

"She was my brother's only love," she finally answered.

Scott then showed the witness every member of the Anderson family, one by one, which she identified. She particularly struggled with her emotions through the presentation of the pictures of Olivia and Nathan.

The jurors tried not to look too intently at the witness who resembled Suzanne Somers with her long blonde hair and tall stature.

"Let me ask you about Christmas of 2007," Scott suggested delicately. "Did you make contact with Judy on December 23, 2007?"

Mary nodded her head.

"We talked over the phone. Judy and Michele were at Target buying Christmas presents. Judy had bought her a Simpsons' movie or something. I remember Michele asking in the background if I would be there on Christmas Eve."

"What did you tell her?" Scott asked.

"I told her, through Judy, that I loved her and I planned on being there. It was a little odd to me since she had ignored me for the prior three months. But, she was my sister and, well, I used to love her," Mary explained.

"I understand," Scott said. He paused a moment. "Were you at the residence on Christmas Eve like you thought you would be?"

She put her head down, wiped her eyes and took a breath before she looked at the prosecutor.

"I was supposed to be there and I planned on being there. It was important to Wayne that we all gather together at his favorite holiday. But, my son got a pretty bad cold. I didn't want to spread his germs to the whole family and make everyone sick. I cancelled at the last second."

"Did Michele ever express that she wanted to harm her parents," Scott asked carefully.

Mary wiped her eyes again.

"Sorry," she said softly. "We were coming back from Monroe a couple months prior. All of the sudden, Michele flipped out. She started saying that she hated mom and dad and she really hated Scott. She said she wanted to kill them. That's how angry she was."

"Did you ever tell Judy, your mother, about it?" Scott asked.

Mary nodded her head. "I told her and we talked about it. We didn't take it seriously. Who would?"

"Did you ever talk about your mother's will?"

"We did but it was just off the wall crazy..."

"Objection!" David Sorenson suddenly interrupted. "Hearsay!"

"Sustained," Judge Ramsdell responded.

Scott O'Toole changed his direction. "Did you ever know Joseph McEnroe?"

"Yes," she said.

"What did you observe about him?"

"I didn't know him all that well. He was my sister's boyfriend," she explained. "Well, they had been living at the lower residence for about a year. My mother and I had discussed their living there rent-free. It was recently decided that she should do her part and pay some rent. I think there was hope that it would inspire her to get out and get a job since she had lost her job a year prior. I don't think Joe had worked for a few months."

"Did you have an occasion when you saw her flip out again?" Scott asked.

"She and Joe were making brownies. Apparently, Joe had not made them perfectly and Michele lost it..."

"Objection!" Sorenson interrupted again. "Irrelevant!"

The prosecutor moved along as the judge sustained the objection. "When did you last see Michele?"

"I can't exactly remember," Mary responded hesitantly. "I would say it would had to have been three months before. We went out for chips and salsa in Monroe."

"And your mother?"

"The last time I saw her was three days before," she answered. She wiped at her eyes with a tissue clutched in her fingers.

"Thank you, Mary," Scott said as he walked to the prosecution table and took his seat.

"Good Afternoon," David Sorenson said as he walked to the podium to cross-examine. "You were talking with Mr. O'Toole about a drive you took with Michele from Monroe to Carnation. Am I right?"

"Yes," she answered.

"That was about three months before the incident on Christmas Eve?" he asked.

"Yes. We were driving back to her home," she said, trepidation in her voice.

"You said she flipped out? That she wanted to kill your parents?"

"Yes?"

"I have to ask you," David remarked pointedly, "why didn't you call the police?"

Mary Anderson lightly shrugged her shoulders. She seemed on the verge of tears. "Why? It's just emotional stuff. People say things. I didn't think she was serious."

"No further questions," the defense attorney said.

It would not be a moment too soon before the jury was relieved of their duty for the day. There were a million thoughts running around in their heads as they made the journey home or to their jobs. The pictures of the crime scene almost paled in comparison to the testimony of Mary Victoria Anderson. Her significance would not elude the jurors.

Few jurors would sleep soundly after their first day. It would be fitful and lonely, their thoughts only to be contained within the deep reaches of their minds, vocalization not allowed by the Court. Images would roll around and resurface with visuals of the day. All would try to avoid thinking too deeply about the last moments of the six victims.

Most of the jurors would not be able to get Erica and Nathan out of their minds as they thought of Scott O'Toole's opening statement and the words of a medical examiner that spoke of 'kissing wounds' and the final moments of a mother and her children.

THERE'S BEEN A MURDER

Colleen O'Connor was already seated at the defense table when I sat down. Moments later, Michelle Morales was followed by Scott O'Toole, wheeling a thick briefcase of files as they entered the courtroom. Michelle took a seat at the prosecution table and began setting up the electronics. Detective Scott Tompkins arrived and took a seat next to her.

Scott O'Toole, dressed sharply in a black suit, white shirt and diamond patterned blue tie casually walked up to Kim, the court reporter and greeted her. He then went to the other side of the bench and greeted Suza, the Court clerk. They had a brief discussion that finished with him smiling warmly at her. He made his way to the front row where the family of the victims were seated and extended his hand and warm wishes to each one.

Judge Ramsdell came out from a door behind the bench and made his way to his seat while the court stood. He asked Scott O'Toole to introduce the proceedings by stating the case, defendant and case number. The judge then asked if the attorneys had anything before the jury was called out.

The prosecutor stated his calendar for the day had two witnesses scheduled.

David Sorenson, however, stood up quickly. He wore a brown suit, beige shirt and yellow and black striped tie.

"Your Honor, the defense objects to the prejudicial testimony that we expect from Pamela Mantle. The jury does not need to hear about character traits or sports the victims played or even their grades in school. It's too prejudicial to our defendant and should excluded."

"The jury needs a complete and accurate depiction of the lives of the victims, which Pamela Mantle can provide. For example, it is important that the jury knows that Scott played football when he went to Cedar Crest High School. Jurors need to know who the victims were," O'Toole argued.

Judge Ramsdell nodded his head.

"I tend to fall on the side of the State. I think we can set parameters but I cannot make a blanket prohibition.

"Thank you, Judge," Sorenson responded. "I suggest that information on Olivia, such as the State's contention that she liked to dance and she liked horses be excluded. It's irrelevant."

The judge thought about it for a moment and then rendered his decision.

"I think it's fair and appropriate that the jury get a sense of who the victims were. I am going to deny the motion. Go ahead and bring the jury."

The first witness was called to the stand and sworn in after the jurors were seated. Pamela Mantle wore pressed blue jeans with a green sweater finished with a red vest. She had shoulder length blonde hair and wore black-rimmed rectangular glasses. While Mary Anderson had carried a countenance of fragility, Pamela contrasted her in her stern confidence.

Scott quickly established that Pamela knew each of the victims as he showed her an array of pictures.

"Erica was my daughter," she stated when she identified a picture taken at Erica's baby shower in 2002.

"How did you know Wayne and Judy?" the prosecutor asked.

"I've known them since 1992. My daughter and Scott had been together for seventeen years. Erica was Scott's high school sweetheart. We would get together three times a year for the big holidays," Pamela said. "Judy worked for the post office in Carnation for many years."

"Can you tell us a little about Scott, your son-in-law?"

"Scott graduated from Cedar Crest High and then went to the University of Washington where he got his business license. I think he originally wanted to be an engineer like Wayne but he was not very good at math so chose business instead," Pamela explained. "He graduated in 1999 and went into the construction business. He worked for Mid-Mountain Construction in Kenmore for the prior six years or so."

"When was the last time that you saw him?"

"Thanksgiving Day of 2007," she answered.

O'Toole picked up a picture of Erica and ensured the jury saw it.

"Tell us a little about your daughter, Erica."

"Well, throughout high school, she had worked at the Kid Smart in Bellevue. She was very driven and had a good head on her shoulders. She was never afraid to work," Pamela said. "After graduation, she went to the Art Institute in Seattle. She was very creative. She got a job at Sportee's, starting out as a baker and then became a bakery manager. After that, she worked in accounting and had moved to being in charge of payroll."

Everyone's head turned when there was a slight commotion at the courtroom doors. My elation turned to chagrin when I saw the Pro se Attorney from the day prior appear. Although I did not make eye contact, I could hear what she was doing. She made no effort to be silent. She unzipped her bag and rustled around for something. She dropped an item on the oak bench next to her. Next, I heard her tapping loudly on her iPad.

"When did she marry Scott?" the prosecutor resumed, once peace and quiet had settled back on the courtroom.

"She got married in 1999. Erica had Olivia on March 10, 2002. Nathan was born on December 10, 2004," she stated.

"When did you last see Olivia and Nathan?"

Pamela pursed her lips slightly.

"That would have been December 22 of 2007. I used to talk to Erica daily. She was not only my daughter, we were best friends," she recalled. "I could not make it on Christmas Eve and planned to see her on the 27th. I did talk to her three times on the 24th. She was going to go do some last minute Christmas shopping at Kohl's and Fred Meyer's. I spoke with her at ten, one-thirty and finally at three-thirty. She was going to be driving from Black Diamond to Carnation so she could arrive around four in the afternoon."

"When did you learn of the murders?" Scott inquired.

"It had been a day and a half since I had last spoken to Erica and that was extremely weird. She and I spoke every day," she said emphatically. "I kept calling her phone and it would go directly to voice mail. Then, I tried to track down Scott and went to Kenmore. Scott had not shown up for work, which was very unlike him, too. Nobody knew where they were. At some point, when I got home, I learned from the King County Sheriff's Department that they had all been murdered."

"Do you recognize this photograph?" Scott asked.

He looked toward Michelle Morales as he signaled for the next picture.

Pamela looked at it for a moment. "The picture was taken in 2002. It was taken in the living room at Christmas time. Scott is on the left seated next to Joseph McEnroe and Michele Anderson. There's Erica with her daughter when Olivia was just a baby."

In the photograph, Michele Anderson did not look wholly different than she did as she sat in the courtroom. It was their first look at Joseph McEnroe. Some might say he resembled Bob Seger, as the rock star looked in the 1970's with his long black hair and dark beard with mustache. Others might say that McEnroe resembled Charles Manson.

"When did you last see Michele Anderson?" O'Toole asked.

"I last saw her at a Target in 2006. She and Joe were looking at video games or something," Pamela answered. "I didn't know very much about Joe."

"Do you recognize Michele Anderson in the courtroom today and can you point her out to us, if you do?"

The witness pointed toward Anderson who wore a mauve blouse and black pants. She did not make eye contact with her brother's mother-in-law and, instead, looked toward her lap.

"I do," Pamela responded. Her voice was flat but her eyes showed discontent.

The prosecutor then walked to the CD boom box located in front of the Court clerk. He put Exhibit #7, a cassette tape, into the player as the jurors looked on. Even though they had already heard the exhibit once, they would listen to it again as if it were the first time.

Pamela Mantle listened with her head down as the eleven-second tape played.

"9-1-1, please state your emergency," the voice said.

At first, one could only hear a hiss in the background of the recording.

"9-1-1," the operator repeated. "Please state your emergency..."

Far away, it sounded like sobbing.

"Hello? Hello?" the operator asked.

The sobbing became clearer and it was of more than one person. Everyone in the courtroom listened intently.

"Hello?" the operator asked again.

One could definitely hear more than one person crying.

"...no, no...not the kids..."

Michelle pressed stop on the recorded call.

"Can you identify the voice you heard on the phone?" Scott asked Pamela.

"Yes, I can," she responded firmly. "It's my daughter, Erica."

The jury would have found Pamela Mantle credible.

Defense attorneys, David Sorenson and Colleen O'Connor, had no questions for Erica Anderson's mother.

A second 911 call was placed forty hours after the first call. It yielded a much different result.

The second caller, Linda Thiele, was the next person summoned by the State to the witness stand; a feisty woman, the same age as Judy Anderson. She revealed in her testimony that it was through Judy that she had come to work for the tiny, but busy, Carnation Post Office for eleven years. She worked six days a week and ten hours a day as a substitute mail carrier. Many a conversation had been shared in the mailroom, so Linda Thiele felt as if she knew Judy's family pretty well. Occasionally, she and Judy got together outside of work to share lunch, visit at each other's house and, sometimes, shop together at IKEA.

Linda Thiele arrived at work at 6:30 AM on December 26, 2007. All the postal workers knew the day after a holiday was extremely busy which was why Linda became extremely concerned when it was almost 7:00 AM and Judy had not arrived. She instinctively knew something was wrong. She could understand Judy being a few minutes late as she had a short route but definitely not a half hour late. The last time she saw Judy was on December 23 and nothing seemed amiss. She told her other coworkers she was headed to Judy's house. Something was wrong.

"So you went to the house," the prosecutor staged, "and where did you park?"

"Well, I pulled up and the gate was locked. I parked my truck in front of it. Even then, I knew something was wrong," Linda stated.

"How so?"

"The gate was locked. If Judy had left to work, the gate would be open."

"What did you do next?" O'Toole asked.

Linda settled in on the stand. Her hands were clasped in her lap as she told her story.

"I got out of the truck and went around the gate on foot. It's about a seven-minute walk up the dirt road. I remember it being very quiet as I walked up the hill. I didn't see anyone at the trailer on the property. I knew that's where her daughter lived. As soon as I got to the front porch, the next thing I noticed was that I didn't see the dog."

"Oh," Scott said to her. "You did not hear any barking?"

"There was just no dog. Normally, he doesn't bark. He waits to sneak up on you and bite your ankles," she answered as she smiled at the memory.

"Then what happened?"

"Right at the door, I got really suspicious. The screen door was ajar and that would have been unlike Judy to leave it that way. I knocked on the door and called her name a bunch of times and, of course, no one answered. I turned the doorknob handle and the door was unlocked! It didn't make sense that the gate would be locked at the end of the drive and this door would be left open. I pushed open the door..."

A short time later, Scott O'Toole pressed the play button on the boom box for the second time. Named as Exhibit #11, the jurors each held a transcript of the call in their hands. They could read along but they could not read ahead as advised by Judge Jeffrey Ramsdell. Although the jurors would one day be able to hear this 911 tape again in the deliberation room, the transcripts would not be allowed in.

The call was clear and the words succinct as Linda Thiele's voice came through the speakers from a time over eight years ago.

"9-1-1, please state your emergency," a female operator asked.

A breathless voice responded quickly. "There's been a murder!"

"How do you know that?"

"There are three bodies that I could see," Linda whispered frantically into the phone.

"What's your name?"

"Linda Thiele," she said. "Oh, my God. Oh, my God."

"Calm down, ma'am," the operator said. "I have police and fire on the way."

"I can't believe this. It was a man, a woman and a baby. They were lying on the floor. I didn't see any weapons."

"Is anyone in the house with you? Do you think someone is still there?"

"I don't know," she whispered hurriedly. "I'm in a back bedroom. All I saw were the bodies. I didn't stop to look at them really."

"Do you know if the bodies are cold?" the operator asked.

"Hold on," Linda said. One could hear the phone as it dropped.

"No, no, no," the operator said quickly but it was too late. "Hello? Hello?"

Soft noises could be heard in the background as everyone assumed she ran to check the bodies.

"Yes, they're cold!" Linda said when she got back on the phone. "It looks like they've been dead a long time. I checked the adults and they're totally cold. I couldn't touch the baby, the poor baby. My God."

"Linda, please don't leave the phone like that until my deputies get there. It's for your own safety," the operator admonished. "Do you know who they are?"

"Yes," Linda whispered. "One has to be Wayne and the other must be Mary. He was shot in the face and she looks like she was shot right where she was seated on the couch. It might be Judy. I can't tell as she's shot, too. She's my best friend. She was supposed to be at work at 6:30. I knew there was something wrong when she was late. I just knew it!"

"Are you in a safe place, Linda?" the operator interrupted.

Linda laughed a little. "Yes. You ought to see me. I'm on the floor in a corner, between the bed and an end table. I don't think anyone is here but I can't tell. I wonder if I should search the house."

"Stay on the phone with me," the operator ordered. "You need to stay right there until the deputies get there. Do you understand?"

"I do. I'm worried someone's going to shoot me, too. Hold on," she suddenly said as she set phone down again.

"Linda? Linda?" the operator called out with some frustration in her voice.

"I locked the door," Linda said when she picked up the phone another two minutes later. "I'm worried about getting my ass killed. Wait! Shh! Shh!"

"What is it? What do you hear, Linda?"

"I don't know. Maybe it was a dog. Maybe the house creaked. I don't know who's on the goddamn property! Where are the police? What's taking so long?"

"Don't worry, Linda. They are on the way."

"What's taking so long?"

"Well," the operator explained. "We did not have a unit in the area so a couple of vehicles are coming from Monroe."

"Monroe?" Linda repeated. "That's almost twenty miles away. Why didn't they send a car from Duvall? Even from Carnation? Isn't there a Sheriff here? Damn! I just heard something!"

"What did you hear?"

"I don't know! Can I go wait in the car? It's parked in front of the gate."

"Stay with me Linda. The deputies know I'm on the line with you. You said your car is in front of a locked gate? What kind of car and what color is it?" the operator prodded.

"Yes, in front of the gate. It's a blue or black Mountaineer. I walked around the locked gate. You better hope the police are in good shape. It's a long walk up the driveway. And tell them to check the house on the left down the road. The daughter, Michele, lives there. Maybe she did this. It has to be someone from the family. She's very unstable."

"You said someone else lives on the property?"

"Yes. One daughter lives out in Black Diamond and another daughter lives in the trailer down the road at 1910. My friend's house is at 1806. Just down the driveway is where Michele lives. Where's the fire department?"

"They are arriving now and staging the area. They have to check the property for intruders," the operator said assuredly.

"Do you know how scary this is? This is like your worst nightmare! My friend and two people are dead in the living room. Oh my God," Linda said as her voice trailed off.

"There is no need to worry, Linda. You are doing a great job. When is the last time you saw your friend?"

"It was just a few days ago. I think it was on Thursday. God, I'm a total coward," Linda added nervously.

"Did you touch anything when you went into the house?"

"No, I did not" Linda answered. "Well, I touched the front door. I saw the bodies on the floor and I just ran out of there. I went into the dining room and then into the kitchen. I couldn't find a phone. I left my cellphone at work. I didn't touch anything until I called you from the back bedroom."

"That's good," the operator offered.

"It must have been a .45 or a .38. The bodies had small bullet holes. The woman is the child's mother. I can't stop thinking about the poor little baby. You know? I'm wondering if there might be other bodies. I'm thinking that one of the children is missing. Maybe the female on the floor isn't Judy. Where are the police? I don't hear anything, yet!"

"I'm still with you," the operator said.

"Can anyone call the Carnation Post Office for me? I'm supposed to be at work. Tell them that I won't be in."

"Yes. Who do we ask for? Do you have a supervisor?"

"Just tell anyone," Linda whispered. "You can ask for Kim or Lori. Let them know that I am okay but won't be back. They need someone to run my route. The mail isn't going to quit because this happened. They can't be thinking postal office workers are dropping off the face of the earth. Where are the police? I don't see them, yet?"

"You're doing a great job, Linda. My deputies have arrived but they are still securing the premises for your safety."

A muffled sound could be heard in the background.

"Linda?" the operator asked.

"Yes?"

"The deputies are in front. They want you to come out now. Can you go outside?"

"Okay," Linda answered.

The call ended with the thump of a phone as it dropped.

Scott O'Toole stopped the tape in the boom box and walked back to the podium. He waited patiently with his hands behind his back as Kenya collected the jurors' transcripts.

"What happened after that, when you went out the front door?" O'Toole asked.

"I walked out the front door," Linda began, "and I put my hands behind my head. There were officers hiding behind trees and vehicles with six guns trained on me. They hollered that I was to make no sudden moves and to walk forward. I did as they said and then told them they needed to look for more bodies. I saw the deceased lady again before I left and it was not Judy. She would never leave her children and she had to be somewhere."

"Who was the lady?" Scott asked.

"Well, it wasn't Judy and I was pretty sure it wasn't Mary. I was all 'shocky'. My head couldn't keep things straight. It was weird. I still thought the other body was Wayne but nothing made sense," she explained.

"Let me ask you this," Scott said. "How long did you stay with the Post Office after the incident?"

The witness shook her head.

"I left about four or five months afterwards. I took over Judy's job. The thing was, I became paranoid. I kept thinking at every turn that someone must have been murdered if they didn't pick up their mail on time or were a few minutes late at work. It drove me crazy. I couldn't do the job, anymore," she responded remorsefully.

"You had mentioned on the call that you thought the daughter, Michele, might have done it. Why did you think that?" O'Toole asked.

"I don't know. Who would think anyone could do that? But, the front door being unlocked along with the driveway gate being locked told me someone didn't want somebody to come up the driveway. Judy told me about the arguments they were having over the rental and bills. Judy told me Michele was upset. It had to have been a family member. Who else would do it?"

"Thank you. No more questions," Scott O'Toole said as he gathered his things from the top of the podium.

"Mr. Sorenson?" Judge Ramsdell queried. "Your witness."

The attorney stood briefly. "No questions, your Honor."

At the end of the day, I realized that whether the jury knew that Olivia liked horses and dancing was not irrelevant. However, the pictures of a family who once lived would impact the jury enough, especially those of two innocent children.

Flanked by three officers, Michele Anderson was led out of the courtroom after the jury had exited.

She wore pink handcuffs.

DAY 7
January 27, 2016

CAUSE FOR CONCERN

When Kenya stepped up in front of the Court clerk at the beginning of the day's proceedings, I instinctively knew she was going to speak on a juror issue. The jury was still in the deliberation room. Kim, the court reporter, tapped on her machine as the bailiff spoke. The judge watched with patience while the defense and prosecution teams listened with interest.

"I just wanted to make the Court aware that I was approached by two Jurors in confidence this morning," Kenya said as she adjusted her glasses. She wore a calf-long black dress with a Zebra patterned blouse. If one did not know any better, she could have been a schoolteacher in the way she carried herself.

"Go ahead," Judge Ramsdell prodded.

"As I understand it, one juror has been bringing in a copy of The Seattle Times. This happened over the last two days. He has been leaving the newspaper out and it bothered these jurors that it was left on the deliberation table yesterday afternoon," Kenya explained.

Judge Ramsdell shook his head and sighed.

"Is there anything in the paper about this case?" he asked the attorneys.

Scott O'Toole spoke up. He wore khaki pants, a light blue shirt and blue silk tie.

"Recently, I can't tell you exactly what day this week, but there was a prominent article in The Times. It was on the cover of the Local page. It is all over YouTube, as well," he added.

"I have to ask, how many ways in the world are there in trying to create a mistrial for us?" the judge commented rhetorically.

He scratched his head thoughtfully.

"I have been handling juries for over fifteen years and the one thing I can say is that they really try and do the right thing. Case in point, the two jurors who came forward are trying to do just that. In the old days, back when we could afford to sequester juries, we had ways to eliminate the threat of contamination. Someone would remove any inappropriate articles from the newspaper ahead of time. But," he said ruefully, "we can no longer sequester. How do we know the juror actually saw the article?"

David Sorenson spoke up. He wore a charcoal gray suit and beige shirt complimented with a green tie.

"We might have to request a voir dire on the jury," he offered.

"If we do question the jury," O'Toole interjected, "we need to ensure that we don't alert this particular juror ahead of time."

"I'm not prepared to make a decision on how we're going to handle this. What I will do is remind the jurors of their admonishment and re-affirm that they need to avoid media at all costs," Ramsdell stated.

He briefly shuffled and organized some papers.

"Thank you for bringing it to our attention, Kenya. Go ahead and bring the jury in," he directed her.

Although a Seattle Times reporter named Sara had been in the gallery the last couple days, her absence was noticed by me today. I would love to have heard her reaction and, instead, kept my thoughts to myself. Whether the interest in the trial had been lost or whether the media could not afford to do it, the gallery was decidedly absent of any semblance of any media except for me. I was a bit surprised that there was no live-stream.

The jury marched in moments later, assuredly unaware of the courtroom drama that had built around one of its own.

The judge rendered an extremely long admonishment. He reminded them to be vigilant in their admonishment.

He looked over the fifteen members of the jury box. "I am reaffirming that you each make your best effort to avoid any and all contact with the media. Any information you get outside this courtroom could impact your ability to be a fair and impartial juror. We lay trust in you to adhere to the rules we have lain before you."

The matter was closed and the first witness of the day was sworn in, Deputy Ron Harrington. The seasoned officer was dressed in his police uniform and it took him a minute or so to fit in the chair with the gear on his belt.

"How long have you been in law enforcement?" Scott asked.

"I've been an officer since 1987. I spent the first third of my career working out of Honolulu," Harrington answered.

"When did you join the King County Sheriff's Office?"

"I joined the King County Sheriff's Office in 1998."

"What do you do now?" Scott asked.

"I drive a fire truck at Boeing Field. It's a responsibility that I am honored to do. Quite frankly, I enjoy it," he answered with a smile.

"Thank you," Scott said. "There came a time that you were called to an address in Carnation on Christmas Eve, 2007. Does that sound familiar?"

"Yes. I was one of the first deputies who arrived at the Carnation residence the night of the dropped 911. The only information I had, while making the twenty-minute drive from Duvall, was that a call had come into 911 and the dispatcher had said it sounded like a party might have been going on."

The jurors knew by then that there was not a party going on but, rather, the wails of a woman, who had made a final call to save her children.

"I need to ask. Had the call not referenced it was a probable party, would you have reacted differently upon your arrival?"

"Well," Harrington responded carefully, "had the call been identified differently, there may have been somewhat less caution toward the barrier the gate provided. If it had been conveyed that someone's life was in danger, there would have been cause to go past it."

"Were you able to elicit any corroborating information from any neighbors?"

"It's really rural out there," Harrington explained. "I was able to speak to one neighbor, the only neighbor within any distance to the home of the incident, who said he had heard nothing out of the ordinary."

"Did you hear or observe anything that might have indicated a party? Or, for that matter, that anyone was in distress?"

"The night had been rainy and it had been quiet outside. Nothing was heard including any sounds of a party. I eventually met with another officer, Deputy Mikael Brakebill, at the base of the gravel road driveway. We stayed about ten minutes and left the scene."

"Essentially, if I have this right, are you saying that you did not have cause to go past the gate?"

"Nothing seemed out of the ordinary," Harrington answered. "If we had heard or seen anything, we certainly would have gone past the gate."

"Thank you," Scott responded. "No more questions."

"Counsel?" Judge Ramsdell queried the defense.

"No questions," Sorenson acknowledged.

It seemed logical for the jury to find that the next witness on the stand was Detective Mikael Brakebill. He was a stocky man who wore a charcoal gray suit, blue shirt and gray and blue striped tie. Through Michelle Morales, the jurors learned that the deputy had been on the job less than a year. He was still in a probationary status due to his short time on the force in 2007.

His testimony regarding the events of visiting the Carnation home confirmed what Deputy Harrington had said. The only neighbors around had heard nothing strange. It was rainy and dark that evening, with no sounds emanating from the residence where the call had been placed from. He and Harrington made the decision not to go through the locked gate because they did not legally have enough of a reason to. The information relayed to them did not have the urgency of a life in danger and the silent environment confirmed they were making the best decision under the circumstances.

Michelle Morales, who wore a charcoal gray business suit, asked the deputy, "In your report, you made a casual observation of something odd. Can you explain your observation for us?"

Some people in the courtroom threw dirty looks at the doors when the Pro Se Attorney entered; an hour after the proceedings had begun.

The deputy straightened himself in his seat and continued.

"I had to make a decent drive to get there. The residence is way out in rural Carnation. It was a pretty long drive to get there. I thought it was odd that the vehicle in front of me was going in exactly the same direction the whole way."

"What kind of vehicle was it?" Michelle asked.

"It was a black S10 pickup."

"Why was that odd?"

"Well, you take a lot of roads to get out there. I thought it was going to the same location I was headed; and then it pulled to the side of the road a short distance from the driveway I was headed to," the deputy responded.

"Did you see how many occupants were in the vehicle?"

"I couldn't tell you."

"Any idea if it was a man or a woman driving?"

"I could not tell that either. There were rural mailboxes where it pulled over so I did not give it another thought. I heard what happened on December 26, 2007 and then I thought it was a strange coincidence."

"No more questions," Michelle said.

"When you approached the residence, did you use your lights and sirens?" Colleen O'Connor asked.

"No," the deputy responded.

"Did the other vehicle display his warning lights?"

"No, Ma'am. The information we had did not warrant their use."

"You talked to a neighbor, didn't you?" she asked as she referenced her notes.

"We did and we received no confirmation of anything out of the ordinary."

"You did not hear a party going on?"

"No, Ma'am."

"No more questions," Colleen said.

While the jurors waited patiently for the next witness, many of them chewed thoughtfully on the black S10 Pickup truck. They would have remembered from earlier testimony that Michele Anderson and Joseph McEnroe owned one. If the murders were in process at 5:13 PM, based on the 911 call, and the deputies arrived at 5:45 PM, based on their testimony, how could the defendant's truck be driving toward the residence? What did it mean?

Sergeant James Gray, a thirty-three year veteran with the King's County Sheriff's Office, took the witness stand wearing a light brown police uniform. It also took him a moment to adjust the gear on his belt so he could sit. He had reddish-brown hair and a long and full mustache.

Scott O'Toole questioned him proficiently and delicately. He and the witness utilized a series of pictures, each entered as an exhibit, as an evidence timeline of events.

"When did you first become aware of an incident in Carnation?"

"A 911 dispatch call came over all of our radios simultaneously at 8:00 AM on December 26, 2007," Gray responded.

"Where were you when the call came in?"

"We were having a meeting at a Starbucks over coffee in Snoqualmie. It's a routine we do every morning before the day begins."

"Where is Snoqualmie?"

"It's a rural city, about a half hour drive, northwest of Carnation," Gray answered.

"Who were the other deputies?"

"It was four of us including myself, Hastings, Walker and Orendorff."

"Thank you," Scott said. "So when the call came in, what did the four of you do?"

"We wasted no time making our way to Carnation immediately. Each of us took our own car and all of us drove in a caravan with lights and sirens the full distance to Carnation."

"Why did you use sirens?"

"The only information we had was fairly limited. A caller had reported three deceased at a residence and it was possible her life was in danger. One of the 911 operators still had the caller on the line. It was hard to tell what kind of situation we were headed into. Plus, all indicators were that the situation was fluid and time sensitive."

"Were you able to come up with a game plan before you got there?" Scott queried.

"I had formulated a plan on how the residence would be approached. Also, I executed a historical search on the computer to see what history the residence had on any prior 911 calls."

"What did you learn?"

"There was not much of a history except that the only call to 911 had been made on Christmas Eve, two days prior. With that limited information, I planned on the team going onto the property at high alert," Gray responded.

"Had anyone arrived prior to the four of you?"

"Yes. I saw the fire department staging the scene when we arrived. They were along the road."

"Had anyone gone past the gate?"

"No one had gone past the locked gate. We took our weapons out at the base of the driveway. As a matter of fact, one deputy carried an AK-47. We went around the locked fence and walked up the driveway in two pairs. We each scanned the woods and our surroundings for a possible shooter. Before we could get to the person who was still in communication with dispatch, we had to clear all the territory behind us," Gray recalled.

"What did you do after you crossed the gate?"

"We walked up the driveway with our guns drawn. We came upon a singlewide trailer, garage and lean-to half way up the driveway. We took the time to search the area before we headed toward the house at the top of the hill. We found nothing to be a threat and pressed forward with our guns raised horizontally to the ground. When we came upon the main residence, we did a cursory search of the property outside before making contact with the caller. It was a priority to get her out of the building and we wanted to make sure she was safe."

"Once you determined that there was no active shooter, what did you do next?" Scott asked.

"I told dispatch to tell the caller to exit the building."

"What happened after that?"

"Linda Thiele had come out with her hands behind her head and into the safety of deputies, despite the raised weapons. One of the officers took imprints of Linda Thiele's soles of her shoes. Although she thought it odd, she did not object. Once she was secure, the three of us cautiously made our way up the steps to the front screen door."

The courtroom was dark, with the only light coming from the series of exhibit pictures that were displayed on a projection screen across from the jury. The deputy spoke in the darkened room while the jurors waited to see the things they did not want to see.

Michelle Morales displayed one picture at a time while the Deputy narrated their first sights inside the residence.

The deputies had entered through the front door. Off to the right, they immediately saw a prostrate body lying on the floor; face up, with the arms stretched out a little to the sides. It was Scott. The first deputy checked the body for any signs of breathing by looking at the chest. It was important not to touch the victim to avoid the risk of contamination. It was soon clear that the victim was deceased.

Just to the left of the front door, a decorated Christmas tree sat in quiet repose. A large wrapped gift was under the tree, along with two Paper Mache stuffed gift bags. Cartoon characters adorned sides of the bags.

Beyond the first body, one could see a living room. Upon closer inspection, one could see a female victim on the floor, her head rested on the front of the loveseat. Some blood was seen and there was no sign of life. Lying almost underneath her, wedged between the coffee table and the couch, and enfolded in her mother's clothes, a small girl nuzzled. Perpendicular to the two embraced victims, Nathan lay face up on the floor.

The coffee table sat in the center of two surrounding couches. Snacks and Christmas candy were on the table ready for guests to enjoy.

Those were images the jurors would never forget. It went far beyond the scope that the imagination could serve with the only respite being the remarkable lack of blood at the scene. It would temper the image but the memory would be in each juror's dreams for a long time to come.

"So, at this point," Scott interjected, "what is your mindset as you are investigating the home?"

"Although we knew the residence was clear of an active shooter, we knew from Linda Thiele that there might have been more victims."

"Did anything in particular get your attention?"

"Well, in the kitchen, toward the back door, one of the deputies discovered blood. It was pink in color as if it had been diluted."

"What did you do next?"

"Before we could follow where the diluted blood led, we had to clear the residence. We searched each room and closet in the residence. We looked through two bedrooms, which included the back bedroom that Linda had hid in. The hallways, the computer room and the craft room were searched. In the craft room, a Christmas paper roll was in the center of the floor. It looked like somebody had been preparing to wrap a box."

"Did that tell you anything?"

"Not much except that this incident was probably a surprise."

"What were your next steps?" Scott asked.

"About thirty minutes later, we checked the perimeter of the forest and the structures in the back yard. We looked through a barn style two-story garage, checked a lean-to, fed the big dog waiting by the doghouse and finally came upon a shed. It looked odd at first sight."

"Why was that?"

"In front of the door, on the wet grass, there was a bundle of old Astroturf-patterned carpet. Underneath, the body of Wayne Anderson was discovered wearing only a T-shirt. He was face down with some blood apparent on the face. His jeans were pulled down to his ankles."

"Was there anything else that drew your attention?"

"Just beyond a partially open shed door, lay the body of Judy

Anderson."

"Was she clothed?"

"She was wearing white socks, jeans and a sweater. She was not wearing shoes."

Scott O'Toole was careful to leave the grisly images on the screen for as short a time as possible. The jurors looked concerned and bothered. The mood was heavy and sad.

It was certain that jurors would steal glances at the defendant. Her reactions would be important. They were sorely denied any emotion as she looked straight ahead while images on her right glowed during the narration of discovery by the sergeant. Each would have wondered how anyone could commit a crime of this nature. It was almost surreal.

"There came a point in time when you saw Joseph McEnroe and Michele Anderson, wasn't there?" Scott asked.

"I saw a black S10 Pickup come up the driveway at 11:00 AM that morning after the property was cleared. I witnessed two occupants getting out whom I later learned was Joseph McEnroe and Michele Anderson."

"Did you make contact with them at all?"

"I never talked to them. With the use of driver's licenses found at the scene, I was kept busy as I tried to match pictures to the faces of the deceased. The people from the black S10 Pickup would interview with someone else."

"No more questions," Scott finished.

After Scott O'Toole had taken his seat, David Sorenson walked up to the podium across from Sergeant Gray as he carried a legal pad in one hand and a pen in the other.

"I only have a couple of things," the defense attorney said. "You testified that the four of you were in the process of clearing the scene and you had gone to the singlewide trailer. Did you knock on the door before you entered?"

"I am not positive I knocked the first time we were clearing the area for any possible threats. There was a sense of urgency involved. The second time there, I knocked loudly and got no response," Gray said.

"Can you give us an idea of the state of the interior of the trailer? Was it neat and tidy? What was it like?" Sorenson asked as he kept his pen readied on his notepad.

"It was pretty bad in there," he answered. "There was garbage thrown about."

"Did you see any dead animals?"

The sergeant thought about it a moment. "Not that I recall."

"Did you maybe see a dead bird?" Sorenson asked.

"I think someone mentioned seeing a dead bird but I don't recall it. I just know the place smelled, it was filthy and I wouldn't want to live in it," Gray commented.

"Thank you," the defense attorney said.

At the conclusion of the late afternoon break, Judge Ramsdell held the jury back.

"Let's go ahead and call Juror #10," he told Kenya.

She walked to the jury room and extricated him from the fellow jurors. He walked briskly to his regular seat in the jury box. A tall man, with gray hair and dressed appropriately, took his seat.

"Thank you for speaking with us," the judge said, as he leaned forward on the bench. "It seems you have been bringing The Seattle Times newspaper into the jury room. Is that accurate and can I ask why?"

"I have a habit of reading the paper every day. I don't have time to read it in the morning," he answered.

"So, you read it when you commute here in the morning?" Ramsdell asked. "Do you take the bus?"

"I do," the juror responded casually.

"I have to ask if you have read anything on the case? How have you managed to avoid reading anything on this?"

"Yesterday, I saw the name Anderson at the top of the page and closed the paper. I didn't read it and I am following your admonishment not to read or see anything on the case."

"You haven't read anything?"

"Did you see any images?"

"No, Your Honor."

"Have any of the other jurors seen it or read any of the newspapers?" Ramsdell asked.

"No, they haven't."

"What do you do with it when you're done with it?" Judge Ramsdell asked. "Should you leave it in the jury room?"

"I'll put it in my briefcase. I will make sure that I do not bring it in again," he offered, contritely.

"I was just about to suggest that. We do not need to be bringing it in and I would suggest you have somebody review your paper before you read it."

"Yes, sir," he answered.

It was cause for concern not only for the life of the trial, but also for justice in the matter of six people who lay dead at the hands of another.

"I still wish we could sequester juries," the judge said as he closed the matter.

DAY 8
January 28, 2016

THE CHRISTMAS PRESENT

The lambs to the law had been corralled and trained. Juror #10 had been returned to the flock unharmed. If he were to bring The Seattle Times back into the jury room, his dismissal would be expected.

A thirty-five year veteran of the King County Sheriff's Department, Mark Orendorff, took the witness stand for the prosecution. He wore brown pants, a pressed green oxford shirt and a brown tie.

"What were you doing when the call came in for the incident in Carnation on December 26, 2007?" Scott O'Toole asked. He wore a crisp black suit complimented with a pink shirt and burgundy tie.

Orendorff looked toward the jury. His hands were clasped in his lap. "The call came over my radio while I was having coffee. It was a little after eight in the morning when the dispatcher alerted us."

"Can you give us an idea of the events that took place after you took the call?"

"At this point, there was some urgency to the matter because we did not know if there was a suspect on the premises," Orendorff explained calmly. "It took about twenty minutes for us to get up there. We used lights and sirens the whole distance. The location was pretty difficult to find as it is rural out there and few residences are marked very well, if at all."

There was a momentary pause as there was a commotion at the courtroom doors. Someone arrived late and I did not have to guess who it was.

"I got there almost at the same time as another officer, Walker," Orendorff continued. "He had a rifle and took cover. I followed suit until there were four of us. We passed the gate by going around it on foot and went up the driveway. We were on the lookout for a suspect on the property."

"Did you ever encounter anyone?" Scott asked.

"No," he answered. "A lot of vehicles were on the property but none were occupied."

"At some point, you entered the main residence?"

Orendorff nodded his head slightly and looked toward the jurors.

"I remember it was hard to see upon first entry. On the right, there was a deceased male on his back. I could see another figure beyond him near the living room couch that looked deceased."

"Why didn't you go up to the other person?" Scott prodded.

"Four of us were working on clearing and securing the residence. When one officer stopped to a safe point, a next officer would then lead the next few steps. We were essentially leapfrogging our way through the house," the officer explained. "I believe it was Walker who confirmed the female deceased by the couch and discovered the two children additionally."

"What did you do next?"

"It took us five minutes to clear the house. We saw a faint blood trail that led out the back door and eventually, through a search of the various out buildings, we came upon two more deceased. A female was behind the closed door of a shed and a male was found in front of the shed under a big piece of old carpet.

"How did you end up with the dog?" Scott O'Toole asked him at one point.

Orendorff smiled bemusedly and then looked at the jurors.

"It was a big black dog, maybe some Labrador in him. He was really skittish at first and distant. It was out by the doghouse while we were securing the property and then he just came up to me and laid down in front me".

"What did you do with it?"

"I realized he must have been hungry. I got some food from the cruiser, fed him, gave him water and he jumped in the back seat."

Some jurors would realize that the dog had lost his family forty-hours prior. It was a heartwarming gesture by Deputy Orendorff. It made him human.

Deputy Scott Walker, whom the jurors would have remembered as the fourth of the four officers who first walked the long gravel driveway the morning of December 26, 2007, followed with his testimony.

Just as Deputies Gray and Brakebill had testified the day prior, Walker confirmed that four officers approached the house on high alert after entering the locked gate, rescued the emergency caller and came upon the horrific scene. They were the first to see the results of an unexplainable event. All of the officers had set aside emotion and approached the situation with attention to safety as well as to detail. Their priority was the protection and integrity of the crime scene.

"Once you were in this house for the first time," Michelle Morales asked, "what did you think happened?"

"I thought it must have been a murder-suicide," he answered ruefully.

"No more questions," Morales finished.

David Sorenson, dressed in a gray suit, white shirt and green tie, stood up and walked to the podium.

"So, you said that you had done a search of the trailer to the left side of the road at 1810?"

"I did," he answered.

The attorney looked at his notepad and back at the witness.

"You testified that you found a dead bird in the mobile home. Is that right?"

"What kind of bird was it?"

"I don't know," Deputy Walker responded. "I don't even know why I remembered it. I had my gun drawn while searching for any threat. I looked down and saw a dead bird on the floor in the hallway. Then, I left."

"Thank you," Sorenson said. "No more questions."

Fire Chief Arthur Cole took the stand and was the most animated witness of the day. He had a large presence in the witness chair. He wore a navy blue suited uniform with five yellow stripes on each of his coat sleeves with various pins and honors affixed to the lapels. He had a gregarious and ingratiating temperament.

"Can you give the jury an idea of your experience with the fire department?" Scott O'Toole asked.

"I began in 1974 as a volunteer firefighter," he started with a booming voice. "In 1980, after three tries on the exam, I was hired for the Bellevue Fire Department. I have been there in various roles since. I retired at 8:01 AM on July 15, 2014."

"8:01?" O'Toole questioned.

"We work twenty-four hour shifts and we work from 8:00 in the morning until 8:00 AM the next. That's why we retire at 8:01," he answered proudly.

Scott smiled. "Very good. So, you don't fight fires anymore?"

"No. I fight fires in the office, not on the street. I'm way too old for that," he said with a chuckle.

Cole testified that on December 14, 2007, the well-seasoned firefighter had been one of the two medics asked to confirm the six DOA's at the Anderson residence. The official and proper way to confirm a death was through the use of two fingers to the carotid artery in the neck, he explained. It required that he move the deceased on a number of occasions. It took him ten seconds to confirm the deaths of each victim. His job on the scene was completed before noon on December 26, 2007.

The jurors' faces revealed that they had really liked Fire Chief

Arthur Cole.

After the completion of the morning break, Judge Ramsdell held the jury back in the jury room. "All right. Welcome back folks. Please be seated," he directed.

"Because it's come to my attention that there have been issues, I want to remind the folks in the gallery," the judge began, "please don't take any photographs in the courtroom without at least letting me know that you intend to do that, and with particularity, there should be no photographs that include the jury members themselves. So, if you are taking photographs, number one: quit."

I had no idea where the admonishment had arisen from as I spent my time with my attention to my notes. I had not even considered taking photographs. My pictures were best painted with words.

"Number two," Judge Ramsdell continued, "if you think you would like to take a photograph, please let me know what you want to take a photograph of first so that I can ensure that jurors are not being photographed because that would be inappropriate. Secondly, although I can't always hear what's going on in the gallery, resist the temptation to make muttering comments or facial expressions that could either be overheard by the jury, the attorneys or anything of that sort. Again, that would be inappropriate, regardless of who is doing it or for whatever purpose."

I had heard mutterings from the tardy guest behind me but had chosen to ignore them.

"So, again, I would urge you to comply with those directives, and if those directives aren't complied with, then remedial sanctions of some sort may have to follow and I certainly don't want to go there," the judge recommended. "So, with that, Mr. O'Toole, I think you are going to a detective; is that right?"

"Yes, thank you," the prosecutor acknowledged.

"Your Honor, can I approach? I'm a person from the gallery that feels that this was directed at me," the tardy lady suddenly said.

The court froze, thankfully outside the presence of the jury. The judge even seemed surprised and one would think he had seen it all.

"And you are? What is your name?" he asked.

"I'm {redacted}. I'm a pro se attorney," she said, a bit louder than probably necessary. "And I'm actually here..."

"Pro se attorney?" Ramsdell interrupted.

"I'm a pro se attorney," she repeated. "So I follow the same rules that any attorney who has a bar license does as far as ethics and what have you."

"Well, you're not involved in this case as a lawyer at all," the judge told her.

"I am a supporter of the defendant. I'm her only support in the room. I'm here as emotional support and so if I'm taking anything as a picture, nothing's being posted anywhere. I don't even have Cloud on this device," she exclaimed.

Judge Ramsdell looked on patiently.

"And just so you know, I'm only doing preservation of evidence on her behalf because I'm aware of the ineffective assistance in many cases, and so I come from that angle. So things might have been purported to you in that meeting that are not quite correct. I do have an interruptive disorder, which is pretty much toned down, and so I, whatever," she explained.

A few people in the gallery had turned around to look at her.

"So the likelihood that you were told somebody's taking pictures and didn't know about it, I didn't know we had to ask. I'm not media. I'm just a person preserving evidence as a spectator and, legally, I can do that," she advised the Court.

The judge did not look happy.

"What do you mean preserving evidence? I have no idea what you're talking about."

"Because depending on the outcome of the case, whether somebody needs appellate information, I'm preserving evidence that may be available to the defendant in the future only. And I can do that as a friend. That's all," she finished.

"Okay," the judge responded. "Well, no more photographs. Okay?"

"Okay," she said.

"You are welcome to stay here and watch the proceedings. No one is going to exclude you. But please resist the temptation to say anything or make facial expressions," the judge advised.

"And I understand that," she replied. "That's part of, you know, having the disability."

"And what was it again, Ma'am?" the judge inquired.

"I have an interruptive disorder. And I also have ADHD and PTSD," she added. "So, I'm documented with a disability. And, let me ask you why would you say I can't do pictures? Because I do know that the pictures are taken with the media."

"Partly because they are media and I am obligated to allow media to take photographs," he said. The judge looked surprised that the exchange continued.

"But regular people can't do it?" she questioned. "I don't, I do not understand that. I don't know that there's a gag order or anything else."

"There is not a gag order," the judge stated. "But this isn't a circus. And if I say everybody can bring in their cameras and take pictures, then all we are going to have is people with their phones taking audio and video recordings and that's not what we are here about."

"Right and I understand that. I'm not doing anything disrespectful," she informed the judge. "As, as, as just so the remainder of the people understood that I was only preserving evidence for Miss Anderson and that's it. That's as far as it goes."

"The bottom line is the evidence being preserved for Miss Anderson is the evidence that's on the Court record here. Okay?"

"And no pictures of the jury," she added. "I respect that one hundred percent."

"Thank you," the judge said as if the matter were settled.

"I sometimes have questions for attorneys on procedural stuff. They got funny about that as well," she said.

"Well, they..." the judge started.

"I merely got admonished for saying hello to her because she knows I'm here for support because my bus brings me late," she continued.

"Okay," the judge said. "The bottom line is..."

She interrupted him again. "I understand where you are, if you understand that what you were told was not quite what was happening."

"I can appreciate that, Ma'am," the judge said as he leaned

forward. "Let me explain to you one thing. My job here is to make sure that Miss Anderson and the State get as fair a trial as humanly possible under the circumstances."

"I understand that," she responded.

"A case like this has gone on for so long that has so many people interested in it, and so many people coming and going on a daily basis, that it makes this job almost impossible."

The pro se attorney again said she understood his position.

"Sometimes I have to remind folks of what they can and can't do, not because I'm trying to thwart their ability to observe what's going on or be attentive to the situation, but because I want to make sure that Miss Anderson gets as fair a trial as she can," he explained with deliberateness in his voice, "and that the State can get a fair trial too, so that nobody is going through this again five years from now. And, so, that's my motivation. If I offended you, I'm sorry."

"I concur with you. I think that how it was brought to your attention was incorrectly done. That's it. We're good," she said as she sat down.

He turned in his chair, straightened some papers and looked toward the Bailiff. The matter was closed when he asked Kenya to bring in the jury.

Scott O'Toole presented his next witness for the State, Detective James Allen, a twenty-six year veteran of the King County Sheriff's Office.

The Detective wore a blue suit, white shirt and green patterned tie and presented well on the witness stand with a calm and intelligent demeanor. He specialized in evidence collection and briefly explained the process of photographing and filming the scene, marking the scene with yellow, numbered stands, bagging and numbering evidence and coding it. He went into general detail about blood spatter collection as well as items to be removed for detailed inspections.

Exhibit #20 was entered into evidence, a live recording of the scene of the assaults.

At this point, the jurors had seen the still pictures of the crime scene throughout each of the four officer's prior testimony of the first arrival on the scene, and it had started to become easier to set emotion aside.

A silent film played on the projection screen across from the jury.

The camera walked slowly up the front steps of the home of Wayne Anderson. A juror would again notice the tin receptacle with an unclasped umbrella, its handle waiting for the next person to pick it up. They would walk through the front door. They would see the first body on the right as the camera panned slowly in the living room.

Some jurors did not look at the bodies but rather inspected things around the body. Whether it was the bloodstains or items that lain randomly on the floor, it all seemed important. Someone's brown, well-worn work boots with untied laces were slightly under the coffee table. Were these the shoes that belonged on Judy outside?

The jury's eyes followed as the camera slowly panned up a living room curtain, the imperfections in the cloth the result of three bullets going through three different spots. The camera came over the coffee table revealing an open box of Wheat Thins, open candy boxes and a variety of other items on the table. The juror would note that the many items on the table were not disturbed. If there had been a struggle, these would have been the first items to end up on the floor, especially given the location of the deceased.

The jurors saw the diluted blood on the kitchen floor and searched the floor for more signs of blood spatter, although most would not be familiar with the latter term. They looked for answers as the camera walked through each room of the house, including each bedroom, the computer room, the craft room and the bathroom. They would notice how undisturbed everything looked.

They looked at the Christmas tree when the camera panned around it and they would wonder whom the gifts were for. The bagged gifts surely must have been for the children. A tall, neatly wrapped Monopoly game-sized box leaned against a chair.

At the completion of the video, Detective Allen and Scott O'Toole discussed the procedures that pertained to the discovery and cataloging of evidence.

Jurors learned that every single piece of furniture from the living room had been removed for a crime reconstruction study.

And then Scott O'Toole entered Exhibit #23.

Nobody saw it coming.

"Do you recognize this item?" Scott asked Detective Allen.

Allen straightened himself in his seat. He held up the brown paper wrapped package and looked at an evidence tag on it. Satisfied, he answered, "I do."

"Where did you get this item from?" O'Toole asked.

"This was recovered by the Christmas tree in the hallway. There were a number of packages in the area. I believe we counted four packages for Nathan and four for Olivia. This was the other one," Allen recounted.

"Will you open it for the Court?" Scott asked.

Kenya gave him a tool to extricate the item from the brown wrapping paper. A sinking feeling would have entered many jurors' hearts when they saw the same wrapping paper as they had seen from the photographs taken near the Christmas tree in the Anderson home. It was a Monopoly game-sized box.

The Detective cut the edges of the brown packaging and then proceeded to remove the Christmas wrapping paper.

"Is there a gift tag on the paper?" Scott asked.

"Yes," the Detective answered after momentarily inspecting it.

"Can you tell us what it says?"

The Detective maneuvered his glasses to read it. "To Michele. Merry Christmas. Love, Judy."

"What is in the box?" the Prosecutor asked, a reference to the unopened gift inside.

"It appears to be a large set of assorted make-ups."

Scott O'Toole walked up to the witness while he asked the judge to approach.

"May I?" he asked as he reached out for Exhibit #23.

The prosecutor held the box by the long end, ensuring it was right side up. He turned toward the jury and slowly walked from one end of the jury box to the other making sure each juror had seen it.

In the moments that he slowly walked, no juror saw the make-up nor cared who had made the product. Instead, they saw a gift that was supposed to be opened the night that the gift-giver was executed.

The gift they saw would never be opened.

It was a stark reminder of the darkness of the crime. It represented what should have been but never was.

A family lost their life on Christmas Eve, as Judy's gift reminded the jurors, and there was something especially wrong with that.

Who could do something like that on Christmas Eve?

DAY 9
February 1, 2016

SIGN CUTTING

The departure of the media in the courtroom precipitated my discussion with my producer, Jarrett Seltzer, of Trial Talk Live. I reported on the proceedings once a day and it occurred to us that there might be an opportunity to set up a live-stream. There was a lot of interest in the trial. I made an informal request to the court the moment I arrived on Monday morning.

The jurors returned from their first three-day weekend feeling refreshed but anxious. At the outset of their weekend, most thought it would be a relief to be away from the trial, a welcome respite from a daily injection of murder. Instead, most found the weekend more troubling than relaxing. Those jurors who returned to work on Friday had to field questions from fellow workers and employers. Other jurors would find that their children and loved ones were curious. There was little peace from the trial despite being away from it. Even more disconcerting, the gerbil wheel of thoughts kept churning in their heads, relentlessly and unceasingly.

"How many days did you spend collecting evidence on the scene?" Scott O'Toole asked the first witness of the day, a continuation of testimony from Detective Allen.

The attorney stood behind the podium, perpendicular to the jury. He wore a black suit, white shirt and blue spotted tie.

Detective Allen, the thirty-one year veteran of the King County Sheriff's Office, wore tan khaki pants, a blue suit coat with a light blue shirt complimented by a yellow patterned tie.

"We collected evidence at the Carnation murder scene from December 27th through the 29th of 2007," Allen answered.

"How many bullets did you recover?" O'Toole asked.

The Detective leaned forward toward the microphone slightly. "We recovered fifteen bullets total."

"When you say total, do you mean just at the scene?"

"We recovered the bullets from both the scene and from the six autopsies," Allen responded. "Eight were found at the scene while six were found by the Medical Examiner. One bullet was never recovered. The bullet that went through the drapes and continued through the dining room window was not found."

Scott O'Toole looked up from his notepad and raised a finger.

"Earlier, it was testified that there were more than forty wounds to the victims, however, there were sixteen bullets to account for including the one never recovered. Can you explain why there is a variance?"

"Some of the bullets were shared between victims," he answered.

"No more questions," O'Toole stated as he made his way back to the prosecution table.

"Miss O'Connor?" Judge Ramsdell said as he looked toward the defense table.

"Just a few questions," she answered. She wore a long-sleeved beige sweater with a black skirt. "When you first arrived, Detective, was the gate open?"

The witness leaned forward. "It was closed. I believe that the lock had been cut at that point. We walked up from there."

Colleen adjusted her glasses. "When you went to 1910, the residence of Joseph McEnroe and Michele Anderson, did you force your way in?"

"We did," he said. "There was no answer. We made a forcible entry for a cursory look."

"Did you find any victims or suspects?"

"We did not."

"What did the trailer look like inside?" O'Connor asked.

"It was, well, messy," the Detective commented.

"Did you come across any dead animals?" the defense attorney asked.

"I don't remember any," he said after a moment of thought.

The attorney glanced at her notes.

"Now, you said you found two guns in the bedroom in your earlier testimony. Is that right?"

"Yes," he said. "A semi-automatic .380 pistol and a Walther Kurt PPK/S 9 MM were recovered."

"Were they loaded?" she inquired.

"Although they were loaded, there were no rounds in either chamber."

"You found a full box of .38 caliber bullets, didn't you?" she asked.

"Yes."

"If I may draw your attention to the Christmas tree room, wasn't there a gun rack with rifles on it?"

"Like the guns, it appeared none were involved with the crime. The rifles had a thick layer of undisturbed dust on them," the Detective stated.

"Can you tell us why ballistic testing was not done until 2009?"

"I do not have an answer for that."

Prosecutor Michelle Morales introduced Fernando Burton as the next witness, a thirty-one year veteran of the King County Fire Department. He was the partner of Arthur Cole, the Fire Chief, who was part of the two-man medic team that made the official medical diagnosis of death on the victims.

He confirmed what Arthur Cole had said, that four gunshot victims were found inside the 1806 residence and two victims were discovered deceased outside.

When it was his turn, David Sorenson asked the fire department veteran whether each, Fire Chief Cole and himself, had checked six bodies and he replied that one medic checked the bodies found outside while the other checked those inside for death confirmation.

"Was the police department already on scene when you got

there?" Sorenson asked.

"Yes," he replied.

"No more questions," Sorenson said as he sat down.

Scott O'Toole called Detective Kathleen Decker to the witness stand. She was a tall, brown-haired woman, with shoulder-length hair, who wore a black suit with a purple oxford shirt style blouse. We learned that she had over thirty years of experience with the King County Sheriff's Office and was a crime scene investigator. She was also a lead search and rescue coordinator.

"Do you have an area you specialize in, additionally?" Scott asked.

"I specialize in human tracking. I am certified as a Master Tracker."

"Can you explain that for the jury," he prodded.

"Whenever we go anywhere, from point A to point B, we always pick up and leave evidence. It can be hair, dead skin cells, fibers, footprints, fingerprints and so on. I specialize in the search for that information to track human's paths," she explained as she looked at the jurors.

"Can you do this inside as well as outside?"

"It can be used in both environments although my job was focusing on the outside of the 1806 Carnation residence."

Scott put up a series of photographs that the jurors had seen multiple times. The pictures of the environment both in and out of the house had become familiar. Yet, somehow, the Master Tracker was able to show them things they had not seen before.

In one instance, a picture of the backyard was presented with its clumpy and uncut grass. One could see a worn path and adjacent to it, there was a trail of flat grass.

"As you can see," she directed with a green laser pointer on the projection screen across from the jury, "the dew is compressed on the grass in this area. You can see the light reflecting on the surface as compared to the dew-laden grass around it. We call it a 'shine'. Now, if we are on a search and rescue operation, we walk the perimeter of the scene and look for evidence such as bent branches or twigs, footprints, disruptions in the grass, etc. This is referred to as 'Sign Cutting'."

"Just so we understand, can you tell us the difference between 'shine' and 'sign'?" O'Toole queried.

She looked toward the jurors.

"Sure, 'Sign' is the evidence left behind when a person or animal passes through a scene. 'Shine', by contrast, is the reflection of sunlight on a surface when an object has put pressure on it. Usually, it is grass we're talking about."

"Very good. Would it be correct to say that when something of weight is dragged across grass, you can make determinations on the 'shine' of the grass?"

"Yes," she answered eagerly. "For example, when a body is dragged across a lawn, the grass that was depressed under the weight of the body will reflect light differently than the untouched lawn. The 'shine' will give investigators information clues as to the direction of travel, the size of the body and so on."

"Thank you," Scott said. "If I may change direction a little, did you have occasion to meet the defendant, Michele Anderson? If you did, where did you meet her?"

"I met both Michele Anderson and Joseph McEnroe on December 26. They were both at the scene with officers in secure locations. I met with Michele Anderson individually. My purpose was to learn what kind of shoes she might have been wearing on December 24. I was able to get pictures, from a variety of positions, of Michele Anderson's boots while the Sheriff's Department forwarded pictures of Joseph McEnroe's boots. They confirmed that they were worn the night in question," she answered.

She was comfortable on the stand and the jury liked her, in part because she looked at them and it seemed to involve them in the discourse between her and the prosecutor.

The screen displayed a disturbed length of pressed grass. Detective Decker used her green pointer to magnify the area.

"We believe two bodies came down these stairs to the lawn in the direction of the shed. One body was carried and the second was dragged."

Exhibits #24 through #27 were entered into evidence despite the objection of David Sorenson. He argued as to the details added to the photographs such as arrows and lines on them.

Scott O'Toole countered that the pictures had not been altered or enhanced, merely that that visual aids were provided. What may be obvious to a witness was not so to the layperson who was in the jury box. Further, the items were previously admitted in the trial of Joseph McEnroe.

David Sorenson was quick to point out that he and Colleen O'Connor were not part of that trial.

Judge Ramsdell overruled the objection, and allowed the photographs into evidence, just before he dismissed the jury for a break. He waited until Kenya, the Bailiff, closed the jury room door behind them.

"There's one other issue I want to address before we go on

break," he told the jury-vacated courtroom. "My understanding is that somebody wants to live stream the proceedings or something like that. I'm not really sure what the request is, but if that person could identify himself."

"Yes, Sir," I said after I stood up. "My name is Paul Sanders and I report for Trial Talk Live."

"What was that again?" the judge asked.

"I work for Trial Talk Live, an online website," I explained. "I'm also an author and write from the perspective of a former juror. I was formerly a death penalty juror so I have an idea of the process and protocols."

Judge Ramsdell nodded his head. "What is it you would like to do, Sir?"

"I essentially want to run a camera and microphone from the corner and just during the proceedings. I don't want to film motions or anything having to do with the jury, which is of primary importance to me, not capturing the jurors," I said.

"So it would be audio and video; is that what you are talking about?"

"Yes, Sir," I answered politely.

"And where would this end up being broadcast?"

"Trial talk Live is a subscription website. It's been around for a couple of years now. We did the Jodi Arias trial," I offered.

"The what?" the judge asked.

"The Jodi Arias trial," I repeated.

It always surprised me when people had never heard of her. The judge was one of the lucky few.

"And so this is your own website, is I guess what you're telling

152

me?"

"Yes."

"So, you are not affiliated with any of the, for a lack of a better term, mainstream broadcast media?" he asked.

"Okay, thank you," he responded. "I think that's..."

The pro se attorney who was seated in the back row suddenly stood up from behind me.

"I have an objection to this because I've been researching online what he actually does and that he's misrepresented both your conversation with me and my conversation with you just the other day and I do have a printout of that," she said.

I stood quietly as the conversation continued. I felt as if I was the bait for the Court hung out to dry.

"I don't want to get into what people are printing on what I say that is taken out of context or misrepresented. If I did that," the judge explained, "I would be spending my entire life doing nothing but reading blog sites and the paper."

"I understand that," the pro se attorney returned. "In the interest of people, and justice, and to save the family and the defendant of any trauma, and your trial to be in a circus that you do not want, I would ask that you deny his motion to you for this because it's already caused me some harm from the things he's written about me."

I wished I had never given her my business card.

"And I've been subjected to the comments from his so-called followers on Facebook and Twitter," she continued. "And so the whole world and, uh, also he published the 911 call. Different things that have happened in this courtroom. And you admonished me for any pictures and this man has been doing it before I even got here."

Had she just accused me of taking pictures? It was not true.

She continued with her rampage.

"So I would request on behalf of the family to not go through more trauma that this man is exactly doing that. He is picking out jurors that he is going to stand with and give them opportunities for his books. That's all he wants!"

"Okay, Ma'am," the judge responded. "Can I ask you, recognizing you from last week, but the record will not reflect who you are. What is your name again?"

"She has my name," the pro se attorney retorted in reference to the Court Reporter.

"Can I get your name again?"

"She has it," she stated obstinately.

"What's that?"

"She has it and he already published it," she said.

"Oh, I know she has it," the judge agreed. "But I just need to make a record."

"Thank you," the pro se attorney responded.

I stood quietly with my hands folded in front of me.

The judge rubbed the bridge of his nose and reseated his glasses. "Because, this is the record that everybody cares about after this trial is over. So, I want to make sure I've got my pieces in place."

"Right. I would just like to see you avoid the circus that you don't want by denying his motion. Thank you, Your Honor. I would like to pass this up so you have it," she said as she raised a packet of paper in the air.

"I don't want it," the judge said firmly. "I don't want to add stuff to the record that isn't relevant."

"No," she said. "This is for your own concern, if you want to take this decision under advisement. That's all."

"I do not," Judge Ramsdell countered. "I'm trying to run a trial here. I'm trying to do it with some kind of dignity and with attention to what needs to be attended to. That's why I'm trying to avoid these problems

that keep cropping up with greater frequency every time I get out here. So, you can have a seat folks."

Thrilled, I took my seat.

"My next order of business," the judge continued, "is that I need to ask the parties what their thoughts are on this. So, Mr. O'Toole, you go ahead first."

"Well, your Honor, if I might," Scott suggested when he stood up, "I should say that taking you out of context is, well, I do it all the time."

The judge smiled.

"I wasn't going to mention names, but, okay," he acquiesced.

"Your Honor, I would say from the observation of the gallery in this courtroom, that Mr. Sanders has been absolutely respectful and unobtrusive," Scott O'Toole explained casually. "I don't think he has in any way obstructed this court or put himself in a position where he drew attention to himself, especially in front of the jury. If, assuming for the sake of argument, Miss {redacted}'s comments are right that what Mr. Sanders has written is somehow inaccurate, he wrote it without any of the trial being streamed by him. So, they are his own personal views and he doesn't have to be right. The law doesn't require for an open courtroom for people to come in and exercise their First Amendment rights that they be accurate or correct or right. I don't know if he is or not."

The prosecutor paused for a moment and raised his finger.

"But Miss (redacted}'s complaint that somehow streaming the trial, results in Mr. Sanders writing, is simply untrue because he has been writing, as I understand it, for a couple of weeks now and he hasn't been streaming anything."

"Right," the judge commented.

"So, I guess my concern is the open court's doctrine, and especially access, it sounds to me that if someone has a legitimate purpose and some history that we, at least, take it seriously, and not dismiss it, and if there's one advantage that Mr. Sanders has, is that he doesn't parachute in as the press does every couple of days or every couple of weeks. At least he is here continually providing a record, however accurate or inaccurate someone wants to claim that it is."

I was honored and humbled to have his support.

"So what is your final position on this request?" Judge Ramsdell asked.

"I don't have a dog in this fight," O'Toole responded. "I don't object because I actually think it's sort of a First Amendment, what the First amendment is all about."

"Okay," the judge said.

He looked toward the defense table. I did not think I would fare as well as I had with the prosecution.

"Mr. Sorenson or Miss O'Connor? What are your thoughts on the request?"

David Sorenson stood up.

"Your Honor, we do object to Live Streaming this trial. The open court's doctrine allows Mr. Sanders to be here. It does not require this Court to even allow one camera in the courtroom. The Court has already entered a media order and it's fairly limited. It is drafted to minimize the intrusiveness of the cameras and adding this camera to the mix is, frankly, unnecessary. Where's the end of it?"

"Okay," the judge said as Sorenson took his seat. "Here's where I'm at and here's the problem. When I'm dealing with broadcast media such as KOMO, KIRO or KING, all of those recognized broadcast entities; I have a mechanism of supervising them. I can enter media orders and if they are not compliant with them, I have a mechanism to monitor them and take corrective action."

I knew where this was headed by the tone of his voice.

"When we have the entire panoply of the public who may or may not have their own blogs, websites or whatever and they come in and say they would like to do this, they are basically asking to be treated like they were broadcast media in the sense that this rule was intended to address. The problem I have," the judge said as he paused to carefully select his words, "is that I have no mechanism for monitoring that. With all due respect to Mr. Sanders."

I nodded my head when he caught my eyes.

"I know he has been professional and so forth in my relationship with him, and in this context, I have no idea what his blog or website says because I'm not monitoring it. I have got another job to do. But, by the same token, I don't have anybody monitoring that stuff. That woman sitting behind him," he pointed out in reference to Miss (redacted}, "has been monitoring him more than I have; but I have a job to do and I have an obligation to make sure that this proceeding is done with dignity. There is an integrity to the process and I think that whenever I lose the ability to control what's happening out there, then I lose my ability to do my job."

"So, with all due respect, Mr. Sanders," the judge directed, "I don't think that I can grant your request at this time. I will tell you up front it's partly because the rules have not caught up with the electronic media that we have and where does it end?"

He had a point.

"I fear that in an effort to be open, we have turned trials into entertainment," the judge continued. "So, Mr. Sanders, I'm saying no to you not because of who you are or anything that you have written but because I fear that if this door is kicked open, it's kicked open to virtually anybody who wants to come in. I think I have to be somewhat cautious to make sure the trial is done correctly so I am going to have to say no."

"Thank you, your Honor," Miss {redacted} responded. She sounded content with the decision.

I did not think the judge was addressing her and it was not the last we would hear from her.

Detective Decker returned to the stand after the recess. The jurors would have respected her. It was clear that she was passionate and fastidious about her work as a Master Tracker. Oftentimes, she gave credit to her mentor, Joel Harden. He was a renowned tracker and considered the founder of the science of human tracking. The Detective was proud to have been trained in a science that was a relatively new field in forensics.

"Is this the picture you took of Michele Anderson's boots?" Scott asked.

"Yes."

"Why is it important to you?"

The detective looked toward the screen.

"I am looking for distinguishing characteristics. Although I have many choices, in this picture, the three small circles that are lined along the center of the sole are significant and prominent to me."

The prosecutor placed another picture on the screen of the sole prints of Joseph McEnroe.

"If you notice the angled grooves along the sides, they become a distinguishing characteristic," Decker explained.

The afternoon was spent looking at multiple photographs of the scene. Many pictures were taken outside and many were taken inside. Jurors quickly learned of the many sightings of small circles within pools and smears of dark blood. Her boot prints seemed to be everywhere on the scene.

Within her set of unique boot prints, the detective testified toward the identification of the other prints, those of Joseph McEnroe. In one example, they went backwards from the base of the stairs at the back door, across the lawn, and to the shed. One trail revealed that he had carried something heavy with Michelle.

A significant amount of attention was spent on the 'shine' of the path of flattened grass, determined not be part of a trail adjacent, and what it represented. The path marked the dragging of Wayne Anderson's body to the front of the shed, where a nearby old piece of carpet was thrown on top of him. Dragged by his hands during the process, the jeans of the victim were gathered at his ankles.

The detective pointed to two boot prints found on the back of Wayne Anderson. They were consistent with the soles of the boots Michele Anderson, which was consistent with those worn on December 24, 2007. Dirty little circles were pressed into the middle of Wayne's t-shirt.

Detective Decker testified that the owners of both sets of boot prints carried Judy Anderson's body from one point to another. Judy was placed in the shed, head first. Her hands were extended above her head. The door would enclose her for the next forty hours.

The shine in the grass revealed significant signs of bloodletting.

"So, you were trained in this field by Joel Harden of Professional Tracking Services?" Sorenson inquired when it was his turn to cross-examine.

"Yes," she answered.

"Is this a private company?"

"Yes."

"Do you work for them?" Sorenson asked.

"No, I volunteer. One day, when I retire, and when Joel Harden retires, it is something I would like to continue to be involved in."

"It's not nationally accredited, is it?" the defense attorney probed.

"No, because it is a new science," she qualified. "Currently, the techniques are used by the military, search and rescue and by police departments."

"But, the science is not accredited by anyone, is it?" he reiterated.

"No, it is not," she answered.

The jurors knew what a duck was and they understood the meaning of sign cutting. The jurors did not have to see every footprint in the path to understand the consciousness of guilt displayed after the killings.

DAY 10
February 2, 2016

DEVIL IS IN THE DETAILS

Three armed guards led in Michele Anderson as the Court, except the jury, waited for her to complete the ritual of being seated between her attorneys.   A strong-armed looking female guard unclicked defendant's pink handcuffs and dexterously put them on her back belt pocket, next to another set of enclosed cuffs.   She packed a variety of tools on her belt and a cannonball weight of keys swung from her hip.   A yellow stun gun could be seen along with a plethora of other gear.   The female guard, with "King County Jail" patches adorning her shoulders, never smiled.

Anderson did not smile, either.   Once the cuffs were removed, she would straighten her mauve blouse, the same one she had worn since the beginning of the trial, and sit down. She never shared a word with her attorneys.

The female guard took her post in her usual spot, a chair just behind the accused. The accompanying male guards, sizable but somewhat more affable, took positions by the Courtroom exit doors. One stood throughout the proceedings, which allowed the other to be seated.

The empty jury box had sixteen office-style black chairs in it. A blue notepad was on each of the fifteen juror's vacant seats, awaiting the notes that would be taken for the day. It was the Court's rule that the assigned notepads not be sent to the jury room until the time came for deliberations. In that, the notes they took could not be read for another five weeks.

There were seven or eight consistent note-takers on the panel.

The survivors of the deceased sat in the front three rows daily. I did not know them and I did not approach them. This was their ongoing journey for justice in the deaths of their loved ones. It was the second trial they had attended daily. They had witnessed the conviction of Joseph McEnroe eight months prior. They were close and they were committed to seeing the road to justice arrive at its eventual destination.

Christopher Hamburg was called to the witness stand by the prosecution. He wore a gray suit, blue shirt and gold and blue-striped tie. Not only had he been a forensic scientist for thirteen years, he had also been an umpire for four years with a minor league baseball team.

"So, you were like a Judge," Scott O'Toole quipped. He was dressed impeccably in a deep charcoal colored suit, blue shirt and red tie.

"I was, actually," the witness said.

Even Judge Ramsdell chuckled.

"Explain for us what you do when you go to a crime scene and what you are looking for," Scott directed.

"When I go into a scene," Hamburg said as he directed his attention toward the prosecutor, "I work from the outside in. I don't look at the obvious things one sees at a scene but rather the things people don't see. I look for particles, fibers, blood, hair and dust. I usually start at the furthest points away from a victim and work inward, looking at such things as blood spatter and blood staining..."

"I'm sorry to interrupt," Scott said with a raised hand. "What is blood spatter? Did you mean splatter?"

"Blood spatter refers to blood that passes through the air and impacts an object. The study of it reveals different types of signs that can be interpreted from blood's paths. For example, when blood falls, like rain falling, it makes a particular pattern. It will be circular with ribbing on the edges. This tells us it fell from a ninety-degree angle," Hamburg explained. "It is sometimes referred to as passive blood spatter."

"What about blood markings that look like teardrops?" O'Toole asked.

"We refer to the markings as elliptical in nature and oblong with a spine," he responded. "If you look at the tail of it, it will tell you the direction blood came from. There is also a pattern we call blood transfer, when blood is moved from one place to another by a foreign source. If someone put their hand in a source and then went to another room to turn on a light, they would leave blood on the light-plate. That's an example of blood transfer."

"You've seen little dots of blood before, haven't you? What kind of pattern would you call that?"

"We refer to it as impact spatter, usually either medium or high-velocity. It can look like a spray pattern," the scientist tutored.

Scott nodded his head. "What if someone were to clean blood up? Is there a way to determine if that happened?"

"We use a solution called Leuco Crystal Violet. When sprayed over a scene, it will react with the presence or past presence of blood by turning purple. For short, we refer to it as LCV. We like it because it generally does not ruin the source allowing for further testing. We can still test for DNA and so on."

"Did you use this in Carnation in your investigation into the events of 2007?" O'Toole asked.

Chris Hamburg responded affirmatively. He spent some time educating the jury on the process of documenting, identifying and preserving trace evidence. Photographs were a very important part of the process and he had an evidence book filled with detailed reports on each of them. His file was 265 pages in length and sat in front of him on the witness stand.

The jury was then taken on a step-by-step visit of his collecting even through the minutest of detailed evidence. Pictures taken of the smallest of bloodstains and ensuing pictures showed the purple images of LCV (Leuco Crystal Violet) as they revealed what the eye could not see, the presence of blood. It was as if jurors were accompanying the forensic scientist as he introduced them to a world that only he saw, a valley of clues camouflaged by the impact of blood.

The forensic scientist testified that he first went to the backyard, to the shed where Wayne had been left under a shoddy piece of carpet. Bare grass was in front of the shed door. His body had been taken to the medical examiner's office before Hamburg's arrival. He opened the door and saw Judy lying on her back in the shed. He took note of the bloodstains on her jeans, sweater, hands and face. There were two wicker chairs and a barbeque set that would require a further detailed review. He observed, took pictures and took meticulous notes.

We then followed him through the screened front door of the main house where the four bodies still lay. He made a cursory look over the living room, took pictures from multiple angles and noted the positioning of Scott, Erica, Olivia and Nathan. True to form, his interest was drawn further away from the scene, where most of his attention would be focused anyway.

Hamburg testified that he looked through the dining room area. His interest was piqued when he saw a bullet hole in the window. He did not run into blood spatter that he could observe with the naked eye.

The kitchen revealed a flurry of activity in days past. Upon first sight, it looked relatively clean except for a pinkish bloodstain on the kitchen tile near a throw rug. However, when he used the LCV, patterns of all sorts appeared like ghosts of the victims.

The refrigerator had children's hand-colored pictures framed with magnets on the doors, once considered prized artwork by a grandmother.

In the first pictures taken by Hamburg, the kitchen had looked fairly clean, considering the violent attacks that had taken place one room away. Yet, when the LCV was applied, blood appeared randomly in many places, mostly in the form of transferred blood. The purple smears of long sweeping and circular wipe marks could be seen. Diluted blood, the sign of adding water to the sample, revealed itself eerily.

The refrigerator revealed telltale signs of having been wiped with a sponge, soaked in blood. Further, a search underneath revealed more blood that was rich and dark, not contaminated by the furious cleaning on the floor and the doors of the refrigerator. The jurors could see the difference between the blood that was wiped and blood that had been missed in the futile clean-up process.

The kitchen counter tests exposed more diluted blood.

The floor by the hallway was marked with two boot patterns the jury had seen the day before: Michele Anderson's, with the tiny circles in the prints, and Joseph McEnroe's, the distinctive angled print impressions. It was clear that both had acquired a lot of blood on the soles of their shoes and had tracked it in many spots at the front of the house.

"Did you have a chance to look at the oven?" Scott O'Toole asked at one point.

"I did," Hamburg replied.

"Did it reveal anything?"

"There was a roast in the oven," he answered. "It was almost burned."

I wondered, as I am sure one or two jurors did, who turned the oven off and who pulled the plug on the Christmas tree? Apparently, the house had power, as we saw the forensic scientist use electrical cords for the high-intensity lights to obtain photographs.

Hamburg testified that the trail led him to the bathroom where the purple reaction of the LCV brought out a lot of blood pooling around the drain of the tub. The bathroom rug near the toilet had tiny specks of blood resting on the weaves of the twisted fibers. His experience told him it was high-velocity impact spatter with thirty stains, one millimeter in size each.

Again, jurors saw the familiar boot print impressions, two different styles, which left multi-directional patterns on the floor with a lot of activity near the bathtub. LCV only exposed prints that had been in contact with human blood. It was why the prints of Wayne and Judy were not seen. They were not alive when the blood was being tracked around during the house cleaning, Hamburg explained.

The small laundry room, with a side-by-side washer and dryer looked clean until the LCV was applied. A long drip of blood that ran down the center of the agitator of the washer told a story to the investigator. Blood was also discovered inside the deck lid. It did not go past the scientist to make note of the bloodstained towels inside. Blood discoloration was present in front of both the washer and dryer.

It looked like some people were pretty busy on December 24, 2007.

The jurors did not have a choice when Chris Hamburg took them into the living room after the return from lunch. It was the one area that the jurors wanted to visit as little as possible. Although the lambs to the law had gotten somewhat adept at setting aside emotion, it was a lot more difficult to keep it at bay while seeing images of Scott, Erica, Olivia and Nathan.

The scientist did not focus on the bodies but rather on the abundance of evidence throughout the room. Samples were taken of almost every example of blood spatter found. Questions would pop in jurors' minds as they tried to figure out how some blood landed on the carpet vertically while other blood was determined to have been horizontal in direction. They did not inspect the large pools of blood with Chris Hamburg. Instead, they journeyed into the minute specks discovered in the living room drapes, only found less than a height of thirty-five inches.

In another spot, three parallel drips of blood were found, recorded and sent to the lab for further analysis. Jurors could not know how this might be important. If the prosecution presented it, they would know someone deemed it important.

They were with the detective when he took samples of elliptical, oblong and directional blood stains. They watched with intense curiosity as he spent time on blood smears, measuring their location and size specifics. The jurors were beside him as he looked at the passive blood droplets found near the Wheat Thins opened box. Underneath the coffee table, next to a pair of hiking boots, tiny bits of spatter were found.

Jurors had the hardest time setting aside emotion when the forensic scientist detailed the hair and skull fragments found in the carpet.

While the jurors were laden with a mountain of evidence, some would steal looks at the defendant in the dark while the exhibits were shown on the projector screen across from the jury. They would not see her pink handcuffs and they could not ignore the guards that stood or sat near her. Although each worked on presuming her innocence, forbidden to make a determination, they could not help looking toward her.

While the details played out their course to the jury from the forensic scientist, and the images were shown on the screen throughout the day, the jurors would notice as she held her hands over her ears, under her hair, despite the horrific pictures of the scene of the crime.

Each juror would reserve judgment until the appropriate time. It was one of the most difficult tasks each had been asked to do.

In spite of it all, a select few jurors thought the day's proceedings were fascinating.

DAY 11
February 3, 2016

BLOOD AND BULLETS

Just as there was a routine for the defendant every day outside the presence of the jury, it followed there would be one for the attorneys.

Colleen O'Connor always arrived thirty minutes early. She would wheel in her bag, unload it and organize her stack of binders on the defense table. A short time later, David Sorenson would arrive, share a few words with her, get settled and he would patiently wait.

When Scott O'Toole and Michelle Morales strolled in, the energy changed, as they both pulled two-wheeled carts behind them. Once they parked their gear, Michelle unloaded the file storage boxes, and got their items situated for the court clerk.

Meanwhile, Scott greeted the defense team and came over to the half- dozen family members seated in the gallery. He was crisply dressed in a black suit, white shirt and navy blue tie. He greeted them as if they were old friends. He listened and offered reassurance just as he had done every day of the trial. Once pleasantries were completed, he checked in with the court clerk for a brief discussion and returned to the prosecution table to assist Michelle. He and Detective Tompkins looked as if they were old friends.

Judge Ramsdell came into the courtroom only moments after 9:00 AM. He always ensured proceedings began on time, which was respectful of the jury's time and commitment. Objections were few and far between and only one sidebar had occurred since the trial had begun.

David Sorenson stood up, after Ramsdell recognized him, and objected to the admission of nine exhibits that were going to be presented by the prosecution. The named exhibits were only a part of the number lined in front of the court clerk.

The defense attorney argued that the exhibits had been used in the trial of Joseph McEnroe and the defense did not want the jury contaminated by it during eventual deliberations.

All the parties decided that the stated items would be renumbered to be consistent with the exhibit numbers of the Michele Anderson trial.

As quickly as the items had been objected to, the judge had found resolution and the proceedings continued when he asked Kenya to bring in the jury.

They took their seats and some could not help but notice the long row of exhibits lined up adjacent to the judge. It was clear that it was going to be a busy day.

Business began with the return of the forensic scientist, Chris Hamburg. Once again, he had his 265-page evidence book, a three-ring binder of records, in front of him. He was dressed in a brown suit, soft blue shirt and a peach tie accented with subtle red linear dots. He maneuvered the microphone and tapped it lightly to ensure it worked properly.

"Do you recognize item number CRH-30?" Scott asked the witness, once the formalities of reintroduction were done.

"Yes," Hamburg responded.

"Can you describe it for us?"

Chris Hamburg held a cigarette-sized box in his hands.

"It is wrapped in brown paper," he said as he scrutinized it by turning it over in his hands. "It is initialed CRH, which are my initials. It is sealed as I placed it on there. It has the evidence seals and has a bar code on it. I will open it."

He reached next to him and retrieved a pair of scissors. Very carefully, he cut along the edge of the longest side. The jury watched quietly, unaware that they would see the protocol play repeatedly throughout the day. It would be repeated every time a new piece of evidence was introduced.

"Can you remove what's inside?" Scott asked.

Chris Hamburg responded affirmatively. He put the box on the table in front of him and set the scissors to his left.

The prosecutor brought him a box of latex rubber gloves and they both shared a moment as they stretch the latex over their fingers. The witness carefully reached into the box and delicately removed a tiny item.

Michelle Morales turned the 50-inch flat screen on in front of the jury. A picture was shown on the screen.

"Where was the origin of CRH-30? Can you show us?" Scott asked.

Chris Hamburg stepped off the witness stand. He picked up a two-foot long pointer. He identified a spot on the television screen.

I could see it was hard for the jury to look at the picture for any length of time.

"Can you identify item CRH-30 for us?" Scott asked in reference to the item in Hamburg's hand.

The scientist held the item at an angle in his open palm. He stated, "It is hair and a piece of skull fragment that came from Erica Anderson's chest."

"Can you show it to the jury?" Scott asked. "Let's go ahead and walk it in front of them. It's a pretty small item."

The scientist obliged the request as he quietly paraded the item from one end of the jury box to the other. He held the piece of evidence at a forty-five degree angle.

The mood was heavy in the courtroom and as subtle as drizzle in fog. The juror's faces were solid as stone as they observed and compartmentalized the evidence in their minds while some would suppress a stab of pain deep inside.

Fortunately, the witness returned to the witness stand and he moved to the next piece of evidence.

The ritual of the introduction of blood evidence to the jury lasted about seven minutes for each item. The forensic scientist was presented with a sealed package or envelope by the prosecutor and the witness would detail all the markings on the box. He would then carefully open it. Before the item was removed, Scott would take the open package and hand it to David Sorenson. Each time, the defense attorney would look inside the box and check the markings on the outside. He verified each exhibit in front of the jurors.

Scott would then take the item to the court clerk while Judge Ramsdell approved the admission of the item into the official trial records. Moments later, Michelle Morales would follow as she handled the logistics of the electronic presentation.

The television screen then displayed a photographic image of the item, sometimes at multiple angles and many with varying degrees of closeness. The witness would confirm the item in his hands matched the exhibit on the screen. Each item presented was shown to the jury, as the witness slowly walked the length of the jury box.

"Why do the dates read 2009 when the evidence was collected in December of 2007?" Scott asked at one point.

"Those dates are on every piece of evidence. It is not atypical for the date of DNA testing to be significantly later than the date the item was packaged," Chris responded casually. "It takes time for evidence to get through the system."

At another point, the jurors saw a napkin with a bloodstain entered as evidence from the coffee table in the living room of the house. A lid from a Planter's Peanuts can that had signs of high impact blood spatter was collected as evidence. Boots had been under the coffee table and each was entered because one boot showed spatter and the other had possible transferred blood on the sole. Under one boot, there was blood in the carpet which had evidentiary value.

The leather armchair in the living room revealed a blood drip that ran from the arm of the chair and into the seat.

Hamburg testified to the attention paid to an old-fashioned wooden Pepsi box situated next to the boots. The antique decorative box had faded colors of two hearts on the top. The forensic scientist did not find value in its age but rather his attention focused on the apparent blood transfer stain on the side.

Evidence number CRH-15 was entered, a bone and tissue fragment found near the prostrate form of little Nathan Anderson. Additionally, a blood weave pattern had been retrieved as evidence from underneath the young boy's head.

The broken television screen had high-impact blood spatter.

The forensic scientist showed the jury a blood swab taken from a smear of blood found on the front door and the front porch gate. It was transferred blood that could only be seen after exposing LCV to it. Images of blue and purple made it clear that this was evidence of someone trying to clean up blood. Attention was paid to the darkened rims of the various bloodstains. This blood, too, had travelled from one place to another.

The images of footprints, both of Joe McEnroe and Michele Anderson, reappeared when LCV was used, found near the cleanup marks.

Chris Hamburg and Scott O'Toole discussed the white fibers that had been retrieved from the dining room area. Some were found on the coffee room table while some were found nearby on the floor. He was not able to conclude their meaning. He had been there to collect.

Bone fragments with blood were found in the dining room while a smear was found on the drapes.

A television remote was entered into evidence. It had transferred blood on it after it was found under the body of Scott

Anderson. It was missing the battery pack and cover, which Chris Hamburg later recovered from a different part of the living room floor.

A Target bag was found with blood spatter on it and it was found in a spot over blood. The bag was deemed important as well as its position at the scene of the murders.

It was significant that two different kinds of boot impression had been found on top of blood. One pattern revealed the characteristic little circles that were of Michele Anderson while the angular lines on the other implicated Joseph McEnroe.

By morning's end, the prosecution team had managed to get almost thirty pieces of evidence in front of the jury. The blood evidence seemed to come from every corner of the front of the house including the hallway, dining room, kitchen, and of course, the living room. Evidence came from the floors, walls, cabinets and household items.

To the jurors, each piece was a tiny part of a puzzle. They knew where the items came from but they did not know how they fit into the picture.

The afternoon was spent on ballistic evidence, evidence that came from a gun or multiple guns. Each piece was entered into evidence in the same manner as the blood, which ended with a tour of the item in front of the jurors. The procedure had become effortless.

A .357 magnum shell casing was found under the love seat. It had brownish stains on it. Under Scott's body, a 9 MM casing was discovered. It, too, had signs of blood on it. Another spent casing was under the television set in the corner of the living room.

The bullet had destroyed the television as it passed through the face of it and then through the working parts of the interior. The forensic scientist had to disassemble the appliance to retrieve the bullet. The recovered bullet, which showed obvious signs of damage, was paraded slowly for the jury to see.

One bullet was pulled from the floor under the carpet. It had been underneath Erica Anderson's head. A wound on her head seemed to match the trajectory of the bullet.

A bullet pierced a wall behind a rack that held Afghan blankets. The scientist had used a trajectory stick to go through the holes found in the blankets. The stick led to the bullet in the wall. The shot was fired at a seventy-degree downward angle.

Another bullet had scratch marks on it its copper jacket. Chris Hamburg explained that this was caused when they had to recover it from a heating duct after it passed through the floor.

Attention was drawn to the curtains in the kitchen and the living room. Bullet impact markings had been found on the other side of the curtains but the curtains showed no ballistic evidence. The lack of holes in the fabric told the investigator that the drapes were partially open when the bullets had been fired.

Within the cushions of the loveseat where Erica had lain, another bullet appeared. It had not gone through the cushion.

"Did you find another bullet near the loveseat?" Scott O'Toole asked Chris Hamburg near the end of the day.

"I did," he answered.

"Where?"

"It was located inside a pillow," he answered.

"Can you tell us where the pillow was found?" Scott inquired.

"It was located over Olivia Anderson's legs in the location of Erica Anderson."

"What did the evidence tell you?"

"There were two bullet holes in the pillow," Hamburg said. "One of the holes is where the bullet passed through and into the heating duct. It likely passed through Olivia before it went through the pillow."

"And what were your conclusions on the other bullet hole?

"In all likelihood, this second bullet also passed through Olivia as she was seated or standing on the loveseat and came to rest inside the pillow."

"Did you note anything of additional significance?"

"Yes, we found red and white fibers at the entrance of the shared wounds."

"What color dress was the Olivia Anderson wearing?" Scott asked.

"Red," Chris answered.

"What color were the fibers?"

"Red and white."

The jurors watched as the witness opened a large package and observed the legal dance it took to be entered into evidence. It was a square pillow that matched the pattern of the loveseat. One side had a velvety texture with printed rose patterns on it while the other side was solid yellow.

Chris Hamburg stepped from the stand and showcased the pillow in front of the jury.

The yellow side of the pillow showed the damage the bullet

caused when it passed through it, as it had exposed the insides of the pillow, blown out through the edges of a black hole.

The jurors were silent as they thought about sixteen bullets and what happened on Christmas Eve of 2007.

The prosecutor had managed to take the analytics of the day and somehow made it come face to face with the emotion that would always be underneath. Olivia and Erica had spoken.

The victims were beginning to raise their voices and the weight of responsibility on the jurors had gotten a lot heavier.

PLEOCHROISM AND THE JURY

Forensic scientist, Christopher Hamburg returned to the stand. It was his third day of testimony. He was dressed professionally in a gray suit with a matching gray oxford shirt complimented with a maroon-striped tie. He leaned toward the microphone as he spoke.

Scott O'Toole wore a tapered black suit coat, brown slacks and a light blue shirt finished with a silk blue tie. He was at ease in front of the jury as he moved from one piece of evidence to the next, almost effortlessly, as Michelle Morales, the second prosecutor, orchestrated the continual stream of slides.

"We were talking about the pillow found over the legs of Olivia and I wanted to revisit one item," Scott began. "You testified that you had discovered a bullet inside the pillow. Is that right?"

"I did," Hamburg answered. "I felt the item but did not remove it."

"Very good," Scott said as he glanced at his notes. "We talked about a number of bullets and casings recovered yesterday. We referred to the bullet found in the window as, Bullet A. The second bullet, found under Erica Anderson and the loveseat was designated to be, Bullet B. The third bullet, recovered from inside the television was called, Bullet C. The undesignated bullet, Bullet D, was the one never recovered. Does this sound accurate?"

"It does," Chris confirmed. "Bullet D was not designated because it exited from the dining room window. The terrain slopes upwards with many trees. Despite many searches, it was not found."

"So, let me ask you this. How do you know that the hole in the window was made from a bullet?"

"We tested the perimeter of the hole for the presence of lead, a component of all bullets," Hamburg stated.

"Was the test positive?"

"Yes," he answered. "We then determined that the bullet came from inside the house instead of outside by looking at the properties of the hole."

"How did you determine the direction?"

"When a bullet hits glass, one side of impact will remain flat while the other will exhibit cratering signs. The flat side of the impact mark was on the inside of the house indicating it was not fired from outside."

Scott directed Michelle Morales to forward the next slide. "The next bullet, Bullet E, was found in the laundry room. Can you tell us how it arrived there?"

"We used a trajectory stick to trace its path. The bullet entered the wall from the kitchen near the refrigerator. After passing through the wall, it came to rest on a wire rack in the laundry room, in between some boxes, and, specifically, inside a Ziploc bag box."

"At what trajectory?" Scott asked.

"It came in at a three to five degree angle downward," the scientist replied.

David Sorenson took the opportunity to cross-examine the witness after Scott completed his questioning. He wore a charcoal gray colored suit with a blue shirt and blue-striped tie. He placed his notes on the podium and adjusted his glasses.

"I have just a couple of questions for you," Sorenson began. "I would like to start by discussing some aspects of your training. In a list of professional courses that you have taken throughout your career, your records indicate you took a course on jury selection. Is that correct?"

"I did," Hamburg agreed.

"Can you tell us a little more about that? What was the intent of the course?"

"It is standard for professionals in my field to take such courses. There is a percentage of our time that involves testifying to our evidence. The course taught us how juries react to a variety of witnesses," Hamburg explained.

"Are the courses meant to teach you how to react in a courtroom?"

"Basically, the course familiarized the student with various techniques on how to interact with those found in a courtroom, whether it be the jury, judge or attorneys."

Sorenson nodded his head. "Moving on, sir, let's talk a little more about Leuco Crystal Violet (LCV). You stated that it can react over time, giving varied results at a scene."

"Yes," Hamburg said. "We use the results of LCV reactions to blood within a short time after it is applied. It does change color over time."

"What is that time frame?" Sorenson asked.

"I would say generally in three days. The existence of light, heat and humidity can expand the color changing properties."

Sorenson glanced at his notepad and then back at the scientist. "Wouldn't that affect DNA results later?"

"Although DNA is not my area of expertise, I would say, no, LCV does not affect DNA testing."

"We spoke of DNA not being tested until 2009 and you told Mr. O'Toole that the length of time for DNA to be tested in this case was not atypical. Why would that be?"

"Given the great demand and sheer volume of testing, factors can push testing times back. Courts have backlogs and many samples are moved ahead of others depending upon a case's appearance in court. Like I said, this is not atypical of DNA testing."

Sorenson paused for what seemed an extraordinary amount of time.

"Weren't you planning on being part of the crime scene reconstruction in this case? At least at the time that you were collecting results at the scene, didn't you anticipate the next step?"

"I did plan on doing the reconstruction. I received a job offer in Oregon in fall of 2008. I moved there so was not further involved in this investigation."

"Other people were chosen to do the reconstruction, I take it," Sorenson concluded. "Is that correct?"

"Yes."

"Do you know Ross Gardner?"

"I do."

"Didn't he do the crime scene reconstruction in this case?"

"He did."

"How did you learn that?" Sorenson queried.

"A former co-worker informed me after I had gone to Oregon."

"Did you ever speak with Gardner about this case?"

"No."

"No more questions," Sorenson finished.

Scott O'Toole accepted the invitation from the judge to question the witness on re-direct examination.

"Do you know where Mr. Gardner is from?"

"I do not know," Hamburg answered.

"Doesn't he teach courses in the study of forensics?"

"Yes, he does. I took a course from him once."

"He has a private company now, doesn't he?"

"Yes."

"Referencing this course that Mr. Sorenson discussed, the course on jury selection, was this class a study in how to present yourself as a witness in court? Is it uncommon to take a course in jury selection?" O'Toole queried.

"We receive training in all aspects of our job. This was part of it."

"Has it ever caused you to change your testimony in front of a jury?"

"No."

"Can you tell the jury what you learned in this course?" O'Toole asked as he pointed toward the jury box.

"The course taught us how we were expected to behave on a witness stand. We learned to avoid saying, "um", when we spoke. We needed to present ourselves professionally and watch our diction. Basically it taught us how to be comfortable on the witness stand by answering questions in a clear and concise manner."

"How many times have you testified in a case in your career?" O'Toole asked.

Chris Hamburg thought about it for a moment.

"Maybe ten times."

"Just one more concern," Scott said. "In your experience, has LCV ever changed DNA after its use?"

"Not that I am aware of," Hamburg responded.

Margaret Barber took the stand after Chris Hamburg stepped down. She was employed with the crime lab in Marysville, Washington. She had twenty years of experience in microanalysis and the study of trace evidence, which focused specifically on the analysis of paint, fibers, hairs and shoe impressions. She was dressed comfortably in dark green pants with a pink blouse and an aqua colored coat. She, too, had a large three-ring binder of evidence in front of her.

Pieces of fiber were presented to her in envelopes much like the evidence that had been presented through Chris Hamburg. The dance of evidence introduction continued like previous days, as the witness carefully inspected each envelope and confirmed the item's chain of custody from the crime scene to the witness stand. Once Barber acknowledged it was the evidence she had examined, a simultaneous picture displayed on the screen while Scott O'Toole brought the item to David Sorenson and then back up to the court clerk. Judge Ramsdell would give his seal of approval on the evidence before the testimony continued.

The lambs to the law were used to the process and waited patiently as each piece of fiber was entered into court records. Although it was often laborious and tedious, the jurors exercised patience.

Margaret Barber testified that fibers from the dining room, recovered from the top of the dining room table and from the floor underneath, had been analyzed. It included a physical examination and focused on microscopic examination. Each fiber was unique to a specific item in the living room. In a close-up look at the fiber, grains of gunshot residue were evident. The fiber was cotton and the lengths of fibers were consistent with holes found on the shirt of Wayne Anderson.

A hot rod decaled t-shirt was displayed for the jurors, the shirt that Wayne had died in. Two holes were in the shoulder while two were in the right sleeve. The shirt, originally white, was stained brown. The shirt had been cut in half with only the front side visible.

The next fibers were recovered from the tip of a hollow-point bullet, found nestled inside a Ziploc bag box, on a wire rack in the laundry room. The fibers were extricated from the tip of the bullet with tweezers and analyzed.

She testified that the fiber's origin was as important as the place it was found. Each fiber, of the hundred found in the tip of the hollow-point bullet, were separated and placed under a variety of microscopes. They were then exposed to a variety of light angles.

"Why, in this sample, are the colors different than from the last sample?" O'Toole asked, while a pink colored fiber was displayed on the screen.

"We use a variety of lights to determine the origin of a fiber, to ensure one fiber is the same or different than the next. We take a control sample and then subject the control sample and its unique characteristics against the specimen being studied. For example, using polarized light, we find that the specimen changes colors from light that comes from a variety of directions. We call it pleochroism."

"Pleochroism? Can you explain that again?" O'Toole asked.

"It is the property of a fiber showing different color reactions when polarized light is shown through it from a variety of angles. It serves to make a fiber specific with itself and fibers that show the same reaction can be interpreted as being a source fiber," she explained.

"What is the definition of a fiber?" O'Toole asked.

"It is an item that is one hundred times longer than it is wide."

Scott nodded, referenced his notes and asked, "So, in the bullet that was found in the laundry room, Bullet E, were you able to determine its source?"

"I was," she answered as she turned a page in her notebook. "The fibers did not match those of Erica but rather of Judith Anderson. The fibers of the blue sweatshirt she was wearing matched the fibers exactly to the fibers found in the tip of the bullet. Scientific and microscopic tests showed them to be consistent with each other."

The prosecutor then walked toward the court clerk and recovered a sizable package and brought it to the witness. She opened the package carefully and then spread the shirt open for the jury to see. The hooded blue sweatshirt clearly evidenced four defects in it with two holes in the front and two in the back. The recovered blue fibers were shown to have fit inside the holes.

The jurors would have remembered Judith's body as it was found in the shed but none had seen the bullet holes until the shirt was displayed in front of them. Again, they did not need an explanation of what the brown stains were on the sweatshirt.

It had been a long morning of fabric analysis and it was certainly not the most exciting testimony that the jurors had seen.

"Your next witness?" Judge Ramsdell encouraged.

"Yes, Your Honor," Scott O'Toole said. He strolled out of the courtroom while the jurors waited silently. He returned moments later. It seemed that the ambience in the courtroom changed almost immediately.

Joel Hardin walked toward the witness stand as he removed his cowboy hat before he was sworn in. He wore a gray suit with a blue shirt. He had black cowboy boots on.

"Can you give us a snapshot of your career?" Scott O'Toole asked once formal introductions were completed.

"I've been in police work for fifty years beginning in 1960 as an Idaho Police Officer. In 1965, I began work with the U.S. Border Patrol, tracking illegals and doing transportation checks. I eventually began working at the Canadian border performing the same sort of tasks. I think that was in 1972 and after ten years, I was hired by the U.S. Attorney's Office," he explained.

I watched the jury as many sat on the edge of their seats. Juries loved evidence that they can see, touch and feel and this witness was a far cry from the tediousness of fabric analysis.

"How long have you been tracking?" O'Toole asked.

"I began learning about it in 1965 with the Border patrol," he said. "I liked the job because it kept me away from the office and in the field. I like putting bad guys in a good place: behind bars."

Some of the jurors smiled.

"Did you go to school to study tracking?"

The witness laughed. "Oh, no. It is all on the job training. You are taught the science of tracking through experienced officers."

"Is there a demand for the study of tracking?" O'Toole prodded.

"There will always be a demand for it," Hardin said. "I have a private company called, 'Joel Hardin Tracking Services' and this is all we do. We train military, police officers, and search & rescue teams how to track someone. We still teach Navy Seals how to do it."

"Is there a process to become certified?"

"Yes," Hardin said. "We are the only company that specializes in this field. There are strict guidelines to advance to each level. We set the standards and are endorsed on a collegiate level, as well as, by police departments and search & rescue teams throughout the country."

"Is there a difference between criminal investigations or missing person's searches?"

Hardin shook his head. "They are usually related. A missing person's search oftentimes has a criminal element to it so the differences are small."

"What is the definition of tracking?" O'Toole asked.

"We follow signs that human beings leave when passing from one place to another."

"Would you consider tracking a science?"

"I would. We use scientific principles in an uncontrolled environment, whether it be outside in the woods or inside at a crime scene. The same principles apply. There was a discussion going back to 1965 when we questioned whether tracking was a science or an art. I think it is a science," Hardin said as he chuckled at the memory.

"Can you give us an idea of what you do?"

"Let me explain it this way," he began. "Our eyes only see twenty-percent of what actually is there. Commonly, one would see a footprint and not recognize it. That's because we do not understand what we are looking at much less whether we are seeing a footprint. We always leave signs of our movement whether we are wearing shoes, boots, socks, or even have a prosthetic leg. We can go back five years to a scene of a crime and find evidence that investigators did not find. It is specific what we are looking for, but one has to learn what to look for. Without training, investigators will miss these things," he said engagingly.

Scott looked at his notes, turned a page and stepped toward the witness.

"You were called to a scene in Carnation, Washington in December of 2007?"

Hardin turned in his chair toward the jurors.

"I was called on Christmas day by Detective Decker. I was informed that there were six homicide victims and she wanted my assistance on the scene. I met her in Carnation along with some of the deputies who were there. We had six trackers and we broke up into three teams of two to search the property."

"What were you looking for?"

"We knew at that time that we had two suspects. We obtained their footwear and made pencil sketches of the soles of the footwear," he explained.

O'Toole cocked his head a little.

"Pencil sketches? Why not use pictures?"

Hardin shook his head as if he was speaking to a naïve novice.

"It does not work that way. We can look at a picture but

glossiness will affect what we see. What we want to do is to commit the pattern to memory and the best way to do it is to draw a sketch of it. The act of drawing betters the memory."

"So, in December of 2007, you were aware of the impressions you were looking for, those of Joseph McEnroe and Michele Anderson?"

"Yes," he said. "They were the only people alive at the scene when the murders occurred. It was logical that we begin from there."

"Did you find foot impressions of the defendant and of Joseph McEnroe at both addresses, 1910 and 1806, in late 2007?"

"We found numerous impressions outside," he answered.

"Did you investigate the inside of the home of Wayne Anderson?" O'Toole asked.

"We did," Hardin answered.

Scott O'Toole looked at the clock.

"I think this might be a good time to recess for the weekend," he suggested toward Judge Ramsdell.

The judge saw it was 4:00, admonished the jury not to investigate the case in any way and dismissed them.

The jurors would have to wait for the continuation of the testimony of Joel Hardin. It would be a cliffhanger for them throughout their three days of respite from murder.

I thought of pleochroism and the value of a witness shining different colors upon the interpretation of the crime scene. Somewhere in the story of the murders of six, this witness would show the jury things they would never have thought to look for.

DAY 13
February 8, 2016

UNEXPECTED EXPERT

The jurors returned from Super Bowl weekend. Many looked forward to the continued testimony of Joel Hardin, the expert in human tracking. They watched with rapt interest as he and Scott O'Toole took them on a journey into the science of human tracking and the picture it painted of his activities on December 26, 2007.

Joel Hardin had received a phone call from Kathleen Decker on the day after Christmas. He oftentimes received calls for assistance at crime scenes nationwide but a call from master trackers always gave him pause. Kathy explained that she wanted a team to come to the scene to assist. The property was rural and encompassed a number of acres.

Joel did not hesitate to offer his help and expertise. He got on the phone and was able to find three volunteers to join him. All of them either worked for Boeing or Kenwood and two of the three were retired engineers. It was an unwritten rule that they support law enforcement when needed and the teams visited free of charge. Many of Hardin's former students were law enforcement professionals and it was a closely-knit community.

The murder scene was not traditional and it was still in an uncontrolled environment.

He arrived with the three other trackers just after 8:00 AM. He climbed out of his truck wearing jeans, well-worn cowboy boots, a heavy jacket and a black cowboy hat. He grasped two 3 x 5 cards in his hand as he walked up the gravel road. He looked at the ground and noted it was damp but not wet. It was good news that it had not rained overnight.

He extended a hand when he saw his other trackers as they waited for him at the top of the hill. Each of the men held 3 x 5 cards in one hand while they shook Joel's hand with the other. It was a reunion of old friends.

They had just gotten down to business when they saw Kathy Decker as she came up the hill. She was dressed in jeans, hiking boots and a warm coat.

"I see you have all done your homework," Hardin noticed when Decker joined them.

"Yes," Brady volunteered. "We have pencil sketches of both boot soles."

Joel smiled. "Glad to see it. Any characteristics stick out to you?"

"The first print shows circles that run the length of the shoe connected by a center line that runs the length of the boot," Dick Walker said. "We're also looking at the intersecting lugs. They will imprint well in the ground, if the ground was wet."

"Couldn't have said it better myself. So, everybody agrees on what we're looking for on the first print?" Hardin asked.

Everyone nodded.

"What about the second print. What is significant? McDuff?"

"There are no circles but there is a "Chevron" looking pattern," he responded. "Also, there is a clipped ribbon on the edges. I think we should look for those open angles when we're looking at impressions."

"The chevron-looking pattern looks like a Christmas tree," Hardin affirmed. They made some additional comparisons but all agreed that they would look for circle patterns and Christmas tree patterns.

The group consisted of five trackers who walked up to Sergeant Toner of the King County Sheriff's Department. They were quickly briefed. Their task was to break up into three teams of two to search the property. They had three goals for the day. They were to further examine the back yard where two victims were found. Next, they needed to secure tracking evidence in the house. Finally, they were delegated to secure a "sign-cut" in the woods. In other words, they needed to define the boundaries at the scene.

The Sergeant gave the tracker team their sixth member, Deputy Troy Chaffee, so they could split into three teams of two. He had shown an interest and the team needed him. Hardin put the rookie tracker with another tracker and dispatched them to search the lower property on the left side of the hill. A singlewide trailer, a cargo trailer, fire-pit and a number of sheds and lean-to's needed to have a better look. The deputy would get on-the-job training from an experienced tracker.

Joel Hardin purposely did not ask about details on the crime scene. He would figure it out with his team.

The other team of two was sent up the hill ahead of Hardin and Decker. That team was to search the border forest for signs and establish a perimeter. It would be a slow and rough hike for them.

Kathy Decker and he walked up the gravel road slowly. Although they talked out loud to each other, neither shared eye contact because their attention was focused on the ground and on the foliage along the side of the road.

He had done his homework the night before. He knew the incident was just a few days old and that was positive news. Hardin had been on crime scenes, sometimes a month to years after the event, and tracking was a lot more difficult. In this case, the temperature and humidity had been static since Christmas Eve, three days prior. Only a trace amount of rainfall had occurred.

They reached a well-worn path that ran alongside the side the house. Hardin took his hat off and wiped the glisten of sweat from his forehead.

"The crime lab is inside," Kathy Decker explained. "They have the scene secure. I have glossy pictures ready for you after we look at the backyard. Do you want to lead the way? I will hang back and let you do your search first."

"Good enough," Hardin said as he made his way around the side of the house. He noted their path was well worn.

As soon as they got to the backyard, he stopped and looked. He saw a shed about twenty yards away that was perched on two pieces of railroad ties. Decker had told him that Wayne Anderson had been found in the front of the shed. His was the only body that had been removed by the medical examiner's office. The shed only held his attention for a moment as he got down on his haunches and removed his hat.

He looked over the surface of the grass carefully. His attention was drawn toward a wide swath of grass. He turned his head at different angles to look at it.

He got up and walked slowly as he inspected the grass and mud on the ground. At one point, when he had reached the wide part of flattened grass, he got back on his haunches while his fingers reached into the thin leaves. He was not pulling out grass. Instead, he felt and inspected it. Something else drew his interest as he moved to look closer at the roots. He withdrew his hand and rubbed fine grains of dirt between his fingers absentmindedly.

Kathleen Decker followed him silently as he made his way to the steps of the back patio. He saw the same broken pieces of fern that she had seen the day before. He looked at the pieces of decayed leaves randomly spread on the surface of the steps and the patio. He reached into his pocket and pulled out his pencil sketches of footprints and closely inspected the wood.

"What do you think?" Decker asked him when he slowly came down the patio steps.

"The flattened grass certainly has my attention," he said pensively. "I figure it's good the temperature has stayed between thirty and forty degrees. I felt the bends in the grass and there is some bleeding which was caused by one or more persons walking on it with additional bruising on the roots because of freezing. That tells me it is consistent with it being damaged on the 24th."

"I agree," Kathy said.

"Plus," he noted, "the grass stayed down because of the dew and since it won't grow at that temperature, it looks remarkably fresh. Look at this," he said as he bent down.

The detective followed suit.

"These are heel prints. They're consistent with the Christmas tree patterned sole. Notice how deep the holes are? Look at the imprints of the lugs. Good detail and obviously something was weighing the heels down. See how defined the impressions are?"

"I do," she said. "It tells me somebody was walking backwards."

He raised his head. "More than one person was walking backwards dragging something. Look at the stride-length," he pointed. "See how short the distance is?"

Kathy Decker knew the importance of stride-length. It was the distance between the toe ends of a foot impression to the heel end of the next foot impression. The distance between prints could reveal whether someone walked, jogged or ran and could even reveal if someone walked backwards. She took note of how deep the heel went into the mud as compared to the front of the foot impression.

They then compared the additional heel prints they found and quickly saw they matched the prints they had drawn to memory, of Joseph McEnroe and Michele Anderson.

"You can see the disturbed grains of mud and sand as it rolled to the base of the grass," he remarked. "Two people were dragging something between them. I can also see another path where they must have been carrying something."

He looked at additional deep markings in the grass and then sign cut his way to the shed. He did not inspect every footprint, but instead, marked the direction ahead and made his way to the end of the path.

Joel Hardin stopped, got on his haunches again and looked at the painted ledge of the doorway. It was as if he did not notice the prostrate body of Judith Anderson as she laid the length of the shed inside. He did not look at her white stocking feet that were at the edge of the doorway. Instead, he removed his hat and looked closely into the paint. He recognized the same boot impressions as he had seen in the mud and on the back patio.

The imprints were significant because they were in blood along the ledge. He saw that the impressions had been walked over repeatedly by the two different sets of boots. He looked at the blood drip that came down the edge and a passive drop within the prints. The blood had fallen from an object and two people had stepped in the blood.

Satisfied that he got all he could from the impressions on the ledge, he made his way around the back of the shed. He did not go inside the shed because the area was cramped and he would learn nothing of value. Along the back of the shed, he and Kathy took note of a set of footprints. They did not show the characteristics of the impressions they were looking for.

Hardin commented to Kathy who was behind him.

"See the edges of the dirt? They have deteriorated. The grass is flat, too."

"There's no shine to the grass," Kathy offered. "I would guess those prints are more than a week old."

Hardin nodded and looked back at the dirt.

"I will bet you these are Wayne Anderson's prints. They look like tennis shoe impressions. The stride length does not show a sense of urgency. I don't think they are part of the night of the 24th."

They walked to the other side of the shed and Joel Hardin stopped again.

"Something here was moved recently. See all that?" he asked as his hand waved to a five by three area. The color of the dirt was significantly lighter than the dirt on its circumference. It was almost dry.

"I think that is where the carpet came from to cover Wayne in front the shed," Kathy said.

"I think you're right," Hardin responded.

It took over three hours of study before Hardin said he had enough information.

That afternoon, the trackers met and discussed each other's findings. Similar tracks had been found outside the second premises with a lot of activity near the fire-pit. Of further note, the utility trailer had a ramp on it. When the ramp was opened, multiple tracks of the familiar foot impressions were found. Like on the back patio and in the backyard, they showed dozens of trips going back and forth.

The team spent the next few hours looking at 8 x 10 photos of the crime scene inside the main house. They saw Leuco Crystal Violet (LCV) stained blood prints located in the living room, kitchen, hallways and bathroom. Once again, the two familiar boot impressions were evident as they crisscrossed pathways throughout the house. The blood smears of the cleanup hid very few of the prints.

None of the team commented on the fact that no bloodied footprints were found of any of the victims. The victims had not walked in blood so their footprints did not show up when induced by the spraying of LCV. More than likely, they were already deceased by the time the multiple bloodied tracks were made.

David Sorenson, dressed in gray suit with a blue shirt and maroon tie, took the opportunity to cross-examine the witness.

"So," he said, a notepad in his hand, "let's talk a little on confirmatory bias. Did Kathleen Decker prepare a report for you?"

"She did," Hardin responded. "She had samples of the prints we were looking for. She also had a layout of the property."

"So, you were briefed by a Sergeant, too?"

"Yes. We determined our tracking objectives," the witness answered calmly.

Sorenson nodded his head. "Now, moving on, did you testify that your company was for profit?"

"Yes, I did. However, we do first visits on crime scenes free of charge. Oftentimes, in the larger scale scenes, we know we are unexpected experts. Usually, law enforcement does not have a budget for us established when they need us. In that, we offer our assistance. Budgets are worked out later. Crime scenes don't wait for budgets."

"When was the last time you were called for a defense?" Sorenson asked.

"Recently, actually. I was called for two different homicides in Arizona."

Sorenson changed gears again.

"Let me ask you about the set of footprints behind the shed. If the set was not from Joseph McEnroe or from Michele Anderson, who were they from?"

"I do not know."

"You also mentioned a "flat" tone and I would like to discuss that further. What do you mean?"

Hardin looked toward the jury. "When a print is first made in grass, it glistens. It will stay like that for only two to twenty-four hours. Of course, it depends upon consistent humidity, temperature and lack of precipitation. After that time, the blades lose that effect. If the blades have been damaged, they will bleed. The damaged areas are very good indicators in determining how much time has passed. The softer and mushier the damage is, the longer the time. It becomes second nature to a tracker to recognize these little clues."

"How do you know the impressions behind the shed were not made at the same time as the drag marks you spoke of?"

"Crime scenes signs deteriorate over time. I could tell the prints were just 72 hours old. Caving could be seen on the edges and the prints were not as clear as the drag path. The definition went away which was not consistent with the grass in front," Hardin explained.

"I don't understand how you know that," Sorenson said. "How do you know the time difference?"

"I've looked at over eighty-thousand impressions. It is something you learn over time and it is what I teach law enforcement how to recognize," he stated patiently.

The jurors would have been satisfied with the credibility of Joel Hardin. They also knew that they would never look at a lawn the same way again.

DAY 14
February 9, 2016

I'M A MONSTER

The jurors knew that something was up when Scott O'Toole passed them each a 112-page document. He was dressed impeccably in a black suit, white shirt and black tie.

"Ladies and Gentlemen," the judge said, "Please resist the urge to read ahead. You must read along while the audiotape is played. The transcript you have in your hands will not be allowed in the jury room nor will its use be allowed in the deliberation process. You will, however, have access to the two-hour tape recording once you are deliberating."

Detective Tompkins had prefaced the tape from 2007 as the one taken after Michele Anderson and Joseph McEnroe had arrived at the crime scene at 11:00 AM on December 26. The pair had driven up in a black S10 pickup and voluntarily approached the detective. Tompkins chose to interview Michele under the impression that he was about to give a death notification and brought her to his unmarked Impala.

Detective Pavlovich had interviewed Joseph McEnroe separately.

Scott O'Toole pressed, "play" on the CD player and the jurors went on a journey into the mind of a killer.

Just as the tape started to play, the pro se attorney barked from the back row.

"Can we use the mike? We can't hear back here!"

For a moment, I saw the judge's face flush. Scott O'Toole went to the witness microphone and tapped it. The dull thumps could be heard from the gallery.

"Very good," the judge said. "Play the tape."

The jury listened intently while some read along. Many jurors would see a painted picture in their minds of Detective Tompkins in the front seat with Michele Anderson while Detective Sue Peters in the back seat.

"Okay," Tompkins said as he looked at Michele. "You and your parents live in a pretty quiet setting out here, correct?"

"Yeah," she answered. One could picture Anderson's hands in her lap while she looked timidly at the floorboards.

"Kind of in the country, so to speak," he said.

"Yeah," she answered. She looked out the window ahead of her.

"When you came home a while ago, what did you see?"

"A row of cars."

Tompkins nodded his head. "Yes? Were there some media

members out front?"

She thought about it for a moment. "There was a van that had a weird thing on top of it."

"Okay," he prodded a little. "And, were there some Sheriff's cars out there?"

"I don't know," she said offhandedly.

"Well, did you see a lot of police cars when you pulled in?"

She nodded her head. "I just saw a lot of these types of cars."

The whirlwind of helicopter blades could be heard overhead while they chatted.

"I'm just saying this is unusual, right?" he asked, looking toward her again.

"Well, yeah," she answered quietly.

"There're people running around in uniforms and things like that," he said as they watched a fire truck make its way up the driveway.

"Yeah," she agreed.

"What's the one question you asked me when we first sat down?"

She thought about it and then remembered.

"I asked if my car was stolen."

"What do you think all these police cars are here for?" he asked.

"I think the house is on fire," she replied hesitantly.

"Why do you think that?"

"The last time I saw helicopters here was when the old house was on fire."

"How did that fire start?" Tompkins asked.

"I think it was a chimney fire and Adolph used to live down there," she said.

Her voice seemed to drag on as if she were intoxicated or as if she had not slept in a long time. Earlier the detectives had learned that she and Joe did not drink or do drugs.

"So, whose house do you think is on fire?"

"Probably my mom and dad's because I wasn't home," she stated.

"Are you at all concerned about them?"

"Yeah," she said.

There may have been an attempt at emotion and then it fell away from her face, a discarded thought.

"Do you think with me wearing this Sheriff's jacket, I'd be in a position to know such a thing?"

Michele picked at something on her knee. She didn't answer.

"Yes or no?" Tompkins asked.

"Yeah," she said.

"Well, why didn't you ask me?"

She shrugged her shoulders. "I'm just. I thought I wasn't supposed to ask any of that. I thought you'd get mad."

"I wouldn't have gotten mad. You can ask me anything you want. Have you ever seen so many police cars in one place at one time?" he asked as he waved his hand in the direction of the windshield.

"When the house was on fire," she quipped. "There were a lot of police and fire trucks here."

"Have you seen one fire truck since you've been here?"

"No," she answered softly.

Dead silence filled the car.

"Michele? Is there anything, anything," he emphasized, "you want to tell us?"

She rearranged herself in the front seat.

"My, my dad might have got a heart attack."

Tompkins dismissed it. "Police don't come out for heart attacks."

Sue Peters asked from the back seat, "Do you think something happened to your family?"

Michele mumbled something. "Maybe."

"Why?" Tompkins asked.

"I don't know," she said, as she looked absentmindedly out the window. Her voice was timid and small. "Because all these cars and I don't know what else it would be."

Neither detective spoke. A commotion from arriving police vehicles could be heard a short distance away. The heater blew warm air through the air vents.

Michele picked at her hands.

"Would you ever harm your family?" Detective Tompkins asked.

"No," she answered softly.

"Would you ever cover up for somebody who did?" he asked.

"No," she responded.

Sue Peters interjected from the back seat. Her voice was confident.

"I think you might know a little more about why we're here; you have to talk to Scott and I about that."

Tompkins focused on Michele.

"Let me tell you a couple of things we're really good at," he began.

He did not get to finish his sentence.

Suddenly, the girl in the black outfit broke down in the front seat. Her face was buried in her hands and her body heaved.

"It's my fault. I'm sorry," she gulped between sobs.

"Tell us what happened," Tompkins asked softly.

Sue Peters reassured her. "It's okay. Sometimes things get out of hand."

"I'm not a bad person."

"No one is saying you are a bad person, Tompkins said. "But, we..."

"It's not Joe's fault. It's all me," she said as she interrupted him.

"Okay. I, I know, honey, but tell me what happened at your parent's house," Peters prodded.

It took Michele a few minutes to compose herself. Her hands were clasped in her lap.

"My brother owes me a lot of money and he refused to pay me back. He knows we've been struggling. And my parents weren't even going to help. They don't care about it. I love my family so much, and it hurt when he took my money and didn't give it back," she explained.

"Okay. Then what happened?"

"Me and Joe went up to the house for help with the lights. My light went out in the kitchen. My mom and dad were up there when we arrived. And then I told Joe to go back to the other house," she said. She paused as she looked out the side window.

"And then?" Tompkins asked.

"I got into an argument with them 'cause they said they're not helping me get my money back from Scott. They threatened to kick me out because they don't believe Scott's a bad person. They want to charge me rent and they changed the rules. They want the rent now. And," she said pensively, "I have too much stuff around here that I gotta sell. There's no way I'd get out in time. And I panicked."

"Yes?" Tompkins prodded gently.

"I went into my truck and got my handgun. I didn't want to live out on the street and I panicked. And soon as I did that, I regretted it," she said as she broke down in tears.

"I know you did," Tompkins said supportively.

"And that's not me because I love them so much. But I was so mad," she emphasized.

"Go on."

"And then I tried to hide it. They were too heavy. And then I got into an argument when Scott came over. I told him I wanted my money and he said 'he doesn't have to listen to this shit' and he came after me. He charged me and he was gonna hurt me. I'm not lying," she said, conviction in her voice.

"I don't blame you a bit."

"I love him but ever since he married Erica, he hates me," she said quietly. "Anyway, I freaked out and shot him. He kept coming and I shot him four times. I thought he would stop when I pointed the gun. I just wanted my car back and the $40,000 that he owed me."

"$40,000," Tompkins repeated. "That is a lot of money."

"I just wanted it back," Anderson stated smugly.

"I can understand why you were upset."

"And they didn't care."

"I understand," Scott responded. "Did you also shoot Scott's wife and kids?"

"They were running to the phone and I freaked out."

"Okay. How many times did you shoot them, Michele?"

She wiped her face.

"One to each kid. I didn't want to do it."

"It's better to talk about this because you have a lot built up in you," Sue Peters offered.

"I'm sorry," Michele said as she nodded her head. "I just wanted my money back and nobody cared. I can't afford to take people to court. After it happened, I thought I would just run. And then I was like, 'I can't do this' and I had to come back."

"You did the right thing," Tompkins responded. "That shows how much you love your family and how big of a mistake this is."

"I loved them so much and I felt so bad. I couldn't sleep or eat."

"Listen," Tompkins said. "Where's the gun right now?"

"I don't know," she said. "I threw it away. Am I a bad person?"

"No. No, you're not."

"I love my family so much. I'm sorry."

"You said that after the killing of your mom and dad, you tried to cover it up. What does that mean?"

"I drug them in the backyard so when Scott came over, I could try to get my money from him and just leave."

"Okay."

"And, as soon as I shot the gun, I felt so bad. Like, what the hell have I done? I'm a monster. I turned into a monster," she said.

"Listen, Michele," Tompkins said. "After what happened to your parents, how long was it before Scott and Erica showed up?"

"I think it was about an hour."

"What were you doing within the hour?"

"I was just cleaning up the blood and drug them in the backyard," she responded matter-of-factly.

"Okay. Did you know Scott and Erica were going to come over?"

Anderson paused momentarily. "Yeah. I didn't know when."

"Was your plan just to confront Scott?"

"All I wanted to do was talk about why they're letting Scott hurt me and not do anything about it," she said angrily. "That's all I was gonna do was confront Scott and say just pay me back. And I just got scared."

"Michele?" Peters asked from the back seat.

"I'm stupid," Anderson mumbled.

"Where was your mom when you first shot her?" Peters asked. "What room?"

"Kitchen."

"What about your dad?"

"The dining room," Anderson stated flatly.

"How did you move those bodies by yourself?" Tompkins asked.

"The rug."

"How come you covered your dad up?"

"Because the dog was freaking out."

"There were a couple of sets of footprints," Peters commented. "Did Joe at least assist in helping with the bodies?"

"And we're not saying he hurt them but did he help you move them?" Tompkins asked after a moment of silence.

"He came up and helped me get rid of the rug," Anderson finally said.

"Where did the rug go?"

"I burnt them."

"Where at?"

"The fire pit in my yard. Joe didn't do anything," she exclaimed. "It was just me. I'm a bad person."

"You're not a bad person," Peters said comfortingly.

"I'm so sorry."

"What room was Scott in when he was shot?"

"Everybody was in the living room," Anderson replied. "It's my fault. I have nothing and they were taking from me."

"What else did you burn in the fire pit?"

"Towels and a rug. I'm sorry. I don't want anything to happen to Joe. I threatened him to help me," she confessed.

"Well, we can understand why you would want to burn those things. Did you throw the gun in there, as well?" Peters asked.

"No. We threw it away and dumped it in a river."

"Well, it's very important because we don't want the gun to get into the hands of a small child," Peters advised. "A lot of times, they find guns and end up being shot."

"I threw both handguns in one river but I don't remember which one," Anderson admitted.

"Do you think you could point it out to us if we took you there?"

"Yes. It's not Joe's fault. I threatened him to help cover, like by not saying anything."

"And that's fine," Peters said. "Joe's up there talking to another detective."

"I'm sorry," Anderson repeated.

"It's okay," Tompkins commented.

"I'm sorry."

Michele would talk about apologies at the end of her interview with Detective Tompkins and Peters.

"It was the stupidest thing ever," she said. "Nothing was worth this. I should've just listened to Joe because he tried to talk me out of it the entire time. It was my idea, not his."

"Did you say any words to anybody else?" Detective Peters asked. "Did you apologize to anyone else?"

It took Anderson a moment to compose her thoughts.

"I apologized to everybody because I didn't want it to turn out like that, but I knew it would. Do you understand? I mean I went up there, knowing, I'd probably shoot these people. But I didn't want to."

"Well," Tompkins interjected, "what did you say or do to show these people you were sorry?"

"I just said 'sorry' before shooting them," she admitted. "It's horrible. I'm a bad person."

"Did you hear Joe do similar?"

"Yeah."

"What did you hear?"

"He said 'I'm sorry'."

"Who did you hear him say he was sorry to?" Peters inquired.

"Erica and the kids," Anderson replied. "We both shot Erica. He shot the kids, not me."

"Okay," Tompkins said softly. "What were they, or how were the kids reacting?"

"Nathan looked like he knew."

"What does that mean?"

"Like, like he knew that he was gonna die and was accepting of it was weird."

"How did that make you feel?" Tompkins asked.

"Awful."

"Did you do anything to prevent it?"

"No."

"Did you have that discussion with Joe about Nathan?" Peters asked.

"We weren't gonna shoot the kids," Anderson stated again.

"But did you have a discussion with him after the fact about what Nathan looked like or what he felt?"

"We felt horrible."

"So you guys talked about that?"

"Yes, but this was all my idea. I pushed him into it," she defended. "We both felt really bad. I should have walked away from it..."

The jurors would go home that night and many would think that they had just heard the most idiotic reason in the world to kill an innocent family of six.

The confession would have been a moment of transcendence in the juror's mind. They learned that not all killers are smart.

Sadly, too, they learned that killers lie and a family lay dead because of it.

DAY 15
February 10, 2016

CAN I HAVE MY TRIAL BACK?

"Let me alert you to something that we are going to take up after the break because I want to give you a little time to think about it," Judge Ramsdell told the attorneys at the start of the day. "Kenya had an interaction with Juror #16 who relayed to her some information about a conversation he had with his mom. I think you will find that Juror #16 didn't do anything outward, but I think you need to know what occurred because he thought it was significant enough to let us know."

The judge had my attention as well as all of the participants in the courtroom.

"So, Kenya," he continued, "do you want to give us a thumbnail sketch of what he shared with you, and we will certainly bring him out separately to chat with us about it after the break."

Kenya wore a black dress, black blouse and long tan sweater shawl as she stood up next to the court clerk, Kim. She was adjacent to the judge and faced the attorneys.

Kim listened intently and worked on her machine silently.

The bailiff held her hands clasped in front of her. "Juror #16 indicated that he was speaking with his mother and he told her that he could not speak about the case. She asked him how much longer he would be serving as a juror. He said a few more weeks or something like that. She then blurted it out that she knew the other defendant had been convicted and she could not wait to talk to him about that because she didn't understand why the woman had to go to trial. He said he then walked away but he had heard her say that."

The judge took his glasses off and rubbed the bridge of his nose. He shook his head.

"Another argument for sequestering jurors," he commented offhandedly. "I think he's been exposed to information that I would have preferred that he had not been exposed to. We will bring him out and chat with him after the break and see if there is any remedial action we need to take. Mr. O'Toole?"

"Before the break or now?" the prosecutor asked.

"I want to do it after the break," the judge answered.

"And you will admonish him to stay away from his mother?" O'Toole asked with a smile.

The courtroom chuckled.

"I might let you do that," the judge cajoled. "I think we just need to talk to him about it. Since we have left the jury back there for thirty minutes already, I want to get the testimony started before we do that. Okay. So, are we ready for the jury, folks?"

The first witness of the day was marked with the return of Detective Scott Tompkins. He wore a gray suit, white shirt and a blue diamond patterned tie.

Scott took a spot to the side of the podium. His charcoal suit and white shirt was complimented with a Christmas Red silk tie. His dialogue with Tompkins was like being part of a conversation. Scott was personable with witnesses, no matter who they were.

We learned that Michele Anderson had been with Detective Tompkins for the entirety of the day, the day after Christmas. After her confession, they got in his car with Detective Peters and drove to the location where she claimed that she and Joe had dumped the guns. In the hours after the murders, she and McEnroe had driven northward, stopping in Monroe for gas. They drove in a northwest direction, passing Everett. When they got to the Stillaguamish River at Exit 208 from I-5 Southbound, she showed the detectives the bridge.

"Where did you go after that?"

Tompkins turned toward the jury. "It was time to have her booked so we drove to the jail."

"Were you still questioning her?"

"It was more like small talk. Here and there we might ask a question," he said as he pondered it. "Most of the time, she just said things."

"Does anything come to mind as memorable or odd to you?" Scott asked.

"She was talking about her father and said she saw him with a skinned cat, or something like that. I think she said she was five. It was horrible to her. I asked if her father was a hunter."

"Why would you ask that?"

Tompkins shifted in his chair. "I think I was being sarcastic. Why would a Boeing engineer be a sadistic animal killer? It had been a long day."

"So you brought her down to the booking station?"

"We did. She got checked in, surrendered her clothes and boots and we kept the boots as evidence," Tompkins recalled. "I think it was around six or seven at night. The boots then went to the evidence room."

The jurors watched as Scott walked over to the court clerk and retrieved a large paper bag. He handed it to his witness and asked him to open it.

The detective verbalized that he recognized his signature, the crime lab seals and the forensics seals. He put on a pair of rubber gloves and used a pair of scissors to extricate the evidence from the bag. One by one, he pulled out two black boots.

Scott followed suit with a pair of elastic gloves and took the boots from the witness. He fastidiously had them entered in the record as Exhibit #44.

The courtroom was silent. One could only imagine what those boots had seen on a tragic Christmas Eve in 2007.

He faced the sole of one to the jury while he paired the other boot in reverse. Slowly, he walked them in front of the jurors and some leaned forward from the back row with interest. They looked for the signature tiny circles on the soles of the boots, the same circles left in blood throughout the house and on the ledge of the

216

shed.

It was a sobering moment for the jury, as they thought of a family of six who had been snuffed underfoot, evidenced by the little circles that recorded the path of a killer.

Robin Cleary took the witness stand after a well-earned court recess. She wore charcoal black pants, a purple blouse and a black coat. She had worked for the King's County Sheriff's Office for the better part of twenty years although she currently worked for Pinkerton Security. She had been a detective in the Major Crimes Division when she was called to the scene on December 26, 2007. Her first assigned task was to go up with the pilot of a helicopter and take aerial photos of the expansive crime scene.

Once her job was completed, she returned to Carnation at 1:00 PM. She reported to the crime lab van and met with Detective Toner who sent her to accompany Michele Anderson for forty-five minutes. Michele had already made a statement and someone needed to be in the room with her.

Detective Cleary walked into the room and sat at a table across from her. Not long after she was seated, Michele timidly spoke. Cleary would refer to it as more a monologue than a dialogue.

"So, what did she tell you?" Scott asked.

"That her brother owed her $40, 000. Her parents had given him $70, 000 for his education and so on.. She was talking like, 'woe is me'," Cleary recalled.

"Did you, or were you," O'Toole clarified, "asking her questions?"

"No," she replied. "I just let her talk. Her tone was intent on telling me her story."

"What did she tell you?"

"She said her brother had guilt-tripped her. She had been living rent-free for a year and suddenly she was supposed to pay rent. She either said she had to be out on December 24th, or she was told on December 24th, to be out of her place. She said she panicked," Cleary explained as she glanced at her documentation gathered eight years ago.

"And then?"

"She told me she argued with her father that night and she shot him. She then said that she and Joe shot everybody. He had a .357 and she had a 9 mm. He was an accessory. Her gun had jammed when she was shooting Scott. She gave the gun to Joe and he continued shooting. He shot both the kids with her 9 mm, in the head."

"What was her demeanor at this time?" O'Toole asked.

"She was whiny and matter-of-fact. She was not tearful," Cleary commented.

"What else do you remember?"

"She said she shot her dad. Her mom came running in from another room. I think she said her mother was wrapping Christmas presents. When her mom saw what happened, she ran to the kitchen and was cowering by the wall and the refrigerator. That's when she said she shot her mother. Scott came home later and she put four rounds in him."

"Are those the words she used?" O'Toole queried.

Detective Cleary checked her report.

"Yes. She also said she put two rounds into Erica."

"What did she say happened next?"

"She said that she and Joe hid the bodies of her parents so that Scott would not see them when he got there. They put her mother in the shed and left Wayne outside under a piece of carpet. After everyone was dead, they used a lot of towels and throw rugs to try and wipe up. They then took the towels and burned them. After that, they drove to a covered bridge in Snohomish and threw the guns in a river. Feeling guilty, she had returned to Carnation to confess because she couldn't live with herself," Cleary finished.

"Did you know she was a suspect?" O'Toole asked.

"I had a pretty good idea that she was after she told me her story."

When it was Colleen O'Connor's turn to question the witness, she asked again if Cleary knew that Michele was a suspect.

"Not at the time," Cleary responded.

"But you knew that the Miranda statement had been done?"

"I did."

Colleen walked toward the podium and looked at her notes. "The defendant said in her comments to you that she had lived in her mobile home for a year on the property rent-free?"

"Yes," Cleary confirmed.

"She also said she panicked on the 24th when she was told she had to move out? That's when she shot Wayne?"

"I believe so."

"She also told you that Joe shot the children with the 9 MM, am I correct?"

"Yes."

O'Connor paused and looked at her notes again. "She also said she shot Scott after he attacked her?"

"She did. As I recall, she told me she went crazy. She was tired of doing everything for them," Cleary answered.

"She also told you that her father was abusive, didn't she?"

Cleary briefly shrugged her shoulders. "Michele Anderson claimed that."

"No more questions," Colleen said as she walked back and took her seat next to Anderson.

The defendant did not acknowledge the defense attorney's presence.

"Just a couple of questions," Scott told the court on re-direct as he walked toward the witness stand. "Michele Anderson told you that she shot Erica two times with the .357 revolver?"

"Yes," Cleary stated.

"She had also told you that she returned to the property to confess, didn't she?"

"Yes."

"Did she mention to you that she lied to detectives for almost two hours?" O'Toole asked with a voice devoid of sarcasm.

"No," Cleary told the jurors. "I don't recall her telling me that."

"No more questions," O'Toole responded.

Although Detective Cleary's testimony had been swift, the jurors would have found that she was a key witness. At the very least, the tale that she told put a lot of the puzzle pieces together. It organized the chaos in each of their heads as they tried to put the timeline of the murders in place. It made sense.

The jury had been dismissed for morning break when Judge Ramsdell held the court.

"I think now might be a good time to have a discussion with Juror #16. Any objections? Counselors?"

Since there were none, Ramsdell asked Kenya, the den mother to the jurors, to retrieve Juror #16 from the jury room.

My stomach muscles tightened as I imagined how uncomfortable it would be for the juror to speak on a private matter in front of everyone.

A young man came out of the jury room from the back of the courtroom and took his regular seat in the jury box. He was dressed casually and neatly. His oxford shirt was pressed. He leaned forward in his seat.

"You're not in trouble," the judge began in a nonthreatening tone. "All we want to do is talk to you about what happened with your mom."

Juror #16 cleared his throat.

"Well, I was on a video chat with my family. My mom said that she couldn't wait to talk. They knew what trial I was on but I haven't told them anything else. She asked when the trial would be over and then she blurted out that the defendant's boyfriend had been found guilty. I stopped her when she said that and told her I could not talk about it. I am not sure where she got her data."

The judge scratched his forehead.

"This would be an argument for sequestering juries. Let me ask you this: Do you think it will impact your decision-making at all?"

"No," he answered. "As far as I know, it's hearsay. I only know what we have seen at the trial. I want to focus on this."

"Mr. O'Toole?" the judge said. "Questions?"

"I keep picturing the Geico commercial where the man is a spy and he's running. Then mom calls," Scott responded. He looked at the lone juror. "Do you think you can base your decisions on only the facts and disregard what your mom said?"

"Absolutely. I should be sequestered from my mom," the juror quipped.

"Mr. Sorenson?" Judge Ramsdell directed.

"No questions," he said.

"I have some information on this that you should know," Miss {redacted} suddenly said from the back row of the gallery.

I could almost hear a collective gasp in the room.

The juror was looking toward the judge.

"The media has reported the conviction of Joe McEnroe everywhere. You should know that," she told the judge. She stood while everyone else was seated.

"Ma'am?" Ramsdell said, cutting her off. "I will not tolerate your behavior from the gallery. This is not your trial! I am here to ensure Michele Anderson gets a fair trial. You are not to blurt things out. I will have you removed if it happens again."

"But I have an interruptive disorder. The court should respect my rights. No one is providing me assistance."

"This needs no more discussion," he said with finality.

He dismissed the juror politely, but quickly.

"Regarding the Juror #16 issue. Do the attorneys have any concerns?" the judge asked after Kenya had secured the door to the jury room.

Scott O'Toole stood up.

"I understand if the defense has a concern. The State sees no harm in what happened."

David Sorenson stood up, as well.

"I know this was a mistake and we appreciate the juror's honesty. It is, however, our opinion that the juror be excused. He heard information that has been excluded in this trial."

"I am not completely sold we should dismiss the juror," Ramsdell commented. "I think I want to reserve on this issue. Let me think about it."

The return from lunch saw the flash of a firestorm that few expected possible.

Scott O'Toole spoke up before the jury was brought in.

"As the Court knows, we invited Juror #16 out to talk about his mother regarding this case. This, so that the record is clear, the court was called upon to address a member of the gallery who spoke out. She blurted out some comments, or started to, as the juror was in the room and that woman's name is Miss {redacted}. She is someone who has addressed the court in the past and to whom the court has directed comments in the past. We are very, very concerned that Miss {redacted} is unwilling and maybe even incapable of controlling what she says in open court, particularly in front of these jurors."

The judge looked back at the prosecutor, his glasses in his hand. He listened carefully.

"I would note that when she addressed the court a week ago, she diagnosed herself as having something called interruptive disorder," he said. "That is of tremendous concern to the State and, I imagine, to the defense as well, with respect to the potential risks of tainting the jury with information they should not hear."

The prosecutor cleared his throat and continued his plea.

"We have advised the court in the past of our knowledge of statements made by Michele Anderson to a witness by the name of Bridgette Brown regarding Miss Anderson's stated intention to disrupt the trial, and by telling the jurors such things as: this is not a death penalty case and telling the jurors that Mr. McEnroe was previously convicted. It is of concern to us that the subject of Mr. McEnroe's previous conviction was a subject on which Miss {redacted} decided to blurt out, or whatever it was she was going to blurt out in front of the Court."

I wondered if Miss {redacted} and the defendant were linked. Had the outbursts been pre-planned? Was it an effort to cause a mistrial?

The prosecutor paused while the judge looked on.

"She has no standing to address the court directly in this case and she is NOT an attorney," Scott continued emphatically. "She represents herself to be a pro se attorney for Miss Anderson, whatever that means. She is not counsel of record and, I would suggest, even off the record. I would note that we have learned in the last few minutes that Miss {redacted} has visited Michele Anderson in the jail as recently as two days ago on February 8 and that is of concern."

It was news to all of us in the gallery. A few were brave enough to turn around and glance at her.

"But to make it clear about whom we are talking, about the prior history, about Miss {redacted}'s own statement that she has interruptive disorder, and about what we all know is potential for prejudice, and the risk of a mistrial in this case, and that she is apparently honed in on Michele Anderson and is visiting her in jail as recently as two days ago, that should this happen again, I will ask on behalf of the State that Miss {redacted} be removed from this court, and barred from this court," O'Toole pointed out, "and not be allowed to attend because of the risks to both parties of a fair trial. Thank you."

The judge looked toward the defense table. "Mr. Sorenson or Miss O'Connor, is there anything you want to state for the record?"

"Yes, your Honor," Sorenson replied. "We agree with the State's concern about Miss {redacted}'s behavior in court, and certainly all those concerns are valid. I think that what needs to be said in addition to that is that in no way, shape or form was Miss Anderson directing or controlling Miss {redacted}'s behavior in this court. Miss {redacted} is not acting on her behalf. She is here for her own unintelligible agenda and I think that that is clear for the record."

"Okay," the judge responded as he made a notation. "Thank you."

Like nails scraping mercilessly along the length of a chalkboard, I heard the unmistakable voice of the gallery guest behind me.

"As I have stated, I did not ever say I was a representative of Michele Anderson," Miss {redacted} said vehemently. "What I said is I am here to preserve appellate evidence and that's exactly what I'm doing! I have an interruptive disorder. It's not self-diagnosed. I actually have ADA rights as a person with a disability."

The judge did not look very pleased.

"I did not blurt out any information, other than where that information got to the juror's mother who he brought forth to the court properly," she continued to the dismay of many. "I was giving you, the media, how it got out and where it came from. Because you, like you have mentioned, that I have been monitoring the media, including Mr. Sanders and the awful comments he made about me, and the other people, and people like that as well."

I am not sure why, at every opportunity, she chose to include me in her conversations with the court. I had not spoken to her since the first day of trial and had never caught her eye since. I had been like a juror, invisible and out of people's way, including hers.

"And so, in that, and we all know the things that have been going on since the last trial. I was not at the last trial and I have no interest in the overhaul. I'm not here to negate the family or to negate her. I'm here because I know things have happened in the jail," Miss {redacted} continued. "I do visit her in jail. I would consider her a friend, and she has no support here from any of these people, and I understand things that maybe somebody else doesn't, but appellate-wise we have attorneys not objecting."

There were plenty of people who wanted to object to her tirade but everyone remained silent, an adherence to standard court protocol.

The look on the judge's face was pure patience but the blush of his ears told me she had raised his blood pressure.

"I wasn't saying anything in front of the juror that he didn't already hear and I wasn't going to blurt out a whole lot of information because, yes, we know that she's not been convicted, yet and that's why we're here in this trial. And," she directed toward Scott O'Toole, "I AM a pro se attorney and have been one for nine years due to the ineffective assistance of other attorneys.

"I have a standing with some judges. You can speak to Judge Rogoff, if you would like to know about my disability and interruptive disorder, and under stress it's a little more concerning and what have you. I notice that the media comes when something juicy is there and not for the other things. I get that. And so it is tampered and tainted with but not because of me.

"And the fact is that preserving somebody's evidence, I have a right as a spectator and I'm not trying to disrupt anything," she explained.

I respectfully disagreed as I took my notes.

"I'm not trying to thwart this trial. But some of the things that I have concerns in some of the rights that are being violated constitutionally and that's where I stand because I know what they are and other people in the gallery may not." she finished.

"Okay," the judge said. He looked as if he was ready to continue when her words trumped him.

"And the fair trial!" she pointed out. "You and I are on the same page. I think everybody else has come around into something else. So, if there is an ADA coordinator and she doesn't work for the court, please give me that information and I will gladly go and do whatever paperwork I need to do under the disability law with the State of Washington to be a spectator in this courtroom to preserve the appellate information for attorneys who are not objecting but should."

"Thank you," Judge Ramsdell responded. "Can I have my trial back? Real quickly, because I have a trial to attend to."

"Yeah," she said.

"Ma'am? You may think you are a pro se attorney. You can be pro se in your cases all day long."

"And I am," she defended.

"But, you are not representing anyone here."

"I never said I was," she responded insolently.

"It sounded like it," the judge corrected. "But, okay. Second thing is that the appellate record is the record that's taken here, and the representation of Miss Anderson is being taken care of by her attorneys. It's not your issue. Thirdly, if you have an ADA accommodation that we have to address, then I guess we might have to address it. As far as I can tell, it's being addressed just fine right now because you are here in the courtroom. There really isn't an ADA issue at present, so I don't need to contact anybody in order to accommodate your needs."

Miss {redacted} began to object but the judge continued.

"Next," he said with an upraised finger, "since you are not a party to this case, you are merely a public spectator, to the extent that you want to raise your hand and participate in the proceedings, and I will not acknowledge that kind of participation. And, last but not least, if you do blurt something out or make any attempt to disrupt these proceedings, number one: I will make sure that you are removed from the courtroom because I have the power and authority to do that in order to control the courtroom."

If I interpreted the judge's words correctly, she had raised her hand in the gallery and in front of jurors. I could bet the jurors wondered who she was.

"Number two," the judge said firmly. "You are on notice that such behavior is inappropriate and I will find you in contempt, and I will have these nice folks," he said as he pointed to the guards, "take you over to the jail for a stay there until we can figure out what to do next. I don't want to do that but that's what I would have to do if this trial gets disrupted. As you've read in the paper, undoubtedly, millions of dollars have been spent on this trial already."

The silence in the courtroom was thick.

"I will not run the risk of having to spend another six months selecting another jury and getting this case off the ground again. We are trying it now. We are going to do it right the first time and leave it at that," Judge Ramsdell admonished.

"And I'm not here to disrupt it," she interrupted. "Again, to confirm, I'm not here to disrupt it. That's not any of the thing..."

The judge took his turn to interrupt her.

"But you understand that I don't want you waving your hand back there asking to be called upon as if you were in school, and I don't want you blurting out anything to the jurors or anybody else at this point in time because that's the kind of thing that's going to require a rather swift reaction on my part, and it's not going to be a good one," he warned her.

"You and I are on the same page," she responded as if she was a well-seasoned team player in the profession of law. "I was not blurting anything. Somebody just took it out of context."

"Okay," the judge said.

He thought they were done.

"And I was letting you know where the media information came from about what was said because it was told to me somebody else knows. I'm a spectator. That's it," she said.

Judge Ramsdell shook his head.

"And, Ma'am? I just want you to understand that I really don't need that kind of help."

"Would you rather have a motion or a note of where the media source is because I'm monitoring them for things that are going wrong?" she asked. "Would that be more appropriate for you?"

"Ma'am? I'm doing my job," he said somewhat impatiently. "I would appreciate it if you wouldn't help me with it. Okay? Thank you! And if we are on the same page, that's terrific but I hope you understand what I'm telling you."

"So, you don't want a motion if there's something that needs media addressing?" she asked, apparently not knowing when to quit. "Is that what I'm hearing you say, your Honor?"

The judge looked toward the attorneys and stopped looking at the self- proclaimed pro se attorney. "Okay, I think we are done now. Thank you very much, Ma'am. So, Kenya, could you invite the jury in?"

"Thank you," Scott O'Toole said.

To the chagrin of the participants in the courtroom, Miss {redacted} would be back like a nasty cold that would not go away.

The jurors spent the afternoon on a tutorship of the science of forensic pathology and the role of the Medical Examiner in a death investigation through the testimony of Dr. Richard Harruff. It would have been new information to most of the jurors. They would have found it clinically interesting.

"Can you tell the jurors what 'autopsy' means?" Scott O'Toole asked the Medical Examiner.

"To see for one's self," he responded definitively.

Most of the jurors were terrified of the next onslaught of evidence.

1. The King County Courthouse (left) nestled within the city of Seattle although the murders occurred at the edge of the county to the east. (Photo: Paul Sanders)

2. The King County Courthouse is located where 3rd Ave and Jefferson cross, coincidentally, the same cross-streets as the courthouse in Phoenix, AZ, where I spent many months covering the Jodi Arias retrial the year before. (Photo: Paul Sanders)

3. Wayne Anderson, a retired Boeing engineer was the first victim killed on December 24, 2007. He was married to Judy, and father to Scott, Michele and Mary. (Photo: Pamela Mantle)

4. Judy Anderson, a carrier for the U.S. Postal Service in Carnation, Washington was the second victim. She was mother to Scott, Michele and Mary. She was married to Wayne Anderson. (Photo: Pamela Mantle)

5. Scott Anderson, who worked for a construction company in Kenmore, Washington, was the third victim. This occurred two and a half hours after the first two murders happened. He was married to Erica and father to Olivia and Nathan.
(Photo: KIRO-TV)

6. Erica Anderson, a baker and a homemaker, was possibly the final victim. She was married to Scott and mother to Olivia and Nathan.

This picture was taken on Mother's Day, 2002 as she fed her first child, Olivia.

(Photo: Pamela Mantle)

7. Olivia Anderson, kindergarten student at Black Diamond Elementary, was the fourth victim. Her favorite things included dancing and a love for horses. Picture was taken as she waited patiently to pet a newborn kitten. (Photo: Pamela Mantle)

8. Nathan Anderson celebrated his third birthday only two weeks prior to becoming the fifth victim. Picture was taken in fall of 2007 while at the zoo in Seattle. (Photo: Pamela Mantle)

9. The Anderson family of Erica, Olivia, Scott and Nathan taken on December 10, 2006 on Nathan's birthday. He had just turned two. (Photo: Pamela Mantle)

10. Scott O'Toole, Senior Deputy Prosecuting Attorney of King County, presented the victims' pictures on placards for the jury. He displayed these pictures to two juries: that of Joseph McEnroe and Michele Anderson. The children's pictures would remain the most painful for all. (Photo:KOMO-TV)

11. Overview of the extensive and rural Anderson property. Right of center is the residence of Wayne and Judy. The dirt road to the left shows the residence of Joseph McEnroe and Michele Anderson. Just out of frame is the gate to the long driveway. No one heard screams or gunshots on Christmas Eve of 2007. (Photo: Google Images)

12. Mailboxes at the base of the long rural driveway which two juries had seen countless numbers of times.
(Photo: Paul Sanders)

13. The gate at the base of the driveway was closed when officers responded to a 911 call made by Erica Anderson at 5:13pm on December 24, 2007. (Photo: Paul Sanders)

14. The exterior of the home at 1806 346 Avenue North East in Carnation, Washington. All six murders took place in the residence. (Photo: King County Prosecutor's Office)

15. The singlewide residence of Michele Anderson and Joseph McEnroe. On Christmas Eve of 2007, they chose to take their truck up the driveway, instead of walking. (Photo: Google Images)

16. "Secret of the Stillaguamish" The Stillaguamish River yielded one gun found by the teenager, Jared Sinnema. (Photo: Paul Sanders)

17. Michele Anderson was flanked by multiple guards as she was led to the crime scene reconstruction. This was on the first floor of the King County courthouse. (Photo: KIRO-TV)

18. Ross Gardner, standing at the back of the room by television set, directed the meticulously created reconstruction crime scene. Detective Scott Tompkins (left) made final preparations before the jurors stepped into the room. (Photo: Paul Sanders)

19. Michele Morales, Deputy Prosecuting Attorney discussed preparations with an intern attorney before the jury came in. (Photo: Paul Sanders)

20. "Blood and Bullets" This is the view of the scene from the approximate location of the doorway where the killers first made their appearance. Only a few of the 14 jurors would walk on the reconstructed scene when given the opportunity. Most jurors thought it to be hallowed ground. (Photo: Paul Sanders)

21. The reconstructed scene from behind where Michele Anderson stood in the final moments of her family's lives. The area around the loveseat is where Erica, Olivia and Nathan were shot. Erica received four bullet wounds with multiple paths. (Photo: Paul Sanders)

22. "Receipts Tell Tales" is Exhibit 165G, a still photograph taken by Bank of America security cameras as Michele Anderson casually made a lien payment on her truck. Jurors would find her affect disconcerting as she had killed her family less than 48 hours prior. (Photo: King County Prosecutor's Office)

23. Scott O'Toole began closing arguments for the jury of Michele Anderson while Judge Jeffrey Ramsdell looked on. (Photo: KIRO-TV)

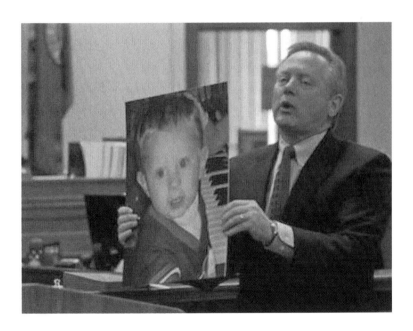

24. Again, in closing statements, Scott O'Toole reminded the jurors who the victims were, which included the youngest, Nathan Anderson. (Photo: KOMO-TV)

25. "Query of the Lambs" Judge Ramsdell and the Bailiff, Kenya, reserved the front row of the gallery to the memory of the six victims: Wayne, Judy, Scott, Erica, Olivia and Nathan with a white Carnation at each seat. (Photo: Pamela Mantle)

26. "Banquet of Consequences" Michele Anderson discussed her final moments in court as David Sorenson and Colleen O'Connor directed her attention to the necessary paperwork that came with her sentence. (Photo: KIRO-TV)

27. "Beyond the Pale" Joseph McEnroe photograph taken on June 28, 2016 at Walla Walla Penitentiary where he will serve life without the possibility of parole. I had always referred to my interview with him as a kaleidoscope of ironies. (Photo: Paul Sanders)

28. Scott, Wayne, Judy and Michele Anderson in a family photograph taken in the mid 1980's. Michele Anderson would presumably have been Olivia's age. (Photo: Pamela Mantle)

29. Taken at Christmas time in 2006 with Scott, Joseph McEnroe, Michele and Nathan. Who could have known that this would be their last Christmas together?
(Photo: Pamela Mantle)

30. A memorial wrapped tree at Black Diamond Elementary School dedicated to the Anderson's. The plaque reads:

"To everything there is a season, and a time to every purpose, under heaven. Your memory is our keepsake, which we'll never part. God has you in our keeping and we have you in our hearts."
(Photo: Pamela Mantle)

31. Pamela Mantle (mother of Erica Anderson) outside the Carnation cemetery with Paul Sanders. (Photo: Paul Sanders)

32. This is Pamela Mantle's favorite picture of Scott and Erica taken on Thanksgiving Day, 2004.
(Photo: Pamela Mantle)

33. Carnation Post Office where Linda Thiele and Judy Anderson were employed. (Photo: Paul Sanders)

34. Judy Anderson Memorial inside the Carnation Post Office. (Photo: Paul Sanders)

35. As was tradition, Erica loved putting her children's pictures on the annual Christmas cards that she would send to family and friends. This was the last Christmas card Erica Anderson would send when she wished her loved ones a 'Happy 2008'. (Photo: Pamela Mantle)

36. Memorial lamppost in Seaside Oregon, which overlooks
Erica's favorite vacation spot. Inscribed at the base:

"Scott, Erica, Olivia & Nathan Anderson
Family and Friends
December 24, 2007 RIP"

DAY 16
February 11, 2016

SALUTE TO A JUROR

The Geico commercial that Scott O'Toole had referenced the day before featured a man in a suit who was running from someone on a rooftop. Another man climbed onto the rooftop as he tried to escape. The man in the suit suddenly turned in another direction. Two more men had joined the chase. The whir of helicopter propellers beat the wind above him.

Suddenly, his cell phone rang. He answered it as he tried to kick off his assailants.

"Where are you?" he asked loudly.

"Well, the squirrels are back in the attic and your dad won't call an exterminator. He says it's personal this time," his mother informed him.

The man shook his head and continued to try and get away from the men who chased him. "Can I call you back, Mom?"

"It's awfully loud there," his mother commented casually. "Are you at a Zumba class?"

The narrator of the commercial then interjected by saying, "If you're a mom, you call at the worst time. It's what you do."

The commercial had captured the awkward position of a juror and the hundreds of random circumstances that could come along and get one thrown off the jury. The juror was always conscious of the possible missteps daily. The threat was always around the corner and the juror lived in fear of it. Whether he or she accidentally saw something on the television, or overheard a conversation, or even when jurors found themselves in the company of principals of the courtroom as they descended on an elevator, jurors always feared making a mistake. It sometimes felt as if a juror needed eyes behind their backs. The omnipresent vibe of paranoia kept the juror in constant awareness of their surroundings.

And, so it went with Juror #16.

"Before we bring out the jury," Judge Ramsdell said after he took care of the morning protocols. He wore black robes over a soft blue shirt with a blue and black striped tie underneath. "I spent a significant amount of time pondering the issue concerning Juror #16. Have the attorney's positions changed for either side?" he asked.

Scott O'Toole spoke pleasantly from a seated position. He wore a crisp light blue shirt and burgundy colored tie.

"The State's position is that we do not believe he has been harmed as a juror. However, we also say that we can understand the defense's position and we would not object." Scott said.

"Ms. O'Connor?"

"Our position has not changed. The juror heard information that was excluded from this trial," the defense attorney said.

I could tell by the tone of David Sorenson's voice that Juror #16 was going to be history. I expected that the outburst of Miss {redacted} the day prior had not helped.

The judge leaned forward on the bench as he clasped his hands and rested on his elbows. "I have put a great deal of thought into this and I truly believe that this juror has not been impacted and I do not believe he has been impaired. However, I am in an awkward position. I am almost cornered on this matter. If I decline on this and it later came up for appeal, the defense has a position in it."

David Sorenson nodded at the defense table.

"The risk is too great for this to be used on appeal which could lead to a reversal and a new trial. My feeling is that it is best to excuse Juror#16 favoring an excess of caution. We are left with two alternates whereas if we were down to a dozen, we might see a different ruling. I just do not believe the Court wants to go down that road," the judge said.

He took his glasses off and quickly wiped the lenses. "I feel really bad for this juror because he did nothing wrong. I don't know how he's going to get along with his mother now," he said as he smiled.

"I hope you have a long speech prepared for him," Scott O'Toole added. "It was his mom that messed up and he's going to feel awful about it. I still can't help but think of that Geico commercial and what happened to the poor juror."

The judge held up a stack of papers. "I agree. It stinks but it is what it is. Kenya?" he asked the bailiff, "will you please bring out Juror #16."

Moments later, the juror, dressed in a pressed checkered oxford shirt and jeans, took his regular seat, the second to the last on the top row.

"I admire you for coming to us and following your admonishment to the letter of the law."

Juror #16 nodded to the judge.

"The court appreciates you and I appreciate your honesty and obligation to your oath. However, I am exercising an overabundance of caution in this trial and find that I must excuse you. I apologize, as I know how much time you have vested in this matter. I need to emphasize that you did nothing wrong," the judge said.

He looked down and referred to his prepared statement in front of him.

"I absolve you from your admonition with only one condition. You are free to talk to anyone about this case, research it, go online and speak to the media if you wish. The media may contact you at some point but you are under no obligation to talk to them or anyone else. You are not allowed to speak with anyone on the jury on this matter. I would suspect you are all buddies by now, or I would hope so, but you will have to refrain from contact until after the trial."

The juror shook his head in acknowledgement.

"I sincerely hope you are okay with your mother. You were selected as a very small fraction of a large pool of potential jurors. You accepted your burden and obligation as a juror and you should be proud that you stepped up. I want you to be proud of honoring your oath," the judge told him with sincerity.

"It makes sense," Juror #16 commented politely.

"Thank you for your service, Juror #16. Kenya will talk with you before you go. Please tell your mom anything she wants to know with my blessing. Do not let this get in the way of your relationship. Thank you."

Then, Judge Ramsdell stood up. "In honor of Juror #16, I would like the court to stand up."

Juror #16 nodded again at the judge and walked past us with his head held up. Kenya escorted him to the jury room to collect his badge and notebook.

When the jury room door opened, jurors were busy chatting. Most of them would not realize that Juror #16 had made his last entry. The last thing he said to them before he left his fellow jurors was, "See you in a bit." Moments later, Kenya accompanied him as he left the courtroom with his jacket in his hand.

Many of the jurors knew that the financial burden on Juror #16 had increased at home. His benefits from Amazon had expired and he was not able to survive on the daily court stipend of ten dollars. The juror's wife had understood civic duty and sacrifice up to the point that the juror had begun to use their vacation savings to pay their bills. Although he was dejected at being dismissed, relief from the financial pressure dimmed the pain.

This juror's commitment had begun on December 11, 2015. It

was the day that his life had turned upside down. He put his family on hold and he rearranged his work schedule to minimal hours. He accepted his ten dollars a day from the State of Washington and had earned $150 since the beginning of jury selection. The first day of jury duty was always free of charge from the citizen.

The unintended consequence of doing his duty was the scar that was left on his soul. One could be sure that he would never forget the names of the victims.

The remaining fourteen jurors watched intently as the Chief Medical Examiner of King County, Washington, Richard Harruff, returned to the witness stand. The jurors knew they were about to journey further into the forensics of the deaths of six. Not one of them looked forward to it however all of them felt they were mentally prepared. Emotion was laid on the back seat as the jurors tried to drive forward and be the fact-finders into the study of the activities on an awful Christmas Eve in 2007.

Scott O'Toole asked the Medical Examiner, "Can you tell us what you, what your job encompasses when you receive a case in your office?"

Richard Harruff looked toward the jury. He was a tall, slight man who wore a black suit, white shirt and gray tie. His glasses seemed to compliment his salt and pepper hair.

"What my office does is make observations relative to understanding the manner and cause of death at a scene," Harruff explained. "We take many pictures, both in and outside the body, do X-Rays, collect evidence

and clean the body. At some point, we open the body, look at each organ, look at body cavities and make a report on our observations. Ultimately, our job responsibility is to determine the manner and cause of death of the decedent so that we may complete a death certificate."

"Can you explain what a 'manner of death' means?" O'Toole asked.

"The manner of death will always fall into one of four categories. It can either be natural, suicide, accidental or homicide. We define homicide as that death that is caused by another. There are times that we will mark a certificate as having insufficient information in determining the manner of death. When we so note, it usually applies to drug, suicide and some accidental deaths."

"Do you recall your office performing autopsies on Wayne, Judith, Scott, Erica, Olivia and Nathan Anderson during the period of December 27th through December 29th, 2007?"

The Medical Examiner nodded his head. "I do."

An organized process was set up for the jury. The Medical Examiner spoke while Scott O'Toole ensured that the sea of pictures that followed created a story on each victim. He and Michele Morales staged the pictures on a fifty-inch flat screen, one chronological picture after another. They began with each victim as they were found at the scene and finished with the final pictures at the autopsy.

Additionally, the testimony on the autopsy of each victim would conclude with Dr. Harruff as he opened a package on the stand. He would identify the item as one he had recovered from the body. Scott O'Toole would then take the item, present it to the defense, enter it as an exhibit with the judge's blessings and then walk to one end of the jury box.

Slowly, cradled in the palm of his latex-gloved hand, he would walk the bullet remains the length of the jury box. Jurors leaned forward as they inspected the lethal items.

Harruff focused on the location Wayne Anderson whose body was discovered outside, in front of the shed, approximately 100 feet from the back of the house. He was covered with a piece of aged Astro-turf carpet.

The Medical Examiner testified that he was more interested in the clothes than the piece of carpet. He observed the blood on the face, dirt on his t-shirt, the fact that it was bunched up and noted the striation marks on Wayne's back. He could also see a footprint on Wayne's shirt, the boot impression mark of Michele Anderson. The pants were down. Those facts combined with the movement of blood suggested the body had been moved and dragged from another position.

His search for wounds yielded a bullet entrance wound in the forehead with a corresponding exit wound coming out the back of his head. The entry wound was defined by a small diameter defect with simple edges. The opposing exit wound was marked by a wider margin of abrasion with signs of scalloping on the edges of the skull. He paid special attention to the marks on Wayne's face near the contact wound. They resembled stippling, telltale marks left when a gun is fired from close range.

The autopsy confirmed most of what he found at the scene. Wayne Anderson had died from a single gunshot wound in the temple. The marks that were thought to be stippling were actually signs of acne. There were also corresponding abrasions found on the underside of Wayne's left arm. Those scrapes were made perimortem; at or around the time of death, and his body being dragged could have caused them. It was determined that Wayne died almost instantaneously when the bullet ripped through his skull.

There were no signs of defensive wounds. Toxicology tests showed no drugs or alcohol in his system.

The jury was somber, but curious, as Scott O'Toole displayed the bullet fragments in front of them.

Harruff testified that Judith Elaine Anderson's body had been removed from the scene on December 27, 2007. She had been examined, as she was lying prostrate in the center and length of the shed prior to her transport. There was very little room to look at her in the shed without disturbing the possible evidence around her. Two chairs, shelving and a barbeque set were in close proximity to her. In that, he made his notes based on observations from the viewpoint of Judith's feet, as he looked forward.

From his standpoint, he could see the wound to her head. However, he noted a large area of bloodstains on her thigh. Harruff was surprised that he did not find a corresponding bullet defect. It appeared to him, despite her position on the floor, the blood from her head had dripped directly to her thigh. It was a discontinuous blood trail. He saw blood on the victim's hand, inconsistent to where the wound was. It seemed that the body had been placed where it was found.

Harruff approved her body to be transported to the King County Medical Examiner's Office once his cursory examination was done. Her hands were wrapped in paper bags; she was covered in a sheet and placed in a body bag.

The autopsy results yielded many hollow-point bullet fragments and multiple bullet holes in her garments, specifically from a t-shirt and sweatshirt Judith had worn at the time of her death. In the end, the Medical Examiner concluded she had died of two bullet wounds although there was evidence that three to four bullets had been fired at her.

The first wound was in the forehead with the bullet found in the back of her skull. The signs of stippling indicated it had been fired at close range and the direction of the bullet was consistent with Judith looking up at her killer when the bullet destroyed her brain. She would have suffered immediate paralysis and an inability to breathe. It was probable that she was conscious when the second bullet hit her.

The path of the second bullet went from an upward to downward direction and went through the victim's neck, through the shoulder and was recovered near the armpit area. The hollow-point with the copper jacket had made a fragment path. He could not determine which bullet was fired first.

Four holes were found in Judith's sweatshirt that did not have a body wound associated with them. It was concluded that one bullet had gone through the shirt, which was bunched, and had missed hitting her.

Abrasions found on the front left forearm, the back of the left hand and on the upper right buttock were of interest as they, too, were perimortem, similar to the wounds found on her husband, Wayne. The wounds were determined not to be defensive wounds but wounds made when the body was moved. The victim had no alcohol or drugs in her system.

Scott O'Toole took the slow walk in front of the jury box. The deadly bullet fragments were cradled in his outward-faced latex-gloved hand.

The jurors would begin to connect the dots, as they matched the forensic evidence against the confession told to Detective Cleary. They could picture the death of Judith. They knew that Judith had run out of the craft room after she heard a gunshot. They would imagine her surprise and fear when she saw her husband as he lay on the floor. She ran to the kitchen and, in a feeble attempt to hide, had crouched in the corner by the refrigerator. She was shot at close range, while she looked up at her killer.

Richard Harruff then testified about his clinical investigation of the body of Scott Anderson.

Scott Anderson had been found as he lay on his back in the living room to the right of the front door. Blood was observed on his face, abdomen and thighs. Closer inspection revealed that he had a head and neck wound, a wound in the abdomen and abrasions to both knees and his right hand.

The autopsy results indicated a bullet had made a path in a downward direction into Scott's chin, through his neck and entered his right front chest. It would appear that the person who fired the shot must have been standing over the victim.

The abdomen wound was made in a different direction. The bullet had entered the stomach and exited the body through the back of Scott. The bullet was found nestled in his t-shirt behind his back. Of concern were the seared marks found at the entrance wound. The blackened edges of the hole in the t-shirt signified the bullet was fired from close range. The Medical Examiner thought that it most likely that this shot had been fired after Scott was dead since there was no bleeding of the wound. The abdomen wound would not have been fatal.

Jurors never received a clear picture of how the abrasions occurred found on both knees and the left hand. They could only surmise. Many of the jurors would wish to hear the opinions of other jurors but they could not. They were encumbered by their strict admonishment.

Nothing could have prepared the jurors for the pictorial sequence that followed on the autopsy of Erica Anderson. In Erica's case, not only had the violence increased in the sequence of deaths, but also the horror was taken to a new level.

Harruff testified that Erica Anderson was found on the floor with her head against the loveseat. Upon first observation, her body was obscured by a coffee table next to her. It was not important that snacks and candies on the table beckoned a guest over for a Christmas holiday. It was important that Olivia, her daughter, lay face down under her. It was disturbing that Nathan lay only a few feet away.

The blood trails found on Erica had changed directions on her face, which told the Medical Examiner that her body moved while she was bled. She had multiple gunshot wounds with some of the wound defects showing re-entry into the body. It was a significantly more complicated autopsy than the prior three victims because of the multiple gun paths. He determined that there were six tracks. It was not possible to tell with any certainty what order they came in except to say they had occurred all within minutes.

 One bullet entered the forehead and was recovered inside the back of her head. There was evidence of stippling, a close range shot from three to six inches away. A second bullet entered the left chest and went through the armpit. A third bullet crossed through her abdomen and was recovered from her back while a fourth bullet went through her thighs. A fifth bullet ripped through Erica's left hip and was found in her abdomen.

The most difficult bullet of the day, the twelfth they were aware of thus far, was the one that entered Erica's right front chest. It was emotional for every juror as they saw the autopsy photo. The Medical Examiner had used tweezers to extricate a piece of skull and tuft of hair found deep inside the victim's chest.

Richard Harruff carefully opened the evidence packet on the witness stand while the court watched silently. He verbally identified the items as those he had removed from Erica's chest, the same as the location of the photograph. Scott O'Toole performed the evidence dance and had it entered as Exhibit #102. He put on a pair of latex gloves.

As he had done eleven times before throughout the day, Scott O'Toole slowly walked the items nestled in his hands in front of the jury. Each juror saw the strands of hair and piece of skull.

"Were you able to make any determinations on the hair?" Scott asked.

The Medical Examiner looked at the jury. "At the time of the autopsy, it was my observation that the hair was from a child. It was very fine hair."

Scott O'Toole allowed the answer to hang in the air while he repackaged the evidence.

As might be expected, there were jurors who would have stolen a glance of Michele Anderson as she sat at the defense table. All they would have seen was a defendant who stared downward as she hid under a blanket of hair. She did not change position all day.

"I think this might be a good time for the Court to recess," O'Toole suggested at 4:00 PM.

The court stood as the jurors exited the jury box for the four-day weekend. I thought of a juror who had been dismissed at the beginning of the day for doing the right thing. I thought of our standing as a salute to the remaining jurors and the task that was still in front of them.

Not one of them looked forward to their return on Tuesday. They had seen the path of twelve of the sixteen bullets.

There were four bullets left.

DAY 17
February 16, 2016

SHORING OF THE HEART

"Let me apologize ahead of time if I have already covered this," Scott O'Toole said.   He looked sharp in a black suit, white shirt and blue and white spotted tie. "Were you able to determine the caliber of bullet found in Judy Anderson?"

"I do not have an opinion on that," Dr. Harruff answered calmly. He wore a black suit, white shirt and gray silk tie. He was on the stand for the third day. "I leave those opinions for firearms experts. I did not give an opinion on any of the bullets recovered."

"Are you able to offer an opinion of the blood-staining on the midriff of Judith's pants?"

Harruff looked toward the jury. "The stain most likely came from her head wound. It would be my opinion that her head was over her lap at some point. The lack of a blood trail on her abdomen was a consideration."

Scott O'Toole turned a page of his notes. "Was she alive when she received her wound to her neck?"

"I believe so."

"What of her head wound? Was she alive when she received this wound?" O'Toole calmly asked.

"Yes. I saw evidence of blood in the bullet path."

"Very good," Scott responded. "Again, I apologize if we already covered it but I would like to draw our attention back to Scott Anderson. Was it your opinion that Scott was likely deceased when he received the wound to the abdomen?"

"Yes, it is unlikely he was alive. I did not see bleeding in the bullet track."

"Was his position, the one he was found in," Scott clarified, "consistent with his lying on his back on the floor?"

"Yes," Harruff responded.

"Regarding the wound to the face, the chin, was this wound incapacitating?"

"As we discussed, the bullet entered the chin, went through his sternal notch and stopped in his left lung. I expect that it was a brisk bleed. He may have been conscious for ten seconds and possibly up to a minute. I would think a shorter time frame than longer."

O'Toole signaled Michelle Morales, who placed a CD in the player. A picture of the Medical Examiner's body schematic was shown on the fifty-inch screen in front of the jury.

"Were you able to determine the order of wounds that Erica Anderson received?" Scott asked.

"The best I can say is that her death was consistent in time with the other deaths. I could not tell the order of the wounds. The head wound, however, would have been immediately incapacitating."

"Can you turn up the microphone?" Miss {redacted} called from the back row of the gallery. She had arrived only minutes before.

The judge did not respond while Scott checked the microphone with the witness. He adjusted some volume settings and continued.

Scott placed another picture on the screen, which the jurors recognized as the hair and bullet seen last week from Erica's chest. "Did you find hair in two locations on the wound track?"

"Yes," Harruff replied. "We found hair at the entrance of the chest wound and, additionally, we found hair and skull fragments in her upper right lung. It is not uncommon for a hollow-point bullet to gather obstacles and then see them separate at a different location within a wound. Some hair was deposited at the entry point of the bullet while some was embedded in the bullet's termination point."

A picture of Erica, taken at her autopsy, appeared on the screen.

Dr. Harruff was directed to come down to the floor in front of the jury and use a pointer on the flat-screen to explain the scenario of the bullet path. "The bullet entered the chest from front to back, left to right and on a downward path. This would have been a fatal shot."

"Aside from the foreign material found in the chest wound, was there anything else you found significant?" O'Toole asked.

"Where the bullet entered the chest, there was a high degree of abrasion around the wound. This told me it was a 'shored' wound.

An object was between the bullet and the skin. As the bullet exits one skin and enters another, it slaps against each other. Sometimes, we refer to it as a 'kissing' wound," the Medical Examiner explained.

"Is it your opinion that Erica Anderson was alive when she received this wound?"

"Yes."

"In your report," O'Toole pointed out, "you make mention of other shored wounds. Can you explain it for us a bit further?"

Dr. Harruff walked to the television screen and, with his metal pointer, showed the path of a bullet as it entered the right medial thigh and went through her abdomen. It changed direction due to body mass, exited the abdomen and re-entered it skin to skin. The re-contact caused the shoring effect with matching abrasions on the edges of both wounds. The bullet then came to rest in her left thigh.

One bullet had effectively caused five wounds.

"Could you make a determination as to what position she was in?" Scott asked.

"This was a complicated bullet path. However, once the wounds were matched to each other, I could comfortably say she was in a squatting position," he explained.

Exhibit #93 was shown on the screen. It was the pencil sketch schematic of Erica's body with enumerated bullet paths detailed along the sides. The jurors inspected the 'L' wound path as it was discussed.

"The bullet entered the left buttock," he said as he drew the jury's attention toward the schematic, "then entered the left hip, went through the abdominal wall, through the colon, through the liver and came to rest in the right lower chest wall."

Scott O'Toole raised his hand slightly while Harruff waited.

"In your opinion, is the bullet track consistent with Erica being bent at the waist and her body facing away from the shooter?"

"I can't say," Harruff said, with a slight shrug to his shoulders.

"How many gunshot wounds were found on Erica Anderson?" O'Toole inquired after a detailed look at the multiple holes found in her clothes.

"There were six wound tracks," Harruff explained calmly. "There were twelve bullet holes. Two of the wounds were perforating wounds; meaning that the bullet went in and out. Another three wounds were penetrating; meaning wounds where the bullet did not exit. One wound was both a perforating and a penetrating wound."

Scott O'Toole nodded his head and casually turned a page on his legal pad. The flat-screen was black. "Aside from the bullet wounds, were there any other signs of injury?"

"There were three areas. She had a left mid-thigh bruise, a scrape on her left leg by the knee and a two-scrape abrasion on her right knee. They were made prior to her death and close to the time of death," Harruff responded.

"Any sign of defensive wounds?"

"No," he answered.

"Were you able to make a determination as to whose hair was found in the chest wound of Erica Anderson?"

"Nathan Anderson," the Medical Examiner responded.

Faces were solemn when Scott O'Toole placed an autopsy photo of Nathan on the screen. It was a sight that no person should ever have to witness.

Harruff testified that his examination had revealed that Nathan had stood thirty-eight inches tall and weighed thirty-eight pounds at the time of his death. The decedent had worn blue jeans, t-shirt, white socks, brown shoes and disposable diapers.

Nathan had a bullet entrance wound on left side and corner of his forehead. There was a corresponding exit wound from the right side of the back of his head. Special interest was drawn to the stippling marks on the face and forehead. The red marks went out in a radius of approximately five inches. He had received the wound from close range, probably less than two feet.

The exit wound in his head showed a 'wide margin of abrasion'; a redness that could appear on the edges of a wound in certain circumstances. It was Harruff's determination that the wound had been shored, or buttressed, by the chest of Erica Anderson.

"What was the cause of death?" the prosecutor asked.

"One gunshot wound to the head."

"What was the manner of death?"

"Homicide."

"How long would Nathan Anderson have lived once he suffered the bullet wound?"

"It would have been instantly fatal," Harruff responded.

The court was silent when Olivia's autopsy photograph was placed on the screen. Once again, it was beyond the pale of what any human being should witness.

Harruff testified that Olivia Anderson had weighed fifty-six pounds and stood forty-six inches in height at the time of her death. She had worn a red dress, a white Christmas blouse and an undershirt. She had been shot twice.

The Medical Examiner could not determine the order of the bullets fired. She was shot once in the abdomen, just above the hip. The other shot had been fired to the back of her head, exiting her right forehead.

Her body was found face down on her mother's body, her mother's arm almost wrapped around her.

"Was there any sign of stippling?" Scott O'Toole asked, in reference to the signature pinprick blood marks left on the skin by gunpowder particles from a close range shot.

"Not that I could see," he answered.

"What did you determine the cause of death to be?"

"The cause of death was from two gunshot wounds. Each wound would have been fatal independent of each other," Harruff responded.

"How long would she have survived if a second wound had not been made?" O'Toole asked.

"It could have been several minutes to several hours with the wound to the abdomen. Although I cannot tell the order of the wounds, I can say that her abdomen showed bleeding in the bullet tracks. Her heart was still pumping blood."

"What did you state was the manner of death on the death certificate?"

Harruff looked at the jury and stated, "Homicide."

I looked at the defendant who had shielded her eyes throughout the day as the autopsy photographs were shown. I did not see any jurors look at her but I knew glances had been stolen.

Scott O'Toole marked the conclusion of a recess in the proceedings as he spoke to the judge and court outside the presence of the jury. "I just wanted to make the court aware that I had an incident with Juror #10," he said.

My interest was certainly piqued.

"Go ahead," Judge Ramsdell directed.

"I was leaving the fifth floor restroom when I accidentally ran into juror #10. I said something like, "oops, I'm sorry." We didn't say anything after that and I thought you all should be aware."

"Thank you, Counselor," Ramsdell responded. He looked toward the defense team. "Do you have any concerns?"

David Sorenson stood up. "No, we don't think so. We appreciate Mr. O'Toole coming forward. Things like that happen."

Angela Van Liew was the second-to-last witness of the afternoon session. She was a slight girl dressed in pressed jeans, a black top and gray tennis shoes. She had medium length brown hair and wore glasses. She had worked in forensics for ten years for the King County Sheriff's Office with a specialty in forensic photography.

"What were you delegated to do?" Michelle Morales asked from behind the podium. She wore a mauve skirt with a black top and black coat.

"We went out to the residence on January 15, 2008 in order to take pictures of the main floor. These pictures would be used to reproduce the floor at some point," Van Liew explained.

"Were you successful?" Morales asked.

"We weren't at that time. We were trying to take 4ft x 4ft pictures. The furniture had been removed and we were using halogen lights and blew the circuits in the house. We tried doing the grid using natural light but it was not acceptable," Van Liew stated.

"Did you go back and try again?" Morales inquired.

"Yes," Van Liew said toward the jury. "On January 30, we returned with new equipment. This time, though, the floor was too fragile. It was starting to rot from underneath. We then returned on February 28 after supports had been put in. This time, we were successful in taking two hundred photographs in 1ft x 1ft pieces."

"Whom were those photographs intended for?" Michelle asked.

"Brian Sherrod," she answered. "He works for the United States Geological Service as a research geologist. He was going to create a mosaic from my pictures."

When Brian Sherrod took the stand after Van Liew, the jurors were treated to one of their more memorable characters in the trial. He was a stocky man with a shiny baldhead. He wore a light blue polo shirt with creased, but worn, blue jeans. He had a deep baritone voice and it was clear that he enjoyed his work.

"I'm the crazy guy you will see camped out in the middle of nowhere,' he explained. "I have a little camper and I sit outside and take pictures. My specialty is in seismology. Part of what goes into that is the tedious process of recording the movement of earth. It moves slower than grass grows. But, when a series of pictures are taken over time, one can track its movement. Through high resolution digital landscaping photography, I create photo mosaics."

Michelle Morales smiled. "In this case, you were asked to create one, weren't you?"

"I was contacted by detective Scott Tompkins. He made me aware of the project and I thought it was something I could do. I was then given a few hundred photographs from Angela Van Liew and was able to create a mosaic grid by lining up a lot of fiduciary marks over an intense period of two days," Sherrod recalled.

"How big is the final mosaic?" Morales asked.

"It is approximately 12ft by 14ft," Sherrod replied.

"In your best estimation, do you believe it is a replication of the living room floor from Carnation?"

"It is an exact replication of the floor from Carnation," Sherrod responded confidently.

"No more questions," Morales said as she walked back to the prosecution table.

Jurors had seen the first signs that a reconstructed crime scene was in their future.

The drive home for each juror would have been consumed with the highly personal and horrific autopsy photos from the prior three days. The visuals were hard to bury. Even those with the most analytical of minds would have had difficulty with the emotion that arose. Each juror would have felt isolated and alone with thoughts that they could share with no one.

When each juror got home, one could be sure that they each would have hugged their children a lot tighter than usual and certainly a little longer. It would have been difficult to quell the tears.

The jurors could never un-see what they had seen and they would never forget those victims who had been murdered with their eyes open.

LOST AND NOT FOUND

Scott O'Toole asked the court for permission to discuss two quick issues at the commencement of the day. He wore a tailored black suit with a blue shirt and red tie.

"First of all," he began, "I want to make sure the Court is aware that we are having some challenges getting the DNA expert in with spring break starting. In that, we will have only three witnesses today."

"I appreciate that, Mr. O'Toole," Judge Ramsdell said. "I saw that she has been rescheduled. What was the other concern?"

"Well, Miss Morales had an incident with a juror," Scott said. "She was walking down the hallway and Juror #4 congratulated her on the new ring on her finger."

"Oh?" the judge queried. "Engagement ring?"

Michelle Morales raised her left hand. She blushed as a band of diamonds glinted in the fluorescent glow of the courtroom.

"Miss Morales continued on without acknowledging the juror," Scott explained. "We just wanted everyone to be aware."

The judge smiled. "Congratulations, Miss Morales. I really don't have any concerns over this. These jurors live with us an extended amount of time and they do not live in a bubble. Things like this will happen."

David Sorenson and Colleen O'Connor did not object.

I thought of the attorneys as they did everything they could to avoid contact with the jurors' daily. It was reminiscent of the Geico commercial O'Toole had referenced.

Judge Ramsdell informed the court that the next day would be a half-day since he was scheduled to be in front of a Senate committee to discuss a legislative bill.

"From rings to bills, let's call in the jury," he directed Kenya.

Kathy Knapp was called as the first witness. She was a stocky lady in her sixties who wore gray pants, a pink top and pink sweatshirt. She had salt and pepper hair.

She stumbled as she sat down and laughed. "Oh I'm so sorry. I've never done this before."

Her energy was infectious and bubbly which was a welcome relief to the many who watched the daily testimony from the gallery, the family included.

Just as the tendrils of murder had reached into all the corners of society to select sixteen strangers for a jury box, it also grasped common people who were just trying to make a living. Sometimes, in the most unexpected ways, witnesses to murder revealed special diamonds.

"What company do you work for?" Scott asked.

"My husband and I own 'Bumble Bee Towing'," Kathy corrected.

"It's a tow truck company?"

"Yes, Sir. Our trucks are black and yellow, painted like a bumblebee."

"Makes sense," Scott said with a smile. "So what do you do?"

"I'm responsible for the paperwork and the phones while my husband, Randy, does the driving."

"Did you receive a call for service on December 26, 2007?"

"I did," she answered. "The phone rang at 5:30 AM. It was a call about a flat tire in Kelso off the I-5. It was an insurance company that called us. Then, I got Randy up. He had to do the service. After that, I talked to the woman in the stranded car. I told her that she better put her flashers on. A lot of bad things can happen out there on the shoulder. People are driving seventy-miles an hour. Let me tell you, I have seen a thing or two."

"Thank you," Scott said. "When you talked to the woman, give us an idea what happened."

"So, I find out that they're getting married in Reno and the truck got a flat. They didn't know how to change it. She was in a big rush. I explained a driver was on the way, told her again to leave her flashers on and that I would contact the State Patrol."

"How was her demeanor over the phone?"

Kathy shook her head. "She got all upset with me about calling the State Patrol. I told her that it's required on the Interstate. She was really agitated."

"Then what happened?" Scott asked.

"I hung up on her," she said as if it were the most obvious thing to do.

Some of the jurors smiled.

"I told Randy have fun with her before he left," Kathy continued. "So, he calls me awhile later to have me run her plates. He thought something was weird. He told me enough to know that something was a little odd, you know? I ran the plates and nothing came back on them. I also sent another driver out there with bolt cutters."

"What did your husband need with bolt cutters?"

"The darn spare tire was locked with some sort of bicycle lock. It would have helped if we knew this on the first call I had with her," she said in reference to the defendant.

"Do you live close to the I-5?"

Kathy laughed. "I could throw a rock and hit it."

"Did you talk to your husband again while he was out there on the tire service?" Scott asked.

"Yeah," she answered. "He called me back forty-five minutes later to tell me they were still on the side of the road. The tire had been changed. You see it's our policy not to leave anyone stranded. I told Randy to tell them to move along."

"We're going to look at some pictures and see if you recognize them," Scott said as he walked to the court clerk and retrieved a stack of papers.

The witness's arm slipped on the arm of her chair. She looked at the jury and chuckled.

"I don't do this, ever," she whispered.

Suddenly, Colleen O'Connor spoke up vehemently from the defense table. "The witness will kindly not speak to the jurors!"

Kathy looked toward the judge and motioned her apology.

The prosecutor continued with a presentation of pictures of the tow service documents that had been completed on December 26, 2007. The documents verified that Michele Anderson had placed the call and was present for the eventual tire change.

Randall Knapp, Kathy's husband, took the stand after she had stepped down. He was a tall thin man who wore blue jeans, a blue decaled 'Bumble Bee Towing' t-shirt and black work boots. He had gold-framed glasses that sat closer to the tip of his nose than to his eyes. One could feel he had been married for years and that he was the worker bee of the household. He was reserved and studious on the stand, and answered each question succinctly.

"You were sent to change a flat on December 26, 2007?" Scott asked.

"Yes," he answered. "I arrived at 5:40 AM, ten minutes after the original call, and was immediately challenged by the locked spare tire and the fact that the two motorists appeared to know nothing about their truck."

"Did anything else strike you as something that was out of the ordinary?"

"Yeah. I thought it weird that they said they were headed to Las Vegas but did not have a piece of luggage either in the front seat or in the flatbed."

"So, the spare tire was locked and they didn't have a key?" Scott asked. "What did you do next?"

"I called my wife to send another driver with a bolt cutter and I requested that it be my cousin Roy," Randall said.

"Why did ask for Roy?"

"He lives close by and I knew he could handle it quickly."

"What did you do while you waited for Roy to arrive?"

"I told my wife to run the plates on the vehicle. Something seemed suspicious," he said.

"Anything come back on the plates?"

"There was nothing to report on the truck."

"What happened when your cousin arrived?" Scott asked.

"It didn't take but a moment to cut the after-market lock. We changed the tire in ten minutes. The driver signed my paperwork and we went back to our trucks."

"Did the truck leave after the tire was changed?"

Randy Knapp shook his head. "It was the darndest thing to me. It was a little bizarre given how anxious she had been at the beginning of the service for us to finish the job and then they just stayed stationary, parked on the side of the freeway. I thought they were in a rush."

"When they pulled back on the freeway, did you see where they went?" Scott O'Toole asked.

"I followed them and they took the first exit. I watched them turn around and get back on the freeway, headed north instead of south," Knapp stated. "The whole thing did not seem right with the lack of luggage, the hurry to get on the road and then to go the other way. It just did not make sense. There was another thing that concerned me later."

"What was that?" Scott asked.

"We went through all this work for a tire that was supposed to be flat. It was soft," he recalled, "but it was not flat."

Scott O'Toole introduced the next witness as Christopher Streeter, who was a manager for Jaffe Jewelry and Loan in Burien, Washington. He was in his early thirties and wore blue jeans, a gray t-shirt and a gray hooded sweatshirt. He had worked for the pawnshop since the early 2000's.

In sequential order, Scott displayed Exhibits #124 - #128, as he questioned the witness. "When is a sales receipt completed in the sale of a firearm?"

"It's done at the point of sale, the day that money is exchanged," Streeter responded.

"How was this gun purchase done?"

"It was paid for by a credit card."

"Can you explain what happens in the process?" Scott asked. "One cannot just walk in and pay money for a gun and walk out can they?"

"No, it doesn't work like that. The buyer has to fill out an application to transfer a gun. They also have to fill out a #4473 notice," Streeter explained. "It has a lot of personal questions that are used for a mandatory background check."

Scott motioned for Michelle Morales to place the next picture on the screen, another signed and dated receipt. "Can you tell us what this is?"

Streeter looked at the screen and nodded his head. "It's an application to transfer a 9 mm firearm to Michele Kristen Anderson dated May 27, 2004. It's a federal document that we both had to sign."

"Did you issue the gun immediately?"

"No," Streeter answered. "The 4473 was submitted and we had to wait for her background check to be approved."

"Did she get the necessary approval?" Scott asked.

"She picked up the gun on June 5, 2004, after her background check was approved."

"At another point in time, did you also handle the sale of a weapon to a Joseph McEnroe?"

"I did," Christopher recalled. "About six months before, I sold a .357 magnum to Joseph McEnroe who was living in Kent, Washington."

"Did he fill out the same paperwork as Michele Anderson had done in her purchase?"

"He did."

"He also had to fill out a 4473, the form for a background check?" Scott prodded.

"Yes, Sir," Streeter responded. "He passed his background check and took ownership of the weapon on January 2, 2004. He had completed his paperwork on December 18, 2003."

"Do you remember that particular weapon?" Scott asked as a picture of a standard .357 was on the screen.

Streeter nodded his head. "Absolutely. It's a popular weapon and I've sold a lot of these. This particular weapon had a holster sold with it but what made it unique was the special handle grip. The grip was not a standard issue thing."

"Very good," Scott commented. "One more thing, when you sell a weapon, do you confirm it is in working order before the customer takes possession of it?"

"Yes."

"In the sale of the 9 MM and the .357 Magnum, were they in working order?"

"Both firearms worked just fine," Streeter responded flatly.

"What was the serial number of the Smith & Wesson revolver?" O'Toole inquired. A picture of the receipt was on the projection screen.

"Model #19-4 with a Serial Number of 57K-2079," he answered

as he read the numbers aloud.

"You said these guns were used when you sold them, and they were both in working order?"

"Yes," he answered. "We always check the hammer, the pulling trigger and ensure that the cartridge and cylinders are working."

The jurors had a pretty good idea that the guns worked when they were used some three years later.

Retired Sergeant James N. Knauss, of the King County Sheriff's Office, took the witness chair as the final witness of the day. He was dressed formally in black suit with a blue shirt and maroon colored tie. His thirty-five years of service had begun in 1980's about the same time that Mount St Helens had erupted, located an hour south of King County. He began his career as a patrol officer and finished as a homicide supervisor in the Marine Unit of the King's County Sheriff's Office. His primary responsibilities included detailed searches of local waters and the search for bodies.

"Who contacted you regarding a search?" O'Toole asked.

"I was contacted by Sergeant Mark Toner of the King's County Sheriff's Office to search for two weapons thought to be in the Stillaguamish River," Knauss replied.

"Where is the Stillaguamish located as far as the investigation is concerned?"

"The point in the river was located approximately forty miles north of Seattle. Its location was at the point where the river crossed the interstate at Exit 208 near Arlington in Snohomish County," Knauss explained.

"It's pretty rural out there?" O'Toole questioned.

"I would call the area farm country with its rolling hills and grazing cows."

"When did you first search for the weapons?"

"We began the first river search on January 3, 2008. Divers swam in the river while a boat hovered above and made a detailed grid pattern of the areas they had searched. It was a tedious job with no visibility in the stirred up waters. The recent rains had swelled the river which forced the divers to feel through the silt and rocks at the base of the river for any objects that might be a gun," Knauss finished.

"Did you recover any weapons?"

"Unfortunately, we were not successful."

"Did you have an opportunity to return to the scene?"

"The marine search team returned on January 23rd and 24th for additional searches. Two full days were spent on a meticulous search going up and down the river. We covered both banks of the river and felt our way through thousands of pounds of mud on the floor of the river."

"Did you recover any weapons on either of the additional searches?" Scott asked.

"I felt like we searched every square inch of that segment of the river and, unfortunately, we had no success. We did not recover any weapons."

When the jurors were dismissed for the day, there may have been some jurors who would toy with the thought that the weapons would never be found.

They would have been dead wrong.

SECRET OF THE STILLAGUAMISH

Scott O'Toole took the jurors on a journey to a summer day in 2011 with his witness, Jared Sinnema.

The heat of the summer was felt on a farm in Snohomish County about an hour's drive north of Seattle. The two brothers had just finished their chores on the raw milk farm. Their dad always said their farm did not produce whitewash milk like the big dairy farms. The milk they sold went directly from the cow into tanks. Although it did not yield as much volume, the quality was much better. It was not easy work and the twelve year-old boys were anxious to go outside and enjoy the warm weather.

Jared called his best friend who lived up the road in Arlington. They were going out to play and he was invited. The friend jumped at the chance and biked his way to the Sinnema's farmhouse.

A half-hour later, the three boys dumped their bikes on the side of the road and walked down the banks of the Stillaguamish River.

The river was low at this time of year because the winter snows had melted from the mountains. It was a great place to fish, especially down the river by the 'fish falls', a rib of waterfalls that ran across the river. The base of the falls always made for a productive fishing day. That day, however, they just killed time and goofed off. Oftentimes, the 'Ker-plunk' of a rock could be heard as it landed in the river after one of the boys threw one in.

The cars that rushed along the bridge of the I-5 overpass got more distant as the boys walked along the river bars. They would walk on pieces of beach-like land formed at the points where the river turned sharply. It was always a good spot to find fishing lures lost on trips past.

Jared had made his way past the first river bar when he saw something shiny sticking out of the mud. He reached down and pulled on it, surprised it was as heavy as it was. He knew it was a gun right away. The holster, though, was rotted and moist. He pulled it off the gun and threw it to the ground.

"Look what I found!" he called to the other boys.

"Cool," his brother said.

"Is that a .22?" his friend asked.

Jared turned it over and over in his hand. It looked like an old gun. It was rusty and the paint was peeled pretty heavily in spots.

He could not tell if it was loaded because the cylinder was stuck. He was familiar with the brand enough to say it was a .357 Magnum. He had learned a lot about guns when he was growing up because his father was a gun dealer.

The gun was cool. He wanted to keep it.

Later that afternoon, as soon as Jared got in the house, it was all he could do to get to a sink. He had all sorts of visions in his head. He could restore the gun or maybe re-blast it. First, he had to clean it and see if he could get the parts moving. He held it under the water while he rubbed and pushed the metal parts until some of the pieces yielded to his pressure. The cylinder fell open and he knew by the lack of tension that the mainspring was broken.

Inside the cylinder, he saw three used shell casings. The other three compartments were empty. He shook the gun and could hear little fragments of debris as they moved around in the handle. The grip would have to be discarded just as he had discarded the holster. It was worthless. The gun must have been in the water a long time.

"Where did you get that?" his father suddenly asked from behind him.

"I found it up the river a ways," Jared answered as he continued to wash the gun in the running water. "I think I'm going to clean it up. All it needs is a new mainspring."

"Hmmm," his father commented. "Are you going to call anyone to let them know you found it?"

Jared shook his head. "What for? It's an old rusty gun."

"I'm not trying to tell you what to do," his father said. "However, if I had found a gun and wanted to keep it, I would probably call the Sheriff first. What would happen if the gun were stolen?"

The boy groaned.

"It's your choice, Jared."

"Okay," he said.

"Would you be more comfortable if I called it in?" his father asked.

"Thanks, Dad."

Jared Sinnema could never have realized the importance of that phone call. He could not have envisioned five years later, that he would be on a witness stand in a murder trial. His friends thought he was cool.

Scott O'Toole presented Jared with a sealed box while the jury looked on with curiosity. The nineteen year-old carefully opened the box and studied at it.

"Does this look like the item that you found on the bank of the Stillaguamish River on July 10, 2011?"

"Yeah, um, it is," he answered.

The prosecutor had the item entered as Exhibit #135. He walked over to the far end of the jury box and slowly walked the length of it. Each juror peered closely as O'Toole held the lid open with one hand and cradled the box in the other.

An old black-colored gun was zip-tied firmly to the inside of the box. The cylinder was open and exposed. The handle looked like raw metal. The grip had been removed.

Jurors thought of Joseph McEnroe, his weapon and what happened to the bullets that were once in the full chamber.

"Did you find another weapon?" Scott O'Toole asked.

"No," Jared answered. "I don't think I ever went back to the river after that."

"Did you discover a jacket or shirt that might be associated with your find?"

"Um, no."

Scott finished with his witness after he walked the three empty bullet casings in front of the jury.

The jurors' faces were somber but intrigued.

Jeff Minor, Deputy Sheriff for Snohomish County, a twenty-three year veteran of the Department, took the stand. He wore a green shirt with a Sheriff's logo, dark green pants and black tie. He had worked the graveyard shift from 6:00 PM until 6:00 AM on the night he received a phone call about a gun that was found on the Stillaguamish River.

"Was that an uncommon call?" Scott O'Toole inquired.

"Not really," the deputy answered. "We actually get a lot of calls on found guns. Plus, people find strange stuff in the river all of the time."

"So you took possession of the gun from the boy's father and then what did you do? Did you run it through the system at all?"

Jeff Miner looked toward the jury. "It is standard to run a search of a weapon anytime one is recovered. Our goal is to return it to the original owner. I ran the serial numbers and nothing suspicious came back on it. So, I logged the weapon and stored it in the evidence room."

"Was that the last you heard on the gun?" Scott asked.

"Actually, no," the witness answered as he scratched his head. "I recall that I was having coffee at a Starbuck's the day after the found gun was put away. All of the sudden, I remembered a conversation with an old partner from three years prior. It was probably in the very same Starbuck's..."

"Objection," David Sorenson interrupted. "Relevance."

"It goes to context, Your Honor," Scott O'Toole noted.

The judge thought about it for a moment. "Overruled. I'll allow it."

"Go on," Scott said to the deputy.

"He had asked me if I wanted to tag along for a weapons search in a river. It was cold and rainy and if I had a choice. I would rather be giving tickets to nice folks like you than traipsing through a river. He had told me it was a search regarding a homicide and some evidence had been thrown into a river."

"So, you did not go on the search?"

"No," Jeff responded. "I remember his saying the homicide was in Carnation, which is in King County. I had done the records check on the recovered firearm in Snohomish County. It occurred to me to call the major crimes division of King County. I thought it would be an odd coincidence that this might be the gun they were searching for considering it was a conversation from three or four years ago."

"What did you do then?" Scott asked. His hands were in his pockets as he conversed with his witness.

"I emailed my Sergeant and asked that this be coordinated with King County. After that, I was not involved in the evidence transfer."

"Can you read the serial number for us?"

The Deputy looked at the projection screen that hung the height of the room across from the jury. "You can see the number on the metal flap when the cylinder is open. The same serial number is located on the frame of the gun at the base of the handle. Five-seven-K-two-zero-seven-nine."

"Thank you," Scott said. "No more questions."

"No questions," David Sorenson responded when he was asked.

The final witness of the day, Catherine Dooley, was a fourteen-year veteran of evidence room storage for the Snohomish County Sheriff's Office. She ensured all transfers of evidence were properly documented.

She did not specifically remember the gun but verified she had processed the Smith & Wesson .357 Magnum in the transfer to Detective Scott Tompkins of the King County Sheriff's Office.

"Why are there two barcodes?" Scott asked her, in reference to the secured gun box.

"One barcode is for the three corresponding bullet casings. The other barcode is for the weapon," she answered.

"Who did you determine to be the owner of the weapon?"

"Joseph McEnroe."

"What is the serial number of the gun?"

"Five-seven-K-two-zero-seven-nine."

"Thank you," Scott O'Toole said as he nodded his head toward the witness. "No more questions."

"No questions, Your Honor," Colleen O'Connor volunteered from the defense table.

Judge Ramsdell informed the jury before they left for the weekend that the trial was moving right on schedule. He advised them that they were expected to go into deliberations on February 29, 2016, only five days away in trial days.

All of them would wonder if that was enough time for the defense team to present their case. Many would wonder when the defendant was going to take the stand.

DAY 20
February 22, 2016

LINES OF DEMARCATION

Richard Wyatt, a supervisor for the Firearm and Tool Marks section of the Washington State Patrol Crime Lab, stood in front of the jury. He was dressed in a charcoal black suit with a black shirt and a vibrant green tie. He had a large black bag at his feet of which he removed an over-sized plastic bullet.

"A bullet is meant to spiral like a football for accuracy and efficiency," he said as he turned the bullet in his hands. "The inside of the barrel of a gun has lands and grooves that spiral inside. Those lands and grooves would make corresponding marks on the jacket of a bullet."

Scott O'Toole displayed a cross-section drawing of a bullet for the jurors to visualize what a 'land and groove' was. He wore a dark navy blue suit, pastel blue shirt and blue striped silk tie.

"The metal is softer on the jacket of the bullet than the metal of the inside of the barrel of a gun. The markings left on the jacket will be specifically unique to only one gun," Wyatt explained. "Even if a manufacturer made ten thousand guns in a row of the same model, each would be subtly different than the next. Further, the marks that the hammer leaves on the bullet jacket would be unique as well."

"With regards to this case, when did you receive the bullets?" Scott asked.

"I received the bullets from the Washington State Crime Lab on September 22, 2010," Wyatt said as he put the plastic bullet in his bag. He returned to the witness stand and sat down.

"What did you do with them first?"

"My first goal was to determine how many guns were used. Each bullet was observed under a microscope and compared to each other. The bullets were in varying conditions and some were just fragments," Wyatt said.

"Did you make a determination as to what kind of gun or guns the bullets came from?" Scott asked.

"It became clear that the bullets either came from a Smith & Wesson .357 Magnum revolver or a Luger 9 MM Semi-Automatic. I would say the majority of bullets came from the .357 Magnum."

"Thank you," Scott responded. "There also came a time that you were asked to look at a gun recovered from the Stillaguamish River. Is that correct?"

"Yes," the tool mark expert replied. "I received a .357 Magnum in my lab on November 17, 2011. "

"What kind of observations did you make?"

"Well, the gun was in not in working order. I took the gun apart and learned that the mainspring was broken. I took a similar gun's mainspring and replaced it on the old weapon. Next, I test fired shots with the gun and the bullets were saved for comparison purposes."

"What did you learn?"

"Once the test bullets were compared with the recovered bullets from the scene of the murders, I was able to see the unique lines of demarcation," Wyatt explained. "The three empty casings matched the three test bullet casings. All three bullets had been fired from the same firearm."

Richard and Scott discussed the .357 Magnum found at the scene. Casings and fragments were discovered in Judith's head, Erica's chest wall and left thigh, and in Scott Anderson's lung. An unfired bullet was found in Scott's clothing. That bullet was determined to have come from the .357 Magnum revolver.

The 9 MM Ruger bullets told its story. One bullet was found under Olivia. Another was found in the north windowsill. A bullet was found in Erica's head and examined. It matched the bullets found in her back, on the sill and the one under Olivia.

"Could you make a determination as to which gun was used to kill Olivia Anderson?" Scott asked.

"No," Wyatt responded.

"In reference to Nathan Anderson, were you able to determine which gun was used?"

"Again, no. The lead fragments I observed had the jackets missing. However, the shell casings found in the pillow and the loveseat were both from a .357 Magnum, in the vicinity of the youngest victims. The bullet that was found in the pillow was determined to have hit something first before it stopped. "

At the conclusion of each bullet study, Scott O'Toole presented his witness with a package. The package was carefully opened entered into evidence. Once the exhibit was entered, Scott would walk the bullet, casing or fragments slowly in front of the jurors. The number of items he paraded for the jurors painted a horrific picture of a night of violence.

The return from lunch saw the jurors held back as Scott O'Toole stood up and spoke to the judge.

"If I may, I want to make you aware of an incident that just came to my attention."

"Go ahead, Mr. O'Toole," Judge Ramsdell acknowledged.

"While Michele Anderson was being transported from the courtroom late last week, she passed members of the family in the hallway. At that point, she mouthed, "Fuck off." I want this on record and I want to remind the court of a no contact order she has in place."

The judge thought about it for a moment. "There are a couple of things to consider. We could open an investigation into this. At the same time, as far as any remedial action, she is already in custody. I am not sure what you would like to do."

"Well, the dynamics in this situation are pretty great. I just want it on record that a no contact order has been in place since July of 2008," Scott proposed.

"Mr. Sorenson?" the judge prodded.

David Sorenson cleared his throat.

"This is the first I am hearing of it. Quite frankly, we are surprised. I wish we would have known."

I noticed that neither defense attorney looked at the offender who sat between them.

"The record is noted," the judge said.

I suspected that the judge would remember such incidents when it came time for the defendant's sentence and whether the defendant was thought to be remorseful.

The afternoon continued with the study of bullets and fragments. The jurors saw dozens of microscopic images of lands and grooves. The images were matched with ten bullets from Joseph McEnroe's .357 Magnum. The most difficult bullet was the one that had red fibers embedded in its tip. Since Richard Wyatt was not a fiber expert, he was unable to say where the fibers came from.

The jurors continued to put puzzle pieces together. They would remember the red dress that Olivia had worn on Christmas Eve.

"Let's talk a little about 'drop-off' distance," O'Toole said. "Can you explain what that is for us?"

"It's a comparison of gunshot residue patterns. We use a test gun and fire into a test paper at varying distances. A pattern shows on the paper and we can determine distance of a gun from the object. In this case, we were using results to determine the stippling effect," Wyatt explained.

"What did you learn?"

"For the 9 MM to create a stippling effect of skin, it had to have been fired from a distance of less than two feet. It is likely that the gun was fired at eighteen inches for it to create the stippling effect as seen on Nathan Anderson."

With a raised finger, Scott asked, "One more question. As far as a 9 MM, could clothes make it jam and would it be usable after it was jammed?"

"Certainly," Richard responded. "Once the clothes were removed from the slide, and the bullet ejected, it could be re-fired."

"No more questions," Scott finished.

Mr. Sorenson stood up. He wore a charcoal gray suit, blue shirt and gold silk tie. He carried his legal pad with him and took a position adjacent to the jurors and faced Richard Wyatt.

"Let me start off by asking you some questions on your training and expertise. I think you told us that you had no formal study in firearms when you were in school in 1998. Is that correct?"

"The science really did not get its start until 2001 or 2002 when the ATF opened a formal academy. I was trained in 1998."

"Have you been through the formal training at the academy?" Sorenson asked.

Wyatt answered, "I teach a course at the academy."

"Some have said that it is not a true science. I'm referring to a study in 1999. Are you aware of that?"

"I am," he responded. "It is a science that has been studied since the 1920's. My goal on examinations is to determine marks that are uniquely tied to a weapon or bullet."

"But there is no minimum standard set in the study, is there?" Sorenson pointed out. "For instance, when we were comparing striation markings, they were not identical from bullet to bullet. There were variations."

"That is why so much time is spent studying the evidence. There will always be a variation between items, however, we are looking for similarities that make those marks unique to that item."

"Do you think formal training would have been beneficial in your ability to recognize differences as well as similarities?" Sorenson asked.

"I have spent hundreds of hours training throughout my career."

"No more questions," Sorenson responded.

Scott O'Toole took the opportunity.

"Can you tell us what a blind proficiency test is?"

"We are routinely tested. We receive a box of bullets and our test is to match them with the correct weapon. I helped make a proficiency test," Wyatt explained.

"Mr. Sorenson mentioned your looking at similarities but that you might have been disregarding differences. What determines uniqueness?"

"Mostly, it comes down to lines of demarcation. Every bullet will fire somewhat differently, even if only seen microscopically. But lines of demarcation and similarities to another sequence of lines of demarcation are overwhelmingly unique to each weapon," Wyatt said.

"Regarding your training, how many years did you study forensic firearm examination?" O'Toole inquired.

"I spent two to three years studying firearms. That was protocol in Texas to be certified. There was a proficiency training program in the science before the ATF put together their program."

"How many years have you been teaching at the ATF Academy?"

"Twelve years," Wyatt answered.

The jurors would go home thinking of lines of demarcation and the damage rendered upon a family of six. The fact that Michele Anderson's gun would likely never be found would not bother the jurors. The treasure in the Stillaguamish had revealed plenty of information. The .357 Magnum connected most of the dots. They were ready for the rest of the story and anxious for it to continue.

The lambs to the law pressed forward in their search for justice.

DAY 21
February 23, 2016

FORENSIC SIGNIFICANCE

Juries love DNA and this jury was no different.

An astute juror would have seen the stack of evidence lined along the rail in front of the court clerk. Thus far, they had seen over five hundred pieces of evidence and more stood ready for Scott O'Toole's perusal.

Megan Inslee took the stand, a DNA scientist and thirteen year veteran of the Seattle Crime Lab. She specialized in molecular biology. She wore a gray business skirt suit with a pink blouse and burgundy colored heels. After an hour-long tutorship of the jurors on DNA and the process of sampling, the jurors would have found her more than credible in her meticulous approach to the science.

"With regards to this case, did you create any reports?" Scott asked. He was dressed impeccably in a charcoal gray suit, white shirt and burgundy tie.

"I created four reports," Megan replied. "First, we reviewed a sequence of blood stains. Second, we created a report on possible blood found on bullets and shell casings. Third, we revisited bullets we had studied from the first case. Finally, we analyzed two pairs of boots."

"Did you have an idea whose blood you would be looking for in the samples given to you?" O'Toole asked.

"We did," she answered. "We created control samples based on the medical examiner's information. Then from various samples throughout the crime scene, we analyzed the DNA in hope of coming up with a match to the victims or suspects."

"Let me ask you this. Had you been to the scene in Carnation?"

"No. I reviewed samples from that location."

"There was an enormous amount of blood at the scene," Scott said. "How do you know what samples to take? I would guess that you couldn't take all the blood."

"That's correct," Megan responded. "We train crime scene investigators to be efficient in what they send to the lab."

"Why is that?"

"The process of testing samples is not only costly, it is time consuming. In that, we need to limit how many samples we are to interpret. There is also an immense demand for testing," she explained.

"Without going into great detail, can you give us an idea of what you might want from a scene such as the one in Carnation?"

"Generally, we want samples collect from various locations. It is important to look for blood patterns that are not consistent with each other," Inslee told the jurors. "For example, let's say a round droplet of blood is adjacent or within a high-impact blood spatter area, it would be suggested that a sample be taken from the cylindrical pattern and from an impact droplet pattern."

"Thank you," Scott responded.

He walked over to the court clerk and delved into the row of evidence. Most of the pieces were in separate envelopes. Each one contained a blood swab with the DNA results enclosed. They were presented to Megan one by one and she verified each item's authenticity in front of the jurors.

"Can you tell the jurors what item this is?"

"Yes," Inslee responded. She held a report in one hand and a small envelope in the other. "We tested the bloodstains found on the curtain at the northeast corner of the house. The long curtain had hung in the living room. The base of the curtain had a large area of blood near the floor while high velocity blood spatter was found further up."

"Did you make a determination of whose blood it was?"

"Yes," she said. "The blood was determined to have been that of Scott Anderson."

"To what degree of certainty?"

"The probability that someone else would share the same DNA is one in 250 billion," she responded as she looked up from her report.

Scott O'Toole replaced and retrieved another exhibit from in front of the court clerk. He returned to the witness. "This is another sample. Do you recognize it?"

"I do. This was from a curtain on the east wall of the dining room.

It was a similar curtain as to that of the living room. It hung to the floor. The area of interest was focused on the blood spatter marks," she explained.

"Did you make a determination as to whose blood it belonged to?"

"The blood matched the reference sample of Wayne Anderson," Megan stated.

"And to what degree of certainty?"

"The probability that someone would share the same DNA is one in 300 billion."

Scott gave her a new exhibit.

Megan scrutinized the envelope and then appeared to verify it to her report. "This sample was retrieved from the refrigerator door."

"What were your conclusions?"

"I could not get a result."

"Why not?" Scott asked.

"In this instance, there was not enough of a sample to be of any forensic significance. The blood had degraded and the fact that it was wiped or diluted blood could have destroyed any usable DNA," Inslee responded.

Scott took the exhibit from her and handed over the next envelope.

"This sample was obtained from the northeast corner of the kitchen by the refrigerator," she said.

"Were you successful in obtaining a result?"

"This blood, in the proximity of the last sample, was determined to have been from Judith Anderson."

"You looked at a sample of blood from the rear door. Is that correct?" Scott asked as he gave her another exhibit.

"The rear door threshold had a blood sample analyzed. It came from an area of transferred blood, blood that came from another object," Inslee replied.

"Did you obtain a result?"

"The DNA profile revealed was the blood of Wayne Anderson."

The exhibit dance continued.

"A spot of blood was found on the floor in the living room located at one end of the coffee table, near the recliner and next to a pair of boots," Megan explained. "It was a stain found almost by itself. It was perfectly cylindrical, the sign of blood after it dropped from straight above."

"Were you able to make a determination?"

"It was a match to Scott Anderson."

The prosecutor handed her another exhibit.

"This sample came from near the boots," Megan said. "One boot was standing up while one was lying on its side next to the drop of blood. The worn boots had blood underneath the right boot. We tested two samples."

"Whose blood was it?"

"Both sets of tests matched Scott Anderson."

"You also tested blood from the recliner?" Scott queried as he gave her another package.

"Yes," Megan answered. "The sample was taken from a brown recliner. The DNA was discovered in the drip of blood that ran from the top right side."

"What did the test results tell you?"

"It was determined to have been that of Wayne Anderson," she replied.

"To what degree of certainty?" O'Toole asked as he had done with every exhibit.

"One in 400 billion."

"You also tested some blood found under the loveseat?"

"Yes," Megan responded perfunctorily. "We determined the sample to match Olivia Anderson."

"Very good," Scott said as he replaced the exhibit in the witness' hand.

She looked at it and her report for a moment.

"We tested a sample from a Pepsi box which had blood spatter on it. Small flecks of blood were discovered within the painting of the two red, white and blue hearts on the box."

"Would you refer to the sample's origin as from high-impact blood spatter?" Scott asked.

"Yes," she said confidently.

"Whose blood did you determine it to be?"

"It was impact spatter from Erica Anderson."

On the next exhibit, the DNA scientist explained that it was retrieved from the coffee table. Specifically, a yellow plastic lid from a Planter's Cashews container drew attention because of the miniscule signs of blood spatter.

"Whose blood was it?"

"Scott Anderson's DNA matched the sample."

"You also tested blood from the cracker box on the coffee table, did you not?"

"Yes," Inslee responded. "Just next to the Planter's container, there was a box of Ritz Crackers. It, too, had tiny flecks of blood on it. Both articles had Scott Anderson's DNA profile on them."

"What of the television screen? Were you able to extract any samples from there?"

Megan briefly glanced at her report. "Yes, we analyzed a tiny spot of blood embedded in the television screen."

"What were your conclusions?"

"It was a match to the blood of Erica Anderson."

"You also analyzed a bullet for evidence of DNA, didn't you?" Scott asked as he handed her another exhibit.

"I think you're referencing a bullet found in the television. I was not successful in obtaining a result. The analyzed sample did not reveal anything of forensic significance with regards to additional DNA determinations."

"You did an analysis on additional bullets submitted to you. Are bullets fairly easy to obtain DNA profiles from?" Scott asked as he walked toward the clerk.

"It is a lot more difficult due to a fall-off factor," Megan Inslee explained. "DNA tends not to stay on casings partly due to additional degrading when a weapon is fired. However, we can get it in certain cases. The tip and the back often yield enough for sampling."

"Did you make a determination on the bullet found in the loveseat?"

"I did," she responded as she glanced at her notes. "The sample matched the profile of Erica Anderson."

"In regards to the flower-patterned pillow found on the living room floor, a bullet was recovered by you from the inside of the pillow. Did you make a determination on the DNA found on the bullet?"

"I did."

"There were red fibers found on this bullet, too, weren't there?" Scott questioned.

"Yes," she agreed. "I did not analyze the fibers because it is not my area of expertise. However, the analysis of the DNA found in the tip of the hollow-point matched the profile of Olivia Anderson."

"You also analyzed some fragments obtained from the medical examiner. They were recovered from the body of Erica. Did they yield any results?"

"I could not get a result on the hair found because it was lacking the root. The shaft does have a sample of DNA that is forensically significant. In that, I had to obtain a sample from the bone fragment. "

"Whose DNA did you determine it to be?" Scott asked.

"It was of Nathan Anderson."

"And you looked at the bullet found in the loveseat?"

"Yes, the DNA profile matched Erica Anderson."

"Did you have the opportunity to test blood found on two shell casings discovered under the recliner?"

"One casing did not yield a result but the other matched the DNA of Scott Anderson on it."

"Did you analyze a casing found in a t-shirt?"

"Yes," Megan said as she turned a page of her report. "A loose bullet was recovered from Scott Anderson's clothes. The casing had his DNA on it."

"Thank you," Scott said as he went back to the diminished row of evidence in front of the court clerk.

The boots of Michele Anderson and Joseph McEnroe re-entered the queue of evidence. Some jurors would feel the element of creepiness upon seeing them again. It was not the little circles on the soles of one set or the diagonal lines on the feet of the other set that bothered them. It was the blood found on them.

"Earlier, we spoke of the difficulty of obtaining results from diluted blood," Scott said as he held Anderson's boots in his hand. "On either the boots of Michele Anderson or those of Joseph McEnroe, was there any evidence of diluted blood?"

"No," Megan responded. "I do not think there was any attempt to clean either pair of boots."

"So, you were able to take samples from both boots. Whose DNA did you recover?"

"I only found evidence of Wayne Anderson and Judith Anderson. It was a mixture of both on all the blood we tested on both pairs."

"Do you know what confirmatory bias is?" Scott asked his witness at the end of the day.

"I do," Megan answered. "It would be a situation where I would look for evidence based on what I was told. In other words, I would know the results before testing."

"Do you think you were impacted by the information you were given ahead of time?" the prosecutor asked.

"No," the DNA forensic scientist answered confidently. "DNA testing is based on numbers. It is not based on opinions. It does not manufacture results."

That was why jurors always loved DNA.

I left the courthouse with everyone else late in the day. I reached the top of the first heart attack hill, nicknamed due to the steep climb. I was a little winded and took a moment to look around me. I was surprised to see the jailer that was responsible for the transport of Michele Anderson in and out of the courtroom.

Out of politeness, I nodded my head at her. She was a husky lady with long reddish brown hair. Despite the fact that she had been in court all day, her uniform still looked crisp and pressed. If one did not read the patches on her arms, she looked like any other police officer on the streets.

"Why does your prisoner wear pink handcuffs?" I asked her.

I think she was a little surprised that I had spoken to her and it took a moment to process the question. Finally, she smiled.

"Those are my handcuffs. I had them custom made. We transport a lot of prisoners and handcuffs tend to get mixed up and lost. None of the guys want the pink handcuffs."

"Thank you," I responded, my query done.

We parted ways when the light changed and I was a little better for the exchange. I should have known that the pink handcuffs were not specific to Michele Anderson. It was easy to forget that she no longer owned anything as she was owned by the State of Washington.

Hopefully, I thought, in a matter of weeks, it would be determined that she would no longer own anything for the rest of her life.

Of course, that depended upon the jury.

DAY 22
February 24, 2016

RECEIPTS TELL TALES

Jennifer Dahlberg from the Colorado Bureau of Investigation's Crime Lab was the first witness of the day. She wore a solid black pantsuit complimented with an aqua blouse.

"You actually have two degrees. Is that right?" Scott O'Toole asked once introductions were completed. He wore a charcoal black suit, blue shirt and a silk blue and maroon colored tie.

"I do," Jennifer responded. "I have one in forensic science with a specialty in DNA. I also have a degree in Astrophysics."

"So, when they say it's not rocket science, you might have a different opinion." Scott quipped. "You are a rocket scientist. I must say that's impressive."

"Thank you," she responded modestly.

"You mentioned that you specialized in DNA study. Is there a particular area within DNA that might make you different than another DNA expert we spoke of, specifically Megan Inslee?"

"My area of study is Y-STR Analysis and it is more specific," Jennifer answered.

"Can you tell us a little more about what Y-STR Analysis is at it relates to your work?"

Jennifer looked toward the jury. "As with DNA testing, my goal was to match or exclude against control samples. My job is to extract and analyze a particular part of DNA with specialized focus on the male chromosomes. The process of extracting the 'Y' chromosome is almost identical to the process of extracting DNA. It's just more particular."

"So, once you extract the chromosome from a sample, what happens next?"

"Once the extraction is done, the samples are run through specialized computer systems. The results yield a variety of graphs and the accompanying numbers are analyzed and compared," Dahlberg explained.

"Did there come a time when you were contacted by Megan Inslee and subsequently received a sample for testing?" Scott asked.

Jennifer glanced down at a notebook in front of her and turned a page. "On July 12, 2011, I received a sample to be tested under the request of Megan Inslee. The item I received was an extract of a sample that Megan had used in her crime lab."

"Were you able to match the profile?" Scott O'Toole asked her. He had his arms crossed on his chest.

"I was. It was a match to a known DNA reference sample from Nathan Anderson."

"Do you know where the extract that you analyzed came from?" Scott asked.

"I did," Jennifer answered. She looked at the jury. "The sample came from a bone fragment recovered from the chest of Erica Anderson."

"Let me ask you this," Scott said as he moved his arms to his sides. "Does the fact that you knew where the sample came from affect the result of your testing?"

"No," she said. "DNA test results speak for itself. Although I like to know the context of what I am testing, it has no impact on the result."

"No more questions," Scott said after he consulted with Michelle Morales.

"Mr. Sorenson?" Judge Ramsdell queried.

"No, Your Honor," the defense attorney responded.

"Call your next witness," Ramsdell directed.

Thien Do, a tall man, was a detective in the Major Crimes Division for the King County Sheriff's Department. He wore a sharp charcoal black suit, white shirt and blue-checkered patterned tie.

"When were you first contacted about this case?" Scott asked.

"I was called by Sergeant Toner December 26, 2007."

"What did he want you to do?"

"The first task I was given by Sergeant Toner was to complete the drawing up of multiple search warrants for the Carnation property. Both of the dwellings and all the vehicles needed separate warrants,"

Thien answered calmly.

"After you completed the warrants, did you go to the scene?" Scott asked.

"I did. When I got there, it was my responsibility to assist with the seizure of a vehicle."

"Was it a black S10 Chevy Pick-Up?"

"Yes."

"What kind of things were you looking for?" Scott asked.

The screen in front of the jury had a crime scene picture of the black S10. Evergreen trees behind it nicely framed the truck. It might just as well have been a Chevy advertisement. It was parked at an angle as sunlight reflected off the window and the hood.

"We look for everything including weapons, documents, ownership papers, receipts, notes, maps and things we see having potential for forensic value," Thien replied.

"Do you look at the vehicle right there or what do you do?"

"As you can see from the picture we took, you'll see police tape around the perimeter of the vehicle. We then seal the vehicle and prepare it for transport to our processing lab in Seattle. The truck went into a bay area and then many photographs of it were taken."

Scott and Michelle Morales entered a series of pictures into evidence as the jurors watched. The bulk of exhibits focused on items found inside the relatively clean cab area.

"Before we go on," Scott said, "was there anything found in the bed of the pick-up?"

Thien Do glanced at his notebook. "We found a couple gas cans and a spare tire. I believe there was some sort of broken cable lock mechanism, as well."

"Did anything catch your attention in the cab area?" Scott asked.

"Aside from the cat?" Thien asked.

"Cat?" Scott asked.

"We didn't notice it until hours after the photographs were taken," Thien explained. "There was a brown cat down in the floorboards. We saw it the pictures when we inspected the photographs."

"What happened to it?"

"We went out to the bay where the S10 was and sure enough, there was a brown cat hiding in it. We retrieved it and turned it over to animal control."

"Now, aside from the cat, was there anything else of interest?" Scott asked.

"Yes. There was an open 'catch all' compartment in the console which had a stack of papers."

A picture of the interior of the truck was on the screen.

"That was particularly interesting?" Scott asked.

"Well, yes," Thien responded bemusedly. "It had a good number of receipts in it. One of our first tasks was to figure out where the truck had been. Receipts can be very valuable."

The jurors watched with interest as each item was entered into evidence.

"What information did you find on this receipt?" Scott asked. A blown-up picture was shown on the screen.

"The receipt was from a Shell Station in Monroe. The time of the transaction was 10:47 PM on December 24, 2007," Thien answered.

Monroe was approximately eighteen miles north of Carnation. Some jurors would ponder that it was not in the direction one would head if the destination were Las Vegas.

"Let me draw your attention to another receipt," Scott said as he replaced the exhibit.

Thien looked at the screen. "It is a receipt for fuel at a Safeway in Kelso, Washington. It was dated December 26, 2007 at 7:52 AM."

Kelso was 144 miles south of Carnation. Certainly, it was in the direction one might head if Las Vegas was the destination.

"Were you able to look at this receipt?" Scott asked after a new one was placed on the screen.

"It is a receipt for fuel in Lake Issaquah, Washington."

"What was the date and time?"

"It was dated 10:25 AM on December 26, 2007," the detective responded.

Lake Issaquah was located just thirteen miles south of Carnation and 130 miles north of Kelso. The direction was away from Las Vegas again.

"Were you able to retrieve another receipt from the console of the truck?" Scott asked.

"Yes," Thien recalled. "It was a teller receipt from a Bank of America. It showed a transaction amount of $306.23. It was dated December 26, 2007. The transaction had occurred in West Issaquah."

West Issaquah was located twelve miles south of Carnation. The receipts traced a path that returned them to the murder scene only fifteen minutes later.

Scott O'Toole entered Exhibit #160, after approval from the defense. He returned it to the witness. "Can you tell us what this item is?"

"It is a folded map of Washington. It was in the compartment with the receipts," Thien answered.

"Did you recover any out-of-state maps?"

"No, Sir," Thien replied.

"Thank you, Sir," O'Toole said. "No more questions."

David Sorenson approached the witness. He wore a charcoal gray suit, blue shirt and black and gold tie. "We were talking about this series of photographs. Those were not all the photographs you took, were they?"

"No," Thien answered. "We took a lot of photographs."

"There is a video of the search, too, isn't there?" Sorenson asked.

"There is. We do all we can to get photographic evidence before it is contaminated. Part of the process includes a video record of the search."

"Very good. Now we also looked at a lot of receipts. Did you collect anything more than the receipts?"

"We did," Thien responded as he looked at the jurors.

"Do you recall recovering some men's boxer shorts?"

The witness furrowed his brow a little. "Do you mind if I consult my report?"

"Not at all," Sorenson said. He waited patiently.

"We did recover men's undergarments. They are on the

evidence log on page four."

Sorenson nodded his head. "And did you recover any women's undergarments?"

"Not that I recall," Thien answered.

"Why did you take in the men's boxers as evidence?" Sorenson asked.

"We felt they might have some trace forensic value. The fact that they were wet might have been significant."

"If we can draw our attention to the receipts; specifically, the Bank of America receipt, it reads for an amount of $306.23. Was this a withdrawal done on December 26?"

"I don't recall," Thien answered. "I think it may have been a payment."

"Thank you," Sorenson responded as he went back to the defense table.

"Just a couple of questions, I promise," Scott O'Toole said as he smiled. "You only took items that were forensically important. You don't take every item for examination. Does that sound right?"

"Yes."

Scott directed Michelle Morales to put a picture on the screen. It was the Bank of America Receipt blown up many times. "If you look on the bottom right, can you tell us what it says?"

Thien nodded. "Ah, a lease payment. I do recall that."

"Would you agree that this is a receipt for a lease payment at a Bank of America in West Issaquah, dated December 26, 2007?"

"Yes."

"The payment was in the amount of $306.23?"

"Yes," the Detective verified.

The path of the Bank of America receipt and its forensic importance continued with the introduction of Andrea Bunch, an Internal Investigation Services officer for B of A. Her responsibilities included investigation of minor time-card offenses to million dollar disappearances. The receipt had landed on her plate of responsibilities after she received a phone call from Detective Scott Tompkins.

"He wanted to see any video associated with the transaction," Andrea explained.

"So when you're asked, what did you do?" Scott O'Toole asked.

"The receipt gave me very specific information. I entered that information into the system and was able to recover a visual record of this specific transaction. This information is accessible from my system at my desk."

Scott entered a video into evidence.

The video played while the jurors watched it, entranced.

Michele Anderson casually walked into a small branch of a Bank of America in West Issaquah. She wore a dumpy black outfit with black boots. A silkscreen could be seen partially on her black shirt but was unreadable. The folds of her black, loose-fitting jacket covered it. She strolled up a carpeted area cordoned off by faux-velvet railings supported with brass poles. Occasionally, she moved some long hair from her forehead, and pulled it back over the top and sides of her head.

She seemed remarkably casual, even though she had recently killed her family.

The video had recorded Michele Anderson as she made a car payment at 10:26 AM. It was strange and it was eerie.

"Did she make the payment in cash?" Scott asked at the conclusion of the short clip. He placed the receipt back on the screen.

"She made it through a check that was not from a Bank of America account. It was a lease payment in the amount of $306.23."

"Were there any other payments made on that account after December 26, 2007?"

"No," Andrea answered. "There were no other payments made after that date."

The jurors went home at the end of the day and many thought about of the B of A receipt. It had not only served to reveal the countenance of the accused, it went deeper. It would make some question her state of mind when she walked into the bank. How could she be sane enough to casually make a lease payment on a vehicle? Was it part of a plan to feign surprise when she arrived at the scene later at 11:00 AM?

There was an element of tension within each juror's minds, too. Some were preoccupied with thoughts of the alternate juror selection. There were fourteen jurors and two jurors would be excluded from deliberations. They knew the selection of the ill-fated jurors would occur shortly after closing arguments. Two jurors would not make it past closing arguments and none of them wanted to be an alternate.

The only jurors that would sleep well were the ones who believed in God's will.

DAY 23
February 25, 2016

NOTHING JUST HAPPENS

Detective Scott Tompkins took the witness stand. He wore a charcoal gray suit, light-gray shirt and a silver and black striped tie. He smiled at the jurors as he sat down while Judge Ramsdell advised him that he was still under oath.

"Welcome back, old friend," Scott said with a smile. He was immaculately dressed in a black suit, white shirt with a blue and red patterned tie.

"Detective Tompkins, if I may remind us where we were at when we last spoke, we had talked about Joseph McEnroe and Michele Anderson returning to the scene. At some point, we heard a lengthy statement from her. If I can, I have just a few questions to cover. We did not get a chance to speak about the three shell casings found from the .357 recovered from the Stillaguamish. Did you have the three casings checked for latent fingerprints?"

"Yes," Tompkins answered. His hands were folded comfortably in his lap.

"Were the casings the only items that you checked for prints?"

Tompkins turned toward the jurors. "Actually, we tested for latent prints throughout the residences in Carnation. We looked at the telephone, the interiors, the shell casings we spoke of, and, oh, the bullet found underneath Scott Anderson."

"Were you able to recover anything of value?"

"The bullets had no recoverable prints. The interior had prints but there was nothing of value since they were the same prints, as we would have expected in the household. They just did not give us any significant information," Tompkins explained.

Scott O'Toole thanked his witness and took a seat in the front row of the gallery behind the defense table.

Colleen O'Connor stood up behind the defense table. She was wore a light lime-green colored dress suit with a beige blouse.

"As the lead detective, you spoke to all of the witnesses, didn't you?"

"For the most part I did," Tompkins replied.

"You interviewed Michele Anderson, as well?"

"I did."

"You also tracked and reviewed all of the evidence?" she asked.

The detective nodded his head. "Over the years, I believe I have."

"Did you complete a Certificate of Probable Cause in this case?"

"Yes."

Colleen looked down at a stack of large three-ring binders that were open in front of her. She licked her index finger and turned some pages slowly. Finally, she looked up.

"Regarding the guns that were purchased, do you agree that Joseph McEnroe purchased his gun in December of 2003 and Michele Anderson purchased hers in May of 2004?"

"I am aware of that."

"We saw a video of the day when Joseph and Michele arrived on the scene. Who was the chaplain at the scene?"

Tompkins pondered it for a moment. "I remember him being there but I don't know who he was. He was wearing a red jacket. Although I did not call him, it is pretty traditional for us to dispatch one to death scenes."

"Did you give Michele Anderson an opportunity to speak with a chaplain?"

"No," Tompkins responded. "Not that I recall."

"You also went into Michele Anderson's trailer on the property, didn't you?"

"Yes."

"Would you agree that the residence was filthy?"

He nodded his head. "I would."

"There was garbage on the floors?"

Tompkins agreed again.

"Food was left out?" O'Connor asked.

"Yes."

"Did you see a dead bird in the trailer?" she asked.

"Actually, I did not. I heard it being discussed amongst a couple of the investigators but I personally did not see it," Tompkins recalled.

"Going back to your interview with her, you did say that she was timid during the interview, didn't you?"

"She began as timid, as I remember."

"You said she was rambling at times, didn't you?" O'Connor asked.

"She did get to rambling."

"She was apologetic?"

Tompkins agreed.

"Would you say she was cooperative?" Colleen pursued.

He agreed again.

"Let's go back to when you first arrived on the scene in Carnation. Didn't you say that you thought early on that you were going to give a death notification? Did you give the notification to Michele Anderson?"

"I did not," Tompkins answered resolutely.

"She was sobbing when she confessed, wasn't she?"

"At times, she was."

Colleen O'Connor turned some pages on the files in front of her. She looked back at the witness.

"Now, Michele Anderson told you she fired at Wayne Anderson and missed. She said that Joseph McEnroe then shot Wayne and Judy. Isn't that right?"

"Yes."

"Michele Anderson also told you that she didn't want to do this, didn't she?"

"Yes."

"She said she argued with Scott and he came at her. Is that correct?"

"That's what she said," Tompkins responded.

"She shot Scott?"

"Yes."

"She told you she was afraid that he was going to hurt her?"

"I recall her saying that."

"Did she also say that Joseph McEnroe shot Wayne?"

The detective cocked his head. "I do not remember that."

Colleen O'Connor directed his attention to a page in the confession transcript. "Doesn't it read, 'Yes, we both shot my dad. I shot him and it hit him.' Do you see that?"

"Yes," Tompkins answered.

"Would it be fair to say that Michele Anderson took responsibility for the murders during your interview?"

"I suppose she did at some point. There was a lot of back and forth on her story."

"She talked about her mother slandering her, didn't she?" O'Connor asked.

"Yes."

"She recalled Wayne being abusive to her mother?"

"She said that."

Again, Colleen O'Connor paused and looked through her three-ring binder. She looked from one book to the next. Finally, she looked up at the witness.

"She also said she gets paranoid and crazy. Do you recall that?"

"I do," Tompkins answered patiently.

"And she said everyone is against her, including Scott?"

"Yes."

"She also said that the crime was not premeditated. She had just freaked out. Do you remember that?"

"I heard her say that," Tompkins responded.

"She began crying when she admitted to the crimes, didn't she?"

"Yes."

"She stated she wasn't planning to shoot?"

"Yes."

"And she told you she had depression. You recall that, don't you?"

Tompkins nodded his head. "Yes."

Once again, O'Connor searched through her legal files.

"Do you have any information on a will?"

The detective frowned. "No. I cannot say I recall a will."

"Thank you," O'Connor said as she sat down. "Nothing further."

Scott O'Toole wasted no time as he walked back to the front of the courtroom from his seat in the gallery. He smiled at the witness and laid his legal pad down on the rail in front of him.

"Do you recall that the defendant said that she and Joseph McEnroe entered the residence armed with their weapons fully loaded?"

"I recall that."

"Do you remember her saying that she killed them all over stupid money and said she should not have done it?" O'Toole asked.

"She spoke of money on a number of occasions throughout the interview," Tompkins conceded.

"In fact, Detective, I believe she mentioned money thirty-eight times in her interview. Does that sound correct?"

"It does," Tompkins replied.

"Was she ever able to explain why the only wound on her was a nick on her finger while Scott Anderson weighed in at two-hundred and seventy pounds when she says he attacked her?"

"No. She never explained it."

Scott turned a page on his legal pad. He marked something with his pen. "Why is a chaplain called to a scene?"

"Typically, he's there to help console the family."

"Would you offer a chaplain to someone who was suspected of murdering their own family?" Scott asked. His voice was calm but the words would sizzle in many jurors' heads.

"I would not expect to do that in this situation," Tompkins replied.

"Why would you choose not to give a death notification in this case?"

"Quite frankly, she had turned into a suspect with her confession."

O'Toole nodded his head in agreement. "She turned herself in at 11:18 AM. How long did it take for her to confess?"

Tompkins thought about it a moment. "It took a while. I think it was thirty-nine pages into the interview before she changed her story into a confession."

"So, she lied to you for thirty-nine pages, didn't she?" O'Toole asked aggressively.

"Yes," Tompkins answered. "You could say that."

"Was she truthful after that?"

"It went back and forth. I wouldn't say she was completely truthful."

"At the end of the interview, on page 111," Scott directed, "she said she was sorry. She also signed the document saying everything she had stated was true and correct. Do you recall that?"

Tompkins looked up from the file he had on his lap. "She signed it saying it was one-hundred percent correct."

"And, when she admitted to killing her whole family, what did she say she was upset about?"

"On a number of occasions, she said she was upset about paying rent and not getting her money from her brother, Scott. Frequently, she mentioned money as her issue," Tompkins replied.

"Did you find any evidence of the abuse Michele Anderson spoke of?" Scott continued.

"No."

"Do you recall Michele Anderson telling you the crime was premeditated?"

"She mentioned it a number of times."

Scott looked down at his legal pad, marked something and turned a page.

"After Wayne and Judy were put outside, we talked about the other four in the family coming home. At that point, didn't she have the .357 Magnum?"

"Yes," Tompkins answered.

"She said that she shot Wayne four times, didn't she?"

"Yes."

"She also said that she shot Erica twice. Does that sound accurate?"

"Yes."

"How many bullets does a .357 Magnum have in it?"

"Six."

"No more questions," Scott said.

The jurors suspected that their world of understanding was about to change dramatically when the next witness took the stand.

Ross Martin Gardner was a tall thin man who walked with an air of importance. He wore a black suit, white shirt and gold tie. In front of him, he held a large file. Once the jurors learned he had authored three books in forensic science; was a world recognized leader in the field, and trained examiners in forensic analysis, his credibility gave them confidence.

The witness' specialty was Crime Scene Reconstruction.

"What were you asked to do for the Carnation scene?" Scott asked.

The witness turned toward the jury. "We knew ahead of time that this was a very complicated scene. My job was to use the data from the scene to define the actions that occurred. With thirty years of experience in the field of forensics, I used multiple data points to reconstruct the scene. I used extensive information from photographs, DNA, Y-STR and firearms to put the pieces together."

"What do you do to reconstruct the crime scene?" Scott asked.

The witness turned his chair toward the jurors. "Nothing just happens. Causal change is always at a scene. I look at the physical evidence in conjunction with the assistance of a sizable team. We do not, however, glean information from witness statements. I don't even want to hear them because it could create a bias. Instead, the scene speaks to the action. Our job is to determine the action and then put it in chronological order. The order of the action is the most difficult."

He took a sip of water while the jurors watched expectantly.

"We define the actions in event segments. The actors in the event are either victims or shooters. The names do not matter to me in the recreation. We are trying to understand a sequence of actions so the names become immaterial. We create a flow chart with simple statements that are conclusions to in-depth studies of a multiplicity of factors. Much of that ties to blood spatter analysis," he explained.

"What did you do in Carnation? Did you focus on the outside and inside?" O'Toole asked.

"Our focus was on the interior with a particular interest on the second event. The first event had clean up and evidence contamination involved. Our thoughts were that it was the event in the living room that was most important. That sequence of events led to another scene outside."

"What did you do to facilitate our understanding of what happened?" Scott asked.

"We recreated the crime scene exactly to a millimeter of scale and have determined, to our best knowledge, the sequence of events that occurred in the living room on December 24, 2007. As we approach this, we are going to look at it with one victim at a time. This event will be in conjunction with a shooter event. For all intents and purposes, the shooter will be listed as 'unknown'."

Much to the jury's chagrin, the day had drawn to a close before they could see the work that Ross Gardner had referenced.

They knew that, to get to the answers they needed, they had to walk into the heart of hell. Ross Gardner would be the tour guide. They were soon going to find themselves in the living room where the horrific murders took place a long time ago and each one of them was nervous.

SCENE OF THE CRIME

"We did not recreate the dining room and the kitchen simply because the scene had been altered," Ross Gardner explained. He wore a black suit, white shirt and thin black tie.

"When you say 'altered', what do you mean?" Scott O'Toole asked. He wore a charcoal colored suit, blue shirt and dark blue, red spotted tie.

"The scene was cleaned up between the first and second event. There was evidence of wiped blood, diluted blood and significant blood transfer."

"There was a gap of time, then?" Scott asked.

"We think it took two and a half hours of time before the second series of events happened. I say this because there was a roast in the oven. The preparations for the holiday dinner had begun but side dishes had not been prepared and the table had not been set. We then had to consider that the process of clean up would have taken a certain amount of time."

Scott directed Michelle Morales to place a slide on the screen. "Can you explain this flow chart for the jury?"

"This is a schematic of the five events that took place within the first event. With regards to the first box, we know that Wayne Anderson's death had occurred in or at the perimeter of the dining room. A shooter had fired from the northeast corner of the living room toward the dining room and the bullet had missed. Before it went through the dining room window, it came so close to Wayne that it took fibers from Wayne's t-shirt and dropped them on the floor with some landing on the dining room table. The bullet that exited the glass was never found," Gardner explained.

"What is the next event?"

Ross referenced his notes.

"An unknown shooter fires on Wayne in the dining room, striking his head. The second bullet was fired from a .357, and hit Wayne in the forehead on a path from left to right and exited. Fragments were found near the threshold of the dining room and kitchen."

"Where was Wayne Anderson's body found?"

"Wayne Anderson collapsed in the dining room. His hair had left marks of his position before he was later moved. There was a corresponding void pattern, illuminated through the lack of color from the LCV test, and no blood was found under him. He had been in that position for some time."

"Did you account for Judy at this time?" Scott asked.

"I would say that close to the time that Wayne was shot the first time, it would have been within seconds that a second action occurred. A .357 shooter fired on Judith from north to south and missed her."

"Where was the bullet found?"

"It was recovered in the Ziploc box in the laundry room. The bullet had come from the dining room, went through the blue hoodie shirt that Judith was wearing in the kitchen and carried the fibers to its resting place in the laundry room."

"What happened next?"

"The .357 shooter fired again and hit Judith in both the shoulder and neck with the final contact in her vertebrae. Judith was standing when the bullet made contact. The evidence pointed to her having had her arm up to protect herself when the second shot hit her."

"Would you say that's indicative of her being in a defensive position?" Scott queried.

"Absolutely," Gardner responded. "The angle of the bullet told us that. The blood evidence said the shot was not immediately fatal, however."

"Which shot was fatal?"

"The fatal shot came from a shooter that was physically close to the victim marked by the stippling on Judith's forehead. She was low and below the shooter. She was probably looking up at the person holding the .357," Ross explained clinically.

"Did you consider this the end of the event?"

"Yes. Wayne and Judith's deaths preceded the next sequence of events by some period. I believe it was a two-hour gap between events."

"Thank you," Scott said. "Your Honor, now it might be a good time to move the jurors."

"Very good, Mr. O'Toole," Judge Ramsdell said.

The judge reminded the jurors of their admonishment and asked them to accompany Kenya to the first floor for a presentation.

The court reassembled a half hour later complete with both teams of attorneys, the family, the press, the court reporter and the jury.

The jurors were staged behind the leather recliner. Slightly to the left, a couch ran lengthwise. The loveseat was perpendicular to the couch. A coffee table, void of holiday treats, was in the center of the seating area. Far to the right, a big screen television faced the room at a forty-five degree angle. A bullet hole could be seen marked on the screen. Far to the left, before the imagined dining room area, there stood a telephone table with a cordless receiver base.

It was a relatively small area that measured only twelve feet by fourteen feet. The floor was bloodied and marked with small yellow scales throughout. A drape hung from floor to ceiling but there wasn't any window behind it. It, too, was marked with signs of blood spatter.

Previously, a remnant of the flow chart had been shown to the jurors. The chart was completed and ran the length of the wall that overlooked the crime scene reconstruction.

The jurors were seated in two rows of seven behind the living room. They knew their position in the scene was where the hallway was. To the direct right of them was the front door. Just behind them, on the right, there would have been a Christmas tree.

There would be no Christmas lights at the crime scene and the jurors would not have been able to take in the smell of a rib roast in the oven.

From where they were seated, they knew that just off to the left, where the defendant was now seated, would have been the dining room.

Michele Anderson was seated just behind the telephone table. She kept her head buried in her hands. I noted that when she had been escorted to the scene, prior to the jury's entrance, she had seemed entranced and intrigued by the re-creation laid in front of her. It had been the home she had grown up in.

When the jury had taken their seats, Anderson buried her head in her hands and never looked up again.

"Let me ask you this," Scott asked from a spot by the leather recliner. "Was it your opinion that the .357 was reloaded in between the two events?"

"The .357 Magnum was definitely reloaded between the conclusion of the first event and the commencement of the second event," Gardner responded from an area by the television set. "If I may, let me set the context of the scene for you."

"Absolutely," Scott encouraged with a wave of his hand.

"It was Christmas Eve to the second four who arrived. Before the event began, the family was in a comfort zone. Shoes were off. There was food out. The clean-up had already been done."

"Where were the shooters at this time?"

"One shooter would have been at the entrance of the living room, to the north of the leather recliner. The first shot that began the second event would have been fired from approximately the front of where the jury is seated," Gardner responded.

"Where was the second shooter?"

"That shooter would have been seated on the couch to the east of Scott. The second shooter had the 9 MM."

"With regards to the .357, how many bullets were fired in the second event?"

"Seven bullets were fired from the .357 Magnum in the next few minutes," Gardner said as he walked to the flow chart on the wall. He pointed to the first event. "We know the shooter fired upon Scott while he was seated on the sofa."

O'Toole stepped back when Gardner made his way toward the end of the couch.

"He may have been leaning forward when the first bullet hit him in the chin, went downward, and into his chest. The blood pool under the coffee table and below him under the couch demanded that he was there. The blood went straight down."

"Would he have been incapacitated?" Scott asked.

"No," Gardner replied. "Evidence showed that he got up and headed in the direction of the shooter toward the window curtains, low to the ground. He collapsed straight back when he got there."

"Would he have been mortally wounded?"

"He was alive when he transitioned from an upright to a supine position in the living room. He would have been alive for a time," Gardner said. "However, he was not alive when the .357 shooter shot him in the abdomen. It was a close proximity shot that probably took place last, after the series of other, almost simultaneous events."

"Would there have been a reload of a weapon during this time?" Scott asked.

"I would say there was a reload before the final shot to Scott's abdomen," Gardner stated.

"There was a 9 MM shooter, as well, wasn't there?"

"Yes. Simultaneously, a 9 MM shooter would have entered the picture. A 9 MM shooter fired from south to north from the sofa and Erica was the likely target. It missed its target. The bullet travelled through an Afghan blanket stand and was recovered from inside the windowsill."

"Would you expect the 9 MM shooter to be standing or sitting?"

"Based on the angle," Gardner demonstrated, "it was likely that the shooter was in a seated position on the couch. There was an unexplained dual hole in Erica's hooded sweatshirt that pointed in the direction of the bullet in the wall. It was probable that Erica had come forward to help her dying husband who lay on the floor."

"What happened next?"

"The next bullet was from the .357 Magnum and came from east to west while she was in the northwest quadrant of the living room. The shooter was positioned in the northeast quadrant of the living room," Gardner said as he pointed toward the living room entrance, near the front door.

"Was Erica standing at the time?" Scott asked.

"Not exactly," Gardner responded. He walked to the end of the loveseat.

"Erica was upright and bent at the waist. Her right side was oriented to the northeast when the .357 shot was fired on her. It made contact with Erica's left shoulder and exited out her back by the armpit area. She had to have been bent down and gunshot residue evidence showed the gun was fired from over Scott."

"Would that have been a fatal wound?"

"No. It was probable that Erica retreated and ended up back near the loveseat. She was still alive. Her torso was bent and her left flank was exposed to the shooter with the .357 Magnum. She was fired upon from the northeast which caused a perforating chest and abdomen wound," Gardner explained.

"Where are Nathan and Olivia at this time?"

"At this point in time," Ross Gardner explained, "the situation has become very dynamic. Things are starting to happen very close to each other. We know Erica is trapped in this area on the loveseat and we know a 911 call was made. It was a cordless phone on the telephone table and the evidence suggests it was not recovered from the cradle but may have been within reach of Erica when she called. One drop of blood was found on the Pepsi crate near the phone stand. It was Erica's blood. She could have been in the proximity. At the same time, Nathan and Olivia are in this scene."

The investigator stopped speaking. He was suddenly choked up.

"I'm sorry," he said.

It was a moment that would have impacted the jury because it had come out of the blue. Suddenly, emotion of the event had come over the witness. The jurors were used to his analytic and meticulous explanation of the sequence of events. Yet, he became human when he cracked. The jurors related to him because they had each shed many a tear in silence over the victims. It was an important impromptu moment.

Everyone waited silently as the reconstruction expert regained his composure.

"Nathan was standing in front of Erica, facing south," the investigator continued after he regained his composure. "The 9 MM shooter was positioned south of both of them when the shot was fired. There was evidence of stippling on Nathan's face. He was on Erica's chest when the bullet hit him in the left side of the face and ended up deep in Erica's chest. The shooter would have been closer than twenty inches from the victim. Nathan would have collapsed to the left of Erica and did not move after the bullet hit him. The 9 MM shooter had killed him almost instantly."

The defendant had her head down on the defense table as her hands covered the sides of her face. The jurors would have ignored her.

"The 9 MM shooter was on the other side of Erica, in front of the couch. The evidence suggests a shot was fired in a downward direction into Olivia's head. Olivia had also been hit in the abdomen by another bullet but it's difficult to tell when it happened in the sequence of events. She had moved after receiving the abdomen wound and was alive when she got the head wound. The hair on her head masked the stippling effect although I am confident the shot was from a close range," Gardner explained.

He paused again and took a deep breath.

"The coup de grace was the shot to Olivia's head. It was followed by a final shot to Erica's head. It is probable that the very last bullet fired at the scene was the shot to the abdomen of Scott who was lying on the floor. I still believe Scott was dead by the time that shot went into him as evidenced by the lack of blood around the wound."

Scott O'Toole paused to speak with Michelle Morales and then told the witness he was done with his questions.

David Sorenson cross-examined the investigator after he was

presented the opportunity. He wore a charcoal colored suit, white shirt and blue striped tie.

"I have just a couple of questions for you," Sorenson said. He held a legal pad in his hands. "Did you have the opportunity to read any statements by Michele Anderson?"

"No, I did not."

"Did you read any statements by Joseph McEnroe?"

"Again, no. I learned of the interviews after my analysis was complete," Gardner responded.

"Did you go the scene?"

"I did not. It would have been cost prohibitive and the scene would have been degraded significantly."

Sorenson turned a page on his notepad. "Earlier you stated that Judy was cooking before the shooters arrived. How do you know Wayne was not cooking?"

"It was an interrupted effort. It is possible Wayne did something to help. However, very little preparation had been done if dinner was anticipated soon. There was no tablecloth out. Side dishes were not cooked or ready. Place settings, as one might expect, would be out."

"You're making assumptions about side dishes," Sorenson countered. "You're assuming when they would eat. Aren't you?"

"No," Gardner replied. "Common sense tells you that side dishes and table preparations for an annual family holiday gathering do not come out five minutes after the roast comes out of the oven."

"Maybe they already ate," Sorenson suggested.

"That's very unlikely. There would be used utensils at the scene."

Sorenson turned a page and looked at Gardner. "What are your sources for the conclusions you made?"

"There are multiple sources including information from the State Crime lab, the Sheriff's Department, DNA reports, bullet analysis and reports from the medical examiner."

"So you relied on their measurements exclusively to make your determinations?"

"I did a significant number of measurements myself."

"Now, if I may, you said you were retained fifteen months after the incident. Is that correct?"

"Is it typical to wait so long?"

"It's routine," Gardner responded casually. "We typically handle cold-cases and we are often asked for assistance long after an incident."

"In regards to Scott Anderson, you can't say that the second shot was immediately after the first shot?"

"No. Scott was seated when he received the first shot. He stood and walked toward the northeast corner and then fell backwards. He would have been supine and alive for a while. However, because there was no bleeding in the bullet tracks from the abdomen, we know he was deceased by the time the last bullet was fired."

Sorenson thought about it for a moment.

"What if someone was behind him when he was first shot?"

"That's not possible," Gardner responded. "No, it could not have been that way."

"No more questions." Sorenson said.

Scott O'Toole stood up. "Your Honor, at some point, you and I discussed giving the jurors an opportunity to look at the scene. I suggest that this might be a good time."

"Thank you, Mr. O'Toole," Ramsdell responded. "As suggested, Jurors, I would like to give you a chance to look at the scene. You may walk on the floor. There is no biohazard concern because the floor is made from ink."

Of the fourteen present, only three or four jurors got up to walk through the living room displayed in front of them. Jurors would tell me later that many did not jump at the chance because they thought the scene was hallowed ground and deserved immense respect.

On the other hand, the jurors who walked within the recreated scene respected it just as well. It was felt that part of their duty was to look closely at every piece of evidence presented.

There was nothing that would ever take away the visuals that had finally come together in their minds. The more perplexing issue was the utter senselessness of it all.

Two selfish shooters had taken six innocent lives. They were taken with premeditation and in a coldness that was nearly palpable. Every shot of the gun was an act of premeditation. Just as the jurors could almost smell the roast in the oven, they surely heard the screams of the victims.

No juror had to be told that the prosecution would rest soon.

It would be time for the defense team to speak. Although they needed to hear some sort of defense, the jurors only wanted to hear from one person and that was the defendant herself. Would she take the stand or would she continue to cower at the defense table with her head in her hands?

SUICIDE BY JURY

"Michele Anderson has decided to exercise her right to testify," David Sorenson told the judge before the jury was called. He wore a charcoal gray suit, white shirt and deep maroon colored tie.

Judge Ramsdell looked a little surprised. "That is certainly her right."

"We have some challenges since Ms. O'Connor and I just learned of her intentions this morning. We have not had a two-way discussion with her in at least a couple of years, although not by lack of attempts. Because of this communication breakdown, we will need some time."

The judge nodded his head. "Go ahead."

"As you know, we have made multiple requests to withdraw. We are in a difficult position," Sorenson stated. "We are concerned about the preclusion of some evidence from the prosecution. Our other issue is that we, quite frankly, do not know what's going to happen on the stand. There have been no rehearsals or mock trial dialogues with the defendant to prepare her. She does not understand the rules of evidence and this puts us in a precarious position."

Ramsdell thought about it for a moment.

"So, what you're saying is that the jury needs to understand her behavior on the stand. She may be mumbling at times and there has been no rehearsal.

"I think it puts the jury in a position where they will think she is perjuring herself. They need a background in why she is appearing on the stand and the circumstances around it. We are most concerned about narrative responses she may give. It would telegraph itself wrong to the   jury," Sorenson pleaded.

"The defendant has a right to testify," Ramsdell stated. "She also has the right not to testify.

"She is aware of her rights."

"I do not think her decision was well advised," Colleen O'Connor said. "She is making this decision in a vacuum without listening to any of our advice."

"I have a right to testify," Michele Anderson suddenly said. Her voice was low-key but clearly irritated.

Judge Ramsdell looked somewhat taken aback. He carried the same raised eyebrows he had when someone had interrupted from the gallery a few weeks prior.

"Ma'am, it is best I don't hear from you."

"You're all talking about me like I'm not here," Anderson said vehemently.

"Ma'am?" Judge Ramsdell warned. "Mr. O'Toole. Do you have any thoughts for the State?"

Scott O'Toole stood up. He was dressed in a deep-blue colored suit, crisp white shirt and a red tie.

"We would have a different story if this was a capital case. I think Michele Anderson would take the opportunity to be a weapon to the jury. At this point, her testifying is of no feasible importance to the jury. I understand it is her right, but her testimony would not be relevant," he explained.

"Go on."

Scott set his notepad down. "I think I need to inform the Court and the defendant that should she testify, there will be questions asked of her. It will be lengthy and in depth. I would also like to make it clear that any cross-examination on our part will be fierce."

The judge looked toward the defense table.

"So, to be clear, you don't have a clue what she will say or do on the stand?"

"No, Your Honor," Sorenson resolutely responded.

"I respect the difficult position that the defense team is in," Scott offered. "The defendant needs to know, however, that there are rules when she is on the stand."

"That's part of the problem," Ramsdell interjected. "It's hard for the defense counsel because they have not had the opportunity to craft questions for her. At the same time, I am also concerned that the defendant may use this trial as an opportunity to make her own statements. Still, I cannot preclude her from testifying."

He took his glasses off and briefly cleaned them as he pondered the situation.

"Ma'am?" he said toward the defendant. "As you have just heard, you will be on the stand for some time should you choose to testify. Not only will it be lengthy, the cross-examination will be not be a comfortable experience."

"They lied to me. My attorneys did!" Anderson exclaimed. "I need an advocate. I need someone to speak for me."

"That is not the issue we are discussing," Ramsdell said. "We are talking about your decision to testify."

"But you're ignoring me," Anderson said. "I have a right to effective counsel. Someone needs to talk on my behalf. My attorneys always lie to me!"

I was amazed at how levelheaded the judge seemed despite the tirade of comments from the defendant.

He decided to think about the issue and review it after Scott O'Toole presented his final witness.

Detective Tompkins was dressed professionally in a gray suit, blue shirt and blue-checkered pattern tie. His hands rested comfortably in his lap.

"I just have some follow-up questions for you, Detective," Scott O'Toole began. "I think there was some concern on the height of the couch and its height in reference to a problem with the legs?"

"Well, yes," Tompkins responded. "The legs were wobbly. As much as we tried to adjust them, the screw holes were ruined. So, I had four-inch pieces of wood cut that were the same size as the originals. We then checked the height of the frilly thing, the blanket, over the back of the couch and it was at the right height."

"Thank you," O'Toole said. He turned a page on his notepad. "We also wanted to revisit why Ross Gardner did not go to the scene. Can you explain why that was?"

"Ross Gardner did not get the case until April of 2009. The property was given back to its owners in 2008," Tompkins told the jurors. "The place had been remodeled by the time we hired Mr. Gardner so the scene was of no value."

Scott nodded his head and picked up a remote control. A picture of the reconstruction scene as the jurors had seen it the day before was placed on the screen.

"The curtains in this exhibit," he said, using a laser pointer. "Are they the same curtains the jurors saw yesterday downstairs?"

"Yes," Tompkins answered.

"Are those curtains the same as they were recovered from Wayne and Judy Anderson's home?"

"Yes."

O'Toole entered the original curtains into evidence as Exhibit #171.

"I want to direct your attention to the television with the bullet hole in it. Is this the same television that the jurors saw yesterday?"

"Yes."

"Is it the same television as was removed from Wayne and Judy Anderson's home?" Scott asked.

"It is," the detective responded.

The television was entered as part of Exhibit #171.

In a quick and expeditious fashion, the prosecutor entered the rest of the inventory recovered from the living room. The television rack, the corresponding Afghans, the magazine rack, five pillows, three blankets, two end tables, two couches, a recliner and a coffee table were officially numbered into the court record.

The final piece was a large white folded painter's tarp. It was presented to the court clerk as a heavy folded bundle. It was the floor recreated by photo image that some jurors had walked on yesterday. It was named Exhibit #141.

"Thank you," Scott O'Toole said. "No more questions. The State rests its case."

The judge looked toward the jury and made the decision to excuse them for a morning break. He waited until Kenya had secured the jury behind the closed doors of the jury room. He looked toward the defense table.

"Mr. Sorenson? Are there any other issues that you wish to review before we proceed?"

"No, Your Honor," he responded.

"Very good. The problem in this matter is the issue of the Michele Anderson testimony," the judge said. "She has the right to ignore the advice of her attorneys and testify…"

The defense attorney interrupted the judge, timidly. "I would like it clear on the record that we did not give advice either way."

"Regardless," the judge responded. "She could choose to testify anyway. The court is aware that she has not communicated with you and aware that it has been a significant amount of time. I have seen the requests to withdraw from the case and I denied each of them. So, I understand the predicament you find yourselves in. But, I will permit her to testify."

Sorenson nodded his head.

"We do this with the understanding that some doors will get kicked in. We will have to deal with each issue as it comes. I think all of us can agree that we do not know what to expect. This step is driven by Michele Anderson and she will have to live with the consequences," he said. It sounded like the matter was closed.

"You can't deny my civil rights," Michele Anderson complained. "My constitutional rights are being violated and you are responsible for it."

The silence was electric.

"Ma'am?" the judge questioned. "I cannot tell you how many things are wrong about the statement you just made."

There would be some in the courtroom who would later say, that the face shown by Michele Anderson in court, must have been the same face the victims saw before she killed them. Her voice was obstinate while her inflections and innuendo's reflected that of a spoiled teenager who was not getting her way.

"I tried to speak to the court. You slandered my credibility. My attorneys slandered me many times. They violated my rights!" she said angrily.

The female jailer with the pink handcuffs on her belt paid a little more attention.

"I don't have legal counsel," Anderson continued. "I am filing charges against you and my attorneys. My legal counsel lied to me. They treat me bad. I am at a disadvantage and they are violating my rights!"

Judge Ramsdell's voice was firm. "Ma'am? That is not the issue on the table. The issue is whether you are exercising your right to testify on your behalf. Are you going to testify?"

Anderson spat back, "I have no effective counsel. They're dishonest."

"You have had two capable attorneys."

"You can throw me out if you want to," she interrupted.

"You have one question to answer," Ramsdell said. "This has been going on for years with your attorneys. You have been given every possible opportunity to speak with your attorneys. In that, we are going to recess. When we return, I only want to hear whether you are testifying or not."

The judge looked toward the three guards. "Take her to jail. This Court is in recess."

Fifteen minutes later, Judge Ramsdell took his seat back on the bench. He looked directly at the defendant.

"Is it your desire to testify, Ma'am?"

"I just want you to know that I have a constitutional right for counsel of choice that I can buy or hire with my own funds," she stated insolently. "I just want you to know that you cannot deny somebody that right."

"Okay, Ma'am," Ramsdell acknowledged. "All I asked you was whether or not you want to testify."

"Or with my choice of attorneys that I want to be represented," Anderson responded.

"That is not my question," Ramsdell simply said.

"It's illegal to have me testify without effective legal counsel," she countered.

"Ma'am? My question is this: Do you wish to testify or not?"

"Yes!" she said adamantly. "I'm going to tell you in front of the jury that I don't have effective assistance of counsel so, my rights are being violated. It has to be on the court record when this is appealed. You can't deny somebody that and retain your job on the bench. You understand that, right?"

"I'm asking you one simple question. Do you wish to testify in your own defense?"

"I wish to stand up there and tell the jury that I have been denied my constitutional right!"

"Well, if that's the extent of the testimony you wish to give to the jury then I am not going to allow you to do that because that's not really relevant to their question of guilt or innocence," the judge stated. "So, as a result..."

Anderson interrupted him. "But you didn't allow me the ability to defend myself and you are denying me my civil rights. You can't keep your job when you do things like that! There's, uh, uh, disciplinary steps..."

Again, the judge asked, "Do you wish to testify on your behalf with regards to the crimes?"

"With effective assistance of counsel!" Anderson retorted. "I am inadequately represented because they cannot take their personal bias out of the picture! I went against my own best interest to stop talking to them because I want to protect myself in malpractice and you're blaming me!" she said as she pointed to herself with her thumb. "They're abusive to me at the meetings so I can't go to those. They lied to me so I'm not getting effective counsel! I bring it up in court and you deny my ability."

"Ma'am?" the judge said with a raise of his hand as he halted her. "I've ruled on these issues many times over. I know you disagree with the rulings but those are over with now."

Colleen O'Connor spoke up. "Your Honor? Can we have just a second?"

"If you wish, Counselor. Go right ahead!"

The two attorneys whispered in the defendant's ear. It was clear that they were trying to interject some sort of voice of reason.

"Are you sure?" Michele Anderson asked the judge after the brief conference. "I just want to know, so it's clear on the record, you're denying me to have the ability to bring in a professional mediator or add a private attorney, to the existing, to, to resolve the problem."

I wondered at that moment whether she had referenced the pro se supporter that had visited her in the county jail recently.

"Ma'am? We're at the end of this trial..."

"You never let me speak in court!" Anderson interjected. "You talk over my head like I don't know what Michele Anderson wants and I'm sitting right here!"

"I'm doing my job, Ma'am," the judge said resolutely. "My job is to find out whether you want to testify in your own defense with regards to the charges. Not whether or not you want to get up here and give a speech to the jury about how everyone's violating your rights. Do you wish to testify in your own defense? Yes or no will do it."

"I just want it on the record that you're denying my ability to have a mediator and to bring a private attorney here to resolve the problem," Anderson repeated.

Ramsdell nodded his head. "She's got it on the record so many times that I don't think anybody will miss it."

"Okay," Anderson acquiesced.

"Do you wish to testify in your own defense with regards to the charges against you?"

"No," Anderson answered. "Not without effective counsel."

Her two attorneys looked straight ahead, as if Anderson was not there.

"We'll re-assert, then, that you don't wish to testify?" the judge queried.

Again, she repeated her discontent at not having effective counsel despite their presence next to her.

It was set in stone, on the record, that Anderson had declined her right to testify.

The jury was called out for the final time of the day after another extended stay in the deliberation room. They seemed to be in good spirits. It was clear that the fourteen random civilians were now friends; bonded in a way only a juror could understand.

Michelle O'Connor stood up behind her desk. "The defense has no witnesses, Your Honor."

Judge Ramsdell did not look surprised.

"The defense rests," she said as she sat down.

"Very good," he responded. He looked toward the jury box. "Ladies and Gentlemen, we are going to excuse you for the day. Just so you have an idea of what's next, I can tell you that we will be reading jury instructions tomorrow and then we will hear closing arguments. Since the alternate jurors are not pre-selected, we will be choosing two jurors after closing arguments," he explained.

Butterflies would once again flutter in the stomachs of some jurors. The exclusion from the deliberating process would be an accepted but difficult cross to bear.

Twelve jurors would soon be at the doorway of justice.

I thought of the defendant and her choice not to testify. It was probably a good idea.

It would have been suicide by jury.

BANQUET OF CONSEQUENCES

"Members of the jury, when I thought about how I would prepare my remarks, I was reminded of an old saying by the author Robert Louis Stevenson," Scott O'Toole said as he began his closing statements, " who wrote that everybody, sooner or later, sits down to a banquet of consequences. I would suggest to you that today is the day, this woman, Michele Anderson, sits down to her banquet of consequences."

He was dressed sharply in a charcoal black suit, soft blue shirt and red tie. He stood behind a podium as he faced the jury. On the angled podium in front of him, he had placed his notes. Along the railing in front of the jury, out of the jury's sight, was a stack of 3x5 ft. poster board outlines and pictures.

"Let me begin by showing you why we are here," Scott said. He picked up one of the poster-boards and presented it to the jury. "This is Wayne Anderson. He was a husband, father and grandfather. He was retired from Boeing. He was an engineer.

"This is a picture of Judith Anderson. She was a wife, mother, grandmother and worked for the United States Post Office for seventeen years," Scott said.

He walked to the railing of the jury box, set the placard down and obtained another.

"This is Scott Anderson. He was a husband, son and father. He was a Huskies football player and graduated from the University of Washington. He worked construction in Kenmore to support his family."

The prosecutor angled the picture so that everyone could see the victim as he had been in life.

"This is Erica Anderson," Scott said as he presented another picture. "She was a wife, mother and daughter. She had two children. She loved to bake."

"This is Olivia Anderson," he presented. "She was five years-old and the daughter of Scott and Erica. She loved horses and loved to dance. For Christmas, she would be given a pink bicycle with trainings wheels. It was a bicycle she would never get to ride."

Scott replaced the victim's picture with that of the sixth. "This is Nathan Anderson. His third birthday was on December 10, 2007. He was the son of Scott and Erica. On Christmas, he was going to get a toy truck, one that he would never play with. He was still in his diapers."

The jurors' faces were somber and serious. Some held back tears.

"On Christmas Eve in 2007, more than eight years ago, two people, Michele Anderson and Joseph McEnroe, walked out of their mobile home, got in their truck and drove up the driveway to her parents' home," Scott continued. "Michele Anderson was the driver of that truck. Her boyfriend, Joseph McEnroe, was in the passenger's seat. They drove up the driveway and they parked. They got out of the truck; concealing two loaded weapons, and walked up the steps to the front porch. They opened the door. She was also armed with the trust of the people inside and carried hatred for them in her heart."

The prosecutor paused momentarily.

"Members of the jury, nobody with the last name of Anderson lives in that house anymore. When this woman," he said with a wave toward the defendant, "and her boyfriend were done, a family that had lived in that home for over thirty years, lay dead. That night, when Michele Anderson and Joseph McEnroe walked through that front door, they were well-prepared, well-armed and knew exactly what they were going to do."

There was a momentary disruption as Miss {redacted} noisily entered the courtroom and took a seat in the back row. Her tardiness had become an established protocol.

"When Michele and Joe were done inside that home, they walked out and got into their truck and she drove back down the driveway," O'Toole resumed. "They returned to their trailer and they talked about what they would do next. They talked about destroying evidence, which they proceeded to do by utilizing a fire-pit outside their home. And, they planned their next move, which was to flee.

The prosecutor paused and glanced at his notes.

"When that Christmas Eve began eight years ago, the victims had been six live human beings whose only misfortune was to be related to Michele Anderson and to have befriended her boyfriend, Joseph McEnroe. This trial is about those human beings and what the defendant and her boyfriend did to them.

"The true measure of a person is what he or she would do when they thought they might never be caught," he continued. "Michele and her boyfriend thought they would never be caught. These were people who chose to operate in the shadows, to operate when their victims were most vulnerable; on Christmas Eve when everyone was sitting down to a family dinner."

He grasped the side of the podium as he looked at his notes. "Remember what Mary Victoria Anderson told you when she testified? How her sister had talked about killing her parents? Then, when Mary was asked on cross-examination, remember her statement? Quote: Who expects a member of your family to slaughter your whole family?"

The prosecutor allowed silence to settle in so the jurors could process his rhetorical question.

"Michele Anderson is someone who chose to terrorize people because they were close to her, because they trusted her. They were victims who thought they would be safe in their own homes, who were unarmed and unsuspecting. Members of the jury, today is the day that the defendant is held accountable, not in the darkness of a Christmas Eve in Carnation eight years ago but in the bright lights of a court of law."

Scott O'Toole's eyes panned the length of the jury box. I would suspect that he made eye contact with many of the jurors' eyes.

He waited when an additional late person entered the courtroom and found a seat in the gallery. The sounds from the crunchy paper bag he carried had attracted the attention of a number of jurors. There were some looks of irritation.

"The fundamental issue in this case is whether the State has proven to you beyond a reasonable doubt that the defendant committed the crimes of murder in the first degree in counts one through six," O'Toole explained. "I am going to appeal to your judgment, your experience and, most importantly, your common sense. In my experience, it seems that jurors have an extra sense that lawyers tend to lose when they go to law school. Lawyers sometimes don't get it but jurors do and that's why we have a jury system. That's why you were called on, to make this very important decision."

He walked over to the wall by the court reporter, picked up a 3 x 5 Ft. placard and placed it on the tripod for the jurors to see.

"Every criminal case, great or small, the burden of proof upon the State is to prove the elements of the crime and, what might surprise you in a case as serious as murder, there are only four elements."

He drew the jury's attention to a line on the exhibit.

"With regards to the first element, which took place on December 24, 2007, is that the defendant intended to cause the death of each victim.

"The second element is that the defendant not only intended to cause the death of six, it was premeditated. The third element," he pointed out on the placard, "that each victim died as a result of the defendant's actions and, finally, that these events took place in the State of Washington."

The prosecutor took a breath, glanced briefly at his notes and continued his conversation with the jury.

"One of the other instructions you are to consider, summarized on this chart, is the accomplice instruction. An accomplice is guilty of a crime committed by another person when he or she is legally accountable for the conduct of that other person," O'Toole explained. "A person is legally accountable for another person with knowledge that will promote or facilitate the commission of a crime when he or she does any of the following."

With a motion of his hand, Scott directed the jury's attention to the placard.

"It means that if you are an accomplice, you are held as responsible as the principal. You don't get a break just because you were an accomplice to the crime. Make no mistake; Michele Anderson was primarily a principal. She is the reason these crimes happened and it was her idea."

Anderson, who wore a blue top with baggy black pants, stared straight ahead from the defense table. Her hands were framed along the side of her face, which shielded her eyes.

"The victims in these murders were all objects of her anger at her brother, her parents and her family. She's the one that began that murder spree on December 24, 2007. She fired that first shot at Wayne and, an hour later, fired the first shot into the face of her brother, Scott, in the second phase. Remember to consider that she is not only responsible as a principal, but as an accomplice. She was the reason why this happened."

Although the jurors had the option to take notes, I noticed that most of them idly held their pens.

"It was Michele Anderson that fired the first shot, not Joseph McEnroe. She, not McEnroe, fired the first shot that hit Erica. She, not McEnroe, is probably the one who fired the first shot that hit Olivia in the abdomen that ultimately went through her body. And she, not Joseph McEnroe, fired the last shot, the 'coup de grace', into Scott's belly as he lay dead on the floor, only inches from his wife and children."

Scott picked up another placard.

"Direct evidence is evidence given by a witness who directly perceives something while circumstantial evidence is evidence based on common sense and experience of which you can reasonably infer something. If you can make decisions, you can make conclusions on circumstantial evidence."

He paused to scan the juror's eyes.

"Why did I tell you this? If you watch enough television, movies or read books such as those by John Grisham, they are always telling you that you cannot convict on circumstantial evidence, that it is somehow not good enough. Yet, the law says to you very clearly that one type of evidence is not necessarily more valuable than the other. You may decide that circumstantial evidence is more compelling and vice versa.

"I think everyone remembers the story of Robinson Crusoe. He was alone on an island for a long time. One day, he sees a footprint. We all know the rest of the story. It was Friday. Well, you may get caught up in what circumstantial evidence is. Your conclusions are based on common sense. Like, when Robinson Crusoe saw the footprint, he knew somebody else was there. In this case, the DNA is circumstantial evidence at the scene. It is evidence they were there. DNA does not tell you why it happened but it does tell you what happened and who was present even though there are no witnesses who saw them there."

Scott casually turned a page on his notes.

"She is the reason why this happened. She and Joseph McEnroe walked into Wayne and Judy's house armed on Christmas Eve sometime in the mid-afternoon. There was a roast in the oven. The Christmas tree was decorated. Judy was in the craft room. She was wrapping presents including one for the defendant. Another present she was preparing to wrap was a toy truck for Nathan. This was Wayne's holiday. The rest of the family was coming over including Mary, Scott, Erica and the children."

The prosecutor's voice was steady and calm.

"She was 29-years old. She admitted thirty-five times that this was all about money. She didn't want to pay rent and she wanted money back from Scott. All she wanted was her "stupid money" as she stated over and over in her interview with Detective Tompkins and Peters. She also made sure both weapons were loaded before they walked in that house on Christmas Eve. She planned an argument with Wayne. She shot at her father and missed. She went to shoot again but her gun jammed. Her accomplice fired the .357 and shot Wayne in the head."

He paused for a moment.

"Judy runs out of the craft room and saw that her husband had been shot in the head. She panics and retreats from the shooters. One shot misses her. The next shot hit her as she had her arms raised in a defensive position. The shot paralyzes her but she was conscious. She was also conscious moments later, when she was shot again, this time in the head by Joseph McEnroe."

O'Toole turned a page in his notes.

"Remember, Michele's gun was jammed. Then, they spent a significant amount of time cleaning the scene and hiding their

362

evidence. She did not want Scott to know, because she would not get her money if he saw the parents deceased at her hands."

"Scott and the children arrived. He sat in his favorite chair after taking his boots off. The kids were playing and Erica was relaxing on the couch. Michele and Joseph sat with them. It must have been a very good cleanup. When asked where Wayne and Judy were, Michele told them they were in the bathroom. It is quite probable that Scott figured out that something had happened to his parents. Scott rose up and was shot in the face. The children and Erica are panicked and struggled to get out of danger. Scott knelt forward and then fell back."

The prosecutor took a sip of water. He did not check his notes. He continued his well-paced dialogue.

"At this point, Erica was the next target. We all know that Erica is the one she really did not like. Both weapons were turned on her. Michele had the .357 and shot Erica twice. Remember the call to 911 at 5:13 PM? It is likely the .357 had run out of bullets. She was reloading while Erica was dialing the handheld. In the background of the call, you can hear Erica screaming, "No! No! Not the kids!"

"So, Olivia was next. Her abdomen shot had probably come from a missed shot at Erica. Olivia had already been hit once. She was burrowing next to her mother. With Joseph McEnroe now standing over the remaining three, Michele orders him to shoot them. She did not want the kids to be scarred forever, she said in her confession. She also minimized the event regarding Nathan by saying that Nathan was at peace because he looked like he knew. Are you kidding me?"

Scott O'Toole abruptly stopped.

He looked much like Ross Gardner had looked when he had

broken down during the crime scene reconstruction. The prosecutor seemed to hold his breath a moment and let the emotion pass. It was not intended to be powerful but it was.

"The children were not at peace," Scott continued carefully. "They were terrified. As you recall, she then went through efforts to burn and destroy evidence. We were witness to the discovery of the gun in the Stillaguamish. She said, and I quote, 'I was tired of everyone stepping on me. I thought about it for weeks. Yes, I was fed up with everything…Yes, it was premeditated.'"

Over the next hour, the prosecutor carefully walked the jurors through the elements of each crime with each death. He spent time on premeditation and he spoke about reasonable human beings and reasonable doubt.

"All of them were shot within minutes of each other and all of them were shot in the head. I would suggest that all of these deaths were part of a common scheme or plan. Go by what the evidence shows you and what logic and reason commands," Scott directed the jurors.

"Don't discount these victims: Wayne, Judy, Scott, Erica, Olivia and Nathan. The evidence established is overwhelming that this defendant, Michele Anderson," he said with a wave toward the defense table, "committed murder in the first-degree and she did it six times. It is your duty to decide the facts in this case and it is your responsibility to accept the law as it is regardless of how you think it should be. You decide how those facts fit within the law.

"Finally, I began my remarks with a quote from Robert Louis Stevenson, 'Everybody, sooner or later, sits down to a banquet of consequences'. There were thirty-eight witnesses, facts and forensics. I suggest to you that you also heard from some other voices as well. Not directly, maybe, but what they left behind in the

DNA that they left on the scene...and in the skull and tissue from Nathan's head into the chest of Erica Anderson."

Each juror would remember the journey they had taken through the sight of each autopsy photograph.

"If Erica had not had the courage to make that 911 call, which told us when the murders occurred, the jumping off point in this investigation, where would we be today?" he asked rhetorically.

"You will decide the facts of the case based on the evidence. Discard both feelings of sympathy and prejudice. This tragedy did not have to happen. Should you have sympathy for Michele Anderson? Should you be outraged over this killing of six? There is no need for either emotion. Look at the facts and you will see that Michele Anderson *did* murder six human beings on December 24, 2007."

His eyes scanned the stoic faces of the jury.

"I ask you to hear all of the voices in this case especially those of the victims. At the end of the day, there's only one voice left and that is your voice."

He turned to his last page of notes.

"I would ask you to consider Wayne, Judy, Scott, Erica, Olivia and Nathan Anderson and how they died on December 24, 2007. Olivia and Nathan may never have fully known what was happening. Is there any sadder image than that of Nathan's head against his mother's chest as Erica tried to protect and comfort him, as a bullet was fired into his head and into Erica's chest?"

The jurors answered his question in their minds.

"Is there a more pathetic claim than Michele Anderson saying to Detective Tompkins, 'Nathan looked like he knew that he was going to die and was accepting of it'? Well," O'Toole continued, "Olivia and Nathan may never have fully known what was happening but Wayne and Judy Anderson did and Scott and Erica did. In the last furious moments of their life, the last person that Wayne, Judy, Scott and Erica saw as they fought for their lives, was the woman who is sitting in this courtroom right now, Michele Anderson."

The silence in the courtroom was thick. The family of the victims sat in the front row of the gallery, their faces resolute. They had waited a long time for this day.

One could have heard a pin drop in the courtroom.

"Martin Luther King once wrote, 'Our lives begin to end the day we become silent about the things that matter'," Scott quoted.

He took a sip of water and set it back down. He took a deep breath.

"Members of the jury, truth matters. Wayne, Judy, Scott, Erica, Olivia and Nathan Anderson mattered," Scott finished. He gathered his things and sat down.

"He's a good actor," I heard Miss {redacted} comment sarcastically from behind me.

All hell broke loose when the jury returned after their break. Like a boil that had festered over time, the pressure had caused an explosion, and it became time for someone else to have a seat at his or her own banquet of consequences.

DAY 26 Part 2
March 2, 2016

FANCIFUL BELIEF

"Have a seat, folks," Judge Ramsdell told the courtroom. The jurors waited behind closed doors.

"Your Honor," Scott O'Toole said as he stood up. "I make this request reluctantly, but I think it's an important request for the Court to consider. I have had it brought to my attention by a number of people following the conclusion of the State's comments just before noon, in closing arguments that Miss {redacted} is making very audible comments that are audible to people sitting at counsel's table. I personally did not hear them because I was focused on the jury."

The judge had his chin in his hands as he listened patiently.

"Apparently," Scott continued, "she made disparaging comments about me. I don't mind that personally but I am very, very concerned about the ability to impact these jurors. I know that Miss O'Connor is about to stand up and give a closing argument. I know that Miss redacted} has some fanciful belief that she is a counsel for Michele Anderson. That's not true."

Scott cleared his throat and continued.

"I am concerned that whatever Miss O'Connor chooses to say would be impacted negatively by Miss {redacted}'s inability to control herself. She says she has an interruptive disorder. She apparently cannot control it. She has been warned and there is a history of this. I am also concerned that she's having animated conversations immediately in front of that jury room door, where that gentleman is now standing. Those doors are not that big," he said in reference to the door at the back of the courtroom. "I'm very concerned about the possibility of misconduct and a mistrial and I've asked that you ask Miss {redacted} to please leave the room."

There would have been no argument from me as I studiously took notes.

"Okay, I'll be very candid with you," Judge Ramsdell commented. "I can't hear from up here. That doesn't mean it's not occurring but I just, frankly, can't hear. So, Mr. Sorenson?"

"Thank you," David Sorenson responded. He wore a tan suit, white shirt and brown striped tie. "I don't think we really have a position or anything to add to Mr. O'Toole's request. I can, factually speaking, say I haven't heard anything. I don't doubt that other people have, but I just haven't heard it sitting here."

"Another point," Scott said, "it's not just from the family members of the Mantle or Anderson family; it's people who have no dog in this fight at all. There's an esteemed member of the defense bar; an elderly member of the defense bar who approached me and indicated to me that he had heard comments. There are others in the audience who also heard comments. I am really concerned. Not only because it may impact both parties right to a fair trial; Miss O'Connor's closing argument; but the position that Miss {redacted} takes right by the jury room door as the jurors come and go is of real concern that she will mutter something. As she says with her disorder, she cannot control it. I am very concerned."

The judge took a breath. "I certainly am, too. And, Mr. Sorenson, you said you had nothing else to say about this?"

"Right," Sorenson responded. "We're in a position where we need to refer it to the court, simply because we do not have enough facts to take a position on the issue."

The judge thought about it for a moment, his eyebrows slightly furrowed.

"To be quite candid about it, my concern, given the current penchant to reverse anything, any action that impedes the public's right to attend, it makes me quite a bit timid about what I need to do in order to make an adequate record for that. Frankly, if I had my way about it, we'd be having a hearing and would be taking testimony from folks in the gallery that have heard what's been said, so that I can make an adequate record; because I suspect Miss {redacted} will be telling me that none of this is true."

"I'm happy to have the person, who is a member of the bar, advise the court as to what he heard and was the first person to advise me immediately after we broke for the lunch hour, if that will help the Court." O'Toole volunteered.

The judge's eyes paused at a location in the gallery. He raised his hand slightly.

"I may not need that. Miss {redacted} is standing there and apparently she wants to say something."

"Yes, Your Honor, thank you for your time," she said from behind me. The whole of the gallery turned around to look at her including members of the family. She wore headphones over her ears and a gray hoodie sweatshirt.

"I do not appreciate him slandering me," she said in reference to the prosecutor. "As far as I believe, I am Michele Anderson's defense lawyer. I'm here for protecting appellate issues only, as I've told you. We've established that. His outrageous claims are incorrect. The person who was there, this person was sitting right in front of me, and overheard something I whispered, four words, to somebody else."

Some would argue that she had not whispered four words but had spoken them aloud.

"They didn't have any, you know, thing about a something about the case. It was," she corrected, "maybe a dig on the prosecutor and his behavior; of how over-the-top his performance was and it wasn't to be heard by somebody else. We've corrected the issue. The prior listening device was very staticky where it was turned up so much, and often I have to remove things from my ear so I'm not getting a headache. You see, some of them are tighter and some are not."

Some would wonder what a headset had to do with her commentary after the prosecutor's closing arguments.

"I think the problem is solved," she explained. "If I owe an apology to anybody, I apologize to family because that's who I would apologize to. I've done nothing that's not different than anybody whispering in court that's happened in time. People are coming in and out, students that are law students and there's nothing that has given anyone any information, indication of bias of anything in the trial."

Her commentary did not get any clearer as she continued her oratory.

"And I think that's where your line is, that what you're supposed to protect, you know. As we know, there's a right to access the courts with TV and her not seeing her discovery and lots of access to court things. And, I think you are correct in reserving the fact that throwing me out as, the inclination that one person stood up, after you were in chambers and said, or repeated what he thought he said or had heard from him out of my mouth that everyone else heard so then it multiplied from there."

I began to suspect that the person speaking was not an attorney although that is not to say that she was not trying to sound like one.

"But, other than that one person that I know of heard it, because these benches are too close in proximity, that's why everyone squishes in between but it was meant for the person next to me and I'm not at the jury door," Miss {redacted} said.

Most of the family had turned their heads back to the front of the courtroom. There were still a few people in the gallery that stared at her, aghast.

Still, she adamantly continued.

"This prosecuting person", Miss {redacted} said as she motioned, "is always standing guard at the jury door. There's media between me; there's the static of media possibly as well. So I think the issue is resolved, and I appreciate you reserving that because I do believe it would be an appellate issue as we've already stated. But, on the record, I would like no more slanders from Mr. O'Toole and the family deserves to finish the trial. Michele deserves to finish the trial."

One had to commend the judge for his patience during her speech.

"And I think this is part of the circus making of Mr. O'Toole, is involved with Mr. Sanders, as well, from what I have seen posted. Thank you, Your Honor," she finished as she sat down.

Once again, I regretted the short conversation she and I had on the first day of the trial.

Scott O'Toole stood up again. "I will advise the Court that I've been advised by Detective Tompkins that Miss {redacted}'s comments were picked up by the media. So, the jury could hear it."

The judge had a concerned look on his face. "Do you have any indication of how many words, how many sentences, duration of time?"

"I do not," O'Toole answered. "I know the court is concerned and we would like to be able to finish this trial. I really don't mean to be difficult."

"No, you're not making my life more difficult," the judge said. "Frankly, the appellate court has made my life more difficult, because they turn this into a field day for anybody who wants to come and go. If I had my way, people wouldn't be treating this like they were at the movies, having little conversations in the background. They'd come in here, sit down and shut up. That's not what happens nowadays."

Judge Ramsdell scratched his head.

"It makes it difficult to control people who come and go. I was giving jury instructions earlier this morning and some gentleman was climbing over people in the back row, loud enough to cause me to interrupt my own instructions. It's making it impossible to do this job the way I think we ought to do it. Right now my best solution to the problem, if I'm going to address it, would be to take testimony to make a sufficient record. Then I think that I would hear from Miss {redacted} that she needs an ADA accommodation, which then would have another set of protocols."

He looked toward the back of the gallery.

"We'll probably have to find her an alternative viewing space and get a Skype set up so she can watch it remotely. Otherwise, I run afoul of ADA accommodations. It gets worse and worse," the judge remarked, "the further we go down this path, and I hope everybody in this courtroom understands that. In the meantime, we are trying to try a very efficient, appellate correct case with a six count homicide, while dealing with all this other static noise..."

Miss {redacted} once again stood up. "I have a solution. I will step outside and use my hearing device if it will suffice for you."

Judge Ramsdell appeared to be interested.

"In the event that I have done nothing wrong, and that I'm not the person to drag out the appellate ADA. I asked for full accommodations and you gave me half, as the record being shown," she suggested in reference to the American Disabilities Association guidelines for the Court. "I will gladly step outside. I'm not going to take your time. Again, I reiterate this to the media circus, of him being blasphemy. He's more worried about his character and why *he* couldn't get Paul Sanders to have that initial feed when the media wasn't here and that is what that is stemming from..."

She could not have been further from the truth. This, in fact, was stemmed from four words she said while the jury was present and, in all likelihood, within earshot of those jurors.

"I will gladly step outside if it pleases the Court and you will not have any more problems that are being brought up from somebody who is sitting right next to me, not everybody *else*, as its been sputtered over the break and I do not ever talk to jurors," she told the judge.

"I wouldn't do something like that until a conviction or appellate process, or what have you, happens after that. I have no intentions of that at this time. So, Thank you," she said with finality.

The judge leaned forward a little.

"So, Miss {redacted}, can you hear?"

"I should be able to. I got, yeah, I got a new device and that's one of the problems and it was. I've solved it with the help of Kenya, actually went and solved it myself with court administration and interpreter services and we're all fine. Thank you, your Honor."

"Okay, so Miss {redacted}?" the judge queried, "I want to make it clear for the record you're voluntarily making this action to move into the hallway to avoid further complications?"

"For the closing arguments," she qualified restrictively. "If there's anything on the record as far as, uh, addressing something after that and the media is out there, are gone or on a break, then I may re-enter the courtroom at my own leisure, if that's okay with the Court, as well; for anything that goes on as far as a motion or the jury is not present."

"I just want to get through closing arguments this afternoon so we can get on to deliberations," the judge commented.

"No problem," Miss {redacted} said. "You and I are on the same page."

"Okay," the judge said carefully.

"Judge?" a male voice prodded from the back row of the gallery. "I want to apologize for this morning. I was..."

Ramsdell interrupted him. "Actually, I don't know who it was. Was it you?"

"Yeah."

"Okay, I appreciate that," the judge said calmly. "I appreciate your apology, Sir, but it's the problem inherent with people coming and going. If we had it my way, we would start the proceeding, close the door and if anybody wasn't here, yet, too bad! And if everybody comes in, they stay until we're done. But I don't have that kind of power and control anymore thanks to my friends at the appellate courts who don't have these problems."

The gentleman from the back row sat down.

I heard a rustle behind me as Miss {redacted} noisily packed her things together and left the courtroom. It was almost as if I could hear a collective sigh of relief from the family and all those seated in the gallery.

"Kenya, call in the jury," the judge directed.

Once the jurors were seated, Colleen O'Connor walked to the podium. She wore a long black dress with a black coat over a white blouse. She placed her notepads on the podium, looked at the jury and adjusted her glasses.

"Ladies and Gentlemen, we know that Michele Anderson was unstable, paranoid and even a spoiled brat. This trial is about her story. Like a movie, it has a plot, a character, a crisis and, unfortunately, a resolution. The State would have you believe that this event was about money and greed. It was not. They had twenty thousand dollars in their bank accounts between the two of them, Joseph and Michele."

Colleen looked at her notes.

"Here is what we know from Mary Anderson. She told us that Michele was a spoiled brat. She said that Michele lived in her own world. She even hung black curtains in her room. We know from Mary that Michele could not keep a job and she was uncomfortable being with other people. And, yes, she flipped out."

"The family knew there was something wrong with her. Judy wanted to protect Michele. Linda Thiele told us that Judy thought her daughter was unstable."

The defense attorney stopped and walked back to the defense table. She looked at a couple pages in one of her three ring binders and returned to the podium.

"In Michele Anderson's interview with Detective Tompkins, she told us that she suffered from depression. It started years ago, this depression. Detective Tompkins spoke of the condition of her trailer. Look at the condition of it. It was cold, damp and filthy. It shows a person who was very disturbed. But, even now, you must presume her innocence. The burden of proof must be applied to every element of the crime."

The defendant had a Kleenex tissue waded to her face with her hand. She might have been crying.

"So, reasonable doubt can arise from evidence or lack of evidence. There are several doubts in this case. The forensic science cannot tell you the state of mind of Michele or Joseph. In her confession, she admits that she is responsible. But her plan was only to confront her parents. The only reason she carried the gun was because she was afraid of Scott. She did not want to hurt anyone. She had an argument. Her shot missed. That proves that she did not intend to kill Wayne. Later, Scott was coming after her. She told us that she defended herself."

Colleen stopped and looked at her notes. She searched through a number of pages before she continued.

"Her demeanor is important. She is not a killer. In her confession, she cried and was apologetic. She was timid and she rambled a lot. She was upset with her parents and her brother. She told us that Scott and her father were abusive. She thought people were stepping on her and she was delusional throughout her confession. That doesn't sound like a killer."

The attorney paused and looked at the jury.

"The State would have you think this crime was thought out but the evidence does not show us that. She went to Monroe that night and drove north. Then she went eastward toward Gold Bar. After that, she bought a map and then threw the guns in the river. When she got the flat tire in Kelso, south, she did not have luggage. She did want to get married. Don't surrender your views on this. It is what the evidence tells you."

The jury waited patiently as the defense attorney went back to her three-ring binders and searched through them for a time.

"So, they came back home on December 26, 2007. They came back to confess. She said that she could not live with herself. You remember that she tried to protect Joseph McEnroe throughout the interview. She also showed great remorse and said that she knew it was wrong. She loved her family. That was why she turned herself in."

Colleen paused as she looked at her notes.

"As far as the law, you are going to discuss the 'accomplice liability'. Remember that you cannot know Joseph McEnroe's state of mind. You cannot make decisions based on him. But, in Count 1, I ask you to find Michele Anderson guilty on second-degree murder as it regards to Wayne. She fired at Wayne but missed. This negates any premeditation. If she planned ahead, she would have hit him. So, she should be not guilty."

The attorney looked through her notes.

"On Count 2, she did not fire at Judy. Joseph McEnroe fired at Judy and shot her twice. She did not do it and that negates premeditation. You cannot convict her for first-degree murder. With regards to Count 3, Scott, she admitted that she shot him but only because he came at her. That is not definitive of premeditation."

I did not see any jurors take notes.

"There is not evidence of premeditation with Erica and Count 4. Michele only reacted. The best you can do is to convict her of second-degree murder on this charge. In regards to Olivia and Nathan, Counts 5 and 6, Joseph McEnroe shot them. Olivia was merely caught in the crossfire. Nobody would shoot a child just because someone told them to do that."

Colleen paused and looked at the jurors.

"We need you to carefully consider all of the evidence. You need to set humanity aside and do your best to consider the evidence and weigh it. During the deliberation process, do not change your mind based on the opinion of others. You must all agree on each element and count. If you find disagreement on any of those factors, you must go to second-degree."

She took her glasses off and wiped them with a tissue and put them back on.

"I am reminded of a movie called, 'A Beautiful Mind'. It is a story of a descent into madness and that's what Michele's story was. You can only hold her accountable for the facts proved. You must find her not guilty for six counts of aggravated murder."

Colleen packed up her belongings from the podium and returned to her seat.

"State's rebuttal?" Judge Ramsdell prompted.

Scott briskly walked to the podium with a legal pad in his hand. He set it down and looked at the jurors.

"Just a few things, Ladies and Gentlemen. When you are in deliberations, you are not surrendering your views. You do, however, have a duty to discuss among your fellow jurors the items that make for a just and fair verdict. In regards to some of the arguments Ms. O'Connor made. She claimed that Michele Anderson was depressed. Yet, in the interview, Detective Tompkins asked the defendant whether she had been through any counseling. The defendant never sought counseling."

Scott grasped the side of the podium.

"What is important is her state of mind on December 24, 2007.

Who told Joseph McEnroe to shoot the kids? In her interview, the defendant said, 'we have to kill everybody because I was afraid.' She directed McEnroe to do her tasks. We do not need to know his state of mind. It is her state of mind that matters. Joseph McEnroe was hired as her back-up man."

The prosecutor absent-mindedly straightened his legal paid on the podium.

"There was a discussion about the defendant being a bad shot. Well, a bad shot does not translate into a lack of premeditation. Remember also that Michele stood there when McEnroe fired at Judy. She fled and McEnroe chased. Judy was frozen in terror and fear when she received the last bullet. Michele Anderson minimized, embellished and lied throughout her confession. She made the confession two days after the killings and the time away had given her time to think and manufacture a story. She did not come back to confess."

The jury's eyes were riveted on the prosecutor.

"If money was not the issue, why did she mention it more than thirty times in her interview? If money was not the issue, why did she take forty dollars from her dead mother's purse and why did she search her dead brother's wallet for more? She was timid in her interview because she did not know if she was a suspect."

Scott directed the jury's attention toward the defendant with a wave of his hand.

"Defendants do not get bonus points for not squeezing the trigger. Joseph McEnroe killed because Michele Anderson told him to. That evening was set into motion by the defendant. There was no dissent into madness because she had planned it at least two weeks prior. They agreed on their story ahead of time and they tried to cover it up."

He turned a page on his notepad.

"Michele Anderson and Joseph McEnroe came back to the scene to 'discover' the murders. They filled the truck, made a car payment and lied to the police for an hour. If she wanted to confess, why didn't she go to a police station? Ladies and Gentlemen, she confessed because she was caught in one lie after another. She is guilty of six counts of aggravated murder."

"All right, folks," Ramsdell said to the jury after Scott took his seat. "Before we excuse you for a break, we are going to select our two alternates. I suspect those selected will be greatly relieved or genuinely upset. It's understandable either way."

The court clerk handed him two pieces of paper retrieved from a hat.

"It looks like Juror #7 and Juror #8 are our alternates," the judge said. "I will ask you to abide by the court rules until after we have a verdict. You will not discuss or research the trial in any manner. We may still need you in the batter's box. Having said that, at least until we have a verdict, you are relieved. Thank you very much for your service and please get with Kenya."

Twelve jurors went to the jury room. A chain with a red sign was placed over their door. Nobody was allowed to enter or exit.

The lambs to the law were now the executors of the law. They would not come out of their room until they had a verdict.

For a time, the voices of Wayne, Judy, Scott, Erica, Olivia and Nathan would be heard again through the passionate voices of the jurors as they deliberated. The lives of six would live once again as they considered the evidence, the law and the route to justice.

The lambs to the law were about to find justice for six while they set aside the banquet of consequences meant for the guilty.

DELIBERATIONS: DAY 1
March 2, 2016

THE ACCOMPLICE
INSTRUCTION

"You may deliberate today until 4:00," Kenya told the jurors, a group of seven women and five men. "It is important to remember that you may only discuss the case when all the jury members are present. That means if someone has to go to the restroom, you must all stop deliberating until the person returns."

"Can we take our notes home and reorganize them?" a juror asked.

"Your notes may not leave the jury room and you may only look at them while the complete jury is present. Although, I appreciate your wanting to do the best job you can," she said with a smile.

"I've never been on a jury before. What do we do? Is there a list or something?"

"The first thing you need to do is chose a Presiding Juror."

"What's that?"

"The Jury Foreperson," someone answered.

"That's correct," Kenya responded. "You will vote on whoever it is and that will be the only person who will sign each of the verdict forms. Just text me when you are ready with the name and I will turn over the jury packet."

The bailiff smiled at the jurors politely and stepped out the room. The door closed and the jury heard the 'Do Not Enter: Jury in Deliberations' chained sign going across the other side of the door.

Somebody sighed. "I never thought I would make it past the alternate selection much less be selected in the first place."

Everybody agreed heartily.

One of the jurors walked along the perimeter of the room as looking at all the boxes of evidence. "I hope we have a list for all of this."

"I took good notes," Greg volunteered.

"Who wants to be the Foreperson?" someone asked.

Nobody seemed particularly excited about the task.

Katie raised her hand. "I could do it if you like."

"Ken might be good, too," someone else said. "Will you do it?"

"I'll do whatever is best for the group," Ken responded.

"Shall we take a vote on it?" one of the jurors asked. "It's between Katie and Ken."

"I think Ken would make a better Presiding Juror than I," Katie said. "I think he would be better able to handle the emotional part of this."

"So it's settled? Ken will be the Foreperson?"

Every hand was raised in agreement.

"Thank you," Ken said. "Let's text Kenya. If you want, while we're waiting, it might be a good time to share your thoughts."

"The thing that keeps me awake at night is the children," Tiffany said. "I have two daughters and one is within just a month of Olivia's age. I can only imagine what Erica must have felt when her family was killed in front of her."

"I agree," Donna responded. "I have kids, too. I couldn't get Olivia and Nathan's face out of my head."

"Anyone else suffer through nightmares?" someone asked.

Almost everyone found common ground. Most of the jurors had family and most of the jurors felt as if they had not had a good night's sleep in months.

Ken answered the light tap at the jury room door. He took a packet from Kenya and closed the door. He looked through the manila folder while the juror's discussion went in all sorts of directions.

"Who could put a gun to a child's head?"

"I don't know much about this McEnroe guy. I don't understand why he didn't stop it," another juror commented.

"The whole story is weird. I'm still not clear what she did after the murders," a juror volunteered. "We know 5:13 pm on Christmas Eve is when the last phone call was made, the 911 call. So, what did Michele do all day Christmas?"

"It's in the confession interview. She went back to the trailer at least three times. The first time was to burn evidence…"

"They must have burned their evidence after the first officers got there and left when they investigated the hang-up."

"Why do you say that?"

"The officers at the bottom of the driveway would have smelled smoke. So, the killers had to have burned it after they were there. She also said they went back to get fruit and then, later, took a nap."

"Yeah," Greg said, "but in my opinion, since she lied in the interview once, we can't trust anything she says in it."

"There were elements of truth in it," a juror responded. "She said she threw the guns in the Stillaguamish and one of those guns was found later.

"Also, Detective Thien Do, found all the receipts verifying her talk about Monroe, Kelso, and Bank of America," remarked another juror.

"However, she said she was getting married," Greg countered. "There is absolutely no evidence of that. I think it is a lie."

"Don't forget," a juror reminded the others, "she and McEnroe went back to the house and stole money from the people they had killed. Remember the forty dollars?"

Ken reined in the conversation after he suggested that they complete their first poll. He tore a couple pieces of paper from his notebook and ripped them into twelve pieces and put them in the center of the table.

"I propose that we only vote if you believe Michele Anderson is guilty or not guilty," Ken said as he picked up a blank piece of paper.

"Are we voting first or second-degree?" one of the jurors asked.

"Well, does everyone here think Michele is guilty of first-degree murder on all counts?"

Although there was a show of hands, not all of the jurors agreed.

"Let's see if we all agree she's guilty of murder. If there are some people here who believe she is innocent, then we need to start there."

Everyone reached to the center of the table and took a scrap of paper. Soon, the folded slips were completed and in a pile. Ken stood by the white dry erase board after he drew three columns. One column said 'guilty'; another read 'not guilty', while the third column had a header that read 'undecided'.

The room was eerily silent as Ken marked the appropriate column and matched it with each juror vote. He discarded one piece of paper at a time as he replaced it with another. He made a check mark in the 'guilty' column.

"Did anyone notice the smell in here?" Tiffany asked.

Half of the room had noticed.

"It's because some of the evidence has dried blood material. That's the smell," Greg said.

Although no one said it aloud, there was a sense that the spirit of a family of six was in the room masked within the musty aroma. It was a subtle and obtrusive reminder of the task in front of the twelve.

The jurors reached their second milestone of the day with a unanimous decision regarding the question of the guilt of Michele Anderson.

"I think someone should read the jury instructions aloud before we begin to go a little more in depth," Ken offered. "Although we could do a more specific poll, is everyone comfortable if we go through the evidence out of respect for all the people who put this case together?"

All of them agreed it was good idea.

Quiet Bill was volunteered to read each page of the instructions aloud.

"Can you read the definition of second-degree murder again?" Greg asked.

Bill nodded his head as he turned a page back. "A person commits the crime of Murder in the Second-Degree when, with intent to cause the death of another person but without premeditation, he or she causes the death of such person or of a third person."

"What's the difference between intent and premeditation?" someone asked.

"I don't think it matters in this case," a juror said. "She went up there to kill her parents and she intended to kill Scott and Erica."

"Maybe or maybe not," Greg said.

"Who has an evidence list?" Donna asked.

"I've got a hand-written list from my notes," a juror said.

"We have one with the blank verdict forms," Ken said as he opened the folder.

He looked at the list and thumbed through the pages. "The list is eleven pages long and has 171 exhibits. Who wants to be in charge of the list and the evidence? This way, we will not mix things up if we only have one person's hands in there."

"I will," Bill volunteered.

"Thank you," Ken said as he handed Bill the list.

Since the jurors' admonishment to speak about the case amongst each other had only been released an hour prior, it was understandable when conversations went off-course.

"Did anyone see the coloring books on our stationery shelf?" a juror asked. "What the heck are they for?"

"I have no idea," someone responded.

"What was up with Anderson having her head in her hands throughout the whole trial?" a juror asked rhetorically.

"Not through all of the trial," a juror interjected. "Did you see how curious she was about the crime scene reconstruction?"

"I saw that," Tiffany commented. "She looked really, really interested in it. It was like she was looking in her own house. I wonder what she was thinking."

"She was awful with a gun," a male juror commented. "Most of her shots missed and she was standing within feet of the people she was shooting at."

"Remember when the defense attorney tried to say that her missing shots was a denial of premeditation?"

"What was up with the defense not giving us an opening statement? That was bizarre," a juror commented.

"I think they were trying to say she was crazy. I believe that although she definitely had mental problems, she knew exactly what she was doing that night. She's very manipulative," Tiffany commented ruefully. "Her covering up the death of her parents says a lot."

"I didn't like that she stepped on her father's back after they dragged his body outside. It tells me she hated her parents."

"She hated everyone including her idiot boyfriend," someone said.

"Who saw her wave at us on the first day?" Donna asked.

Almost everyone had seen it and all had dismissed it.

"I don't understand how somebody could do something so horrible," said Rio, the eldest gentleman on the jury. He had been the only juror to have ever been on a murder trial. "I can't get my head wrapped around it. Why did she do it?"

"For the money," Enrique, the Hispanic juror answered. "That's all she wanted was money. She said it in her confession. She didn't want to pay rent and her brother owed her money."

"You can bet Wayne's property was worth at least a quarter of a million. Who's to say that is not part of the motive?" a juror questioned.

Rio was concerned. "But why shoot the kids?"

"I don't think we'll ever know," Donna said. "Our job isn't to answer that question. We have to determine the degree of the murder charges. You have to put the emotion and the motive aside. It's not our duty to figure that out."

Rio thought about it for a moment. He rubbed his forehead.

"What is it?" Ken asked.

"If she didn't shoot everybody, then she's not guilty of all the murders. Is she?" he asked.

For a while, it became a discussion of which of the victims were shot by Joseph McEnroe and of those Michele Anderson shot.

Ken raised his hand and motioned everyone to quiet down.

"We should read the part of the law that applies to what Rio is talking about," Ken suggested. "Look at your jury instructions and go to instruction number nine. Who wants to read it?"

A rustle of papers could be heard as everyone silently read along once they found the right page.

"A person is guilty of a crime if it is committed by the conduct of another person for which he or she is legally accountable. A person is legally accountable for the conduct of another person when he or she is an accomplice of such other person in the commission of a crime," Bill read carefully.

"A person is an accomplice in the commission of a crime if, with knowledge that it will promote or facilitate the commission of a crime, he or she either: 1. solicits, commands, encourages or requests another person to commit the crime."

"Like Michele did with Joseph," a juror volunteered. "It was her plan and her scheme to kill her parents and her brother and sister-in-law. She told Joseph to shoot them that night after her gun jammed!"

Rio nodded his head that he heard but he still did not look sold.

Bill resumed reading aloud.

"A person is an accomplice if: 2. they aid or agree to aid another person in planning or committing the crime. The word 'aid' means all assistance whether given by words, acts, encouragement, support or presence. A person who is present at the scene and ready to assist by his or her presence is aiding in the commission of the crime. However, more than mere presence and knowledge of the criminal activity of another must be shown to establish that a person present is an accomplice."

"She was definitely present when it happened," a juror commented. "She had a gun and he had a gun. They were accomplices to each other. "

"If we can, let's try and keep McEnroe out of the discussion. Our job is to handle her," Ken suggested.

"It was her family, not his," Donna said. "I don't think he would have done it without her.

"Awful."

"The way I see it, we have a number of tools we can work with. We have our notes, the law, the jury instructions and the exhibit list. We need a strategy. What we need to clarify is the difference between premeditation and intent. Does everyone agree?" Ken asked.

"We do."

"It looks like we will not reach a verdict today because of our getting back here so late. To that, let's look at the exhibit list and see what we would like to review for tomorrow. Since we all agree on the murder segment, we should look for evidence that will help decide the murder charges."

"I'll read the list aloud and you tell me what we should set aside and what we should keep," Bill said.

"Very good."

"The first list has a lot of photographs and DVD's. Things like the driveway and interior shots of the 1806 address."

"I don't want to see the mailboxes again," a juror said. "We saw the bottom of the driveway a thousand times."

"Speaking of the bottom of the driveway, do you think it was Anderson's truck they saw when the police first got there on Christmas Eve?"

"If that's true, it's really creepy that she and McEnroe were driving around right after the murders."

"I think Greg is right. I don't think they were going to go get married," a juror said. "There was no ring and no luggage. I think they drove around in circles because they did not know what to do."

"Let's get back to the list," Ken said.

"There're a number of 911 calls as CD's on this list. Do we want to hear them?"

"I don't know," Ken said. "Will they help us get to where we're going?"

"Maybe not the Linda Thiele call but the 911 calls prior to it could be important."

"I loved Linda Thiele," Tiffany said. "Can you imagine going to look for your best friend and co-worker only to stumble upon that?"

"Just awful," someone said.

"Remember when the operator kept telling her to stay on the phone and she kept leaving? That poor lady."

"I am not sure that will help us but let's flag Erica's 911 call."

"Good idea," a juror said. "I could never really quite hear it."

"There's a ton of swab and DNA evidence on this list."

"I don't think we will need any of it," Ken commented.

"The Christmas present is on the list."

"That was so sad," Katie commented. "It was the make-up kit from her mom."

"We won't need that although it was pretty powerful when Scott showed it to us. Judy had no idea what was coming. The CD of Anderson's interview with Cleary and Tompkins is on the exhibit list. There's no transcript of it, though."

"Let's see what we can do about that," Ken said. "Does everyone agree that the interview is something we'll have to hear again?"

It was unanimous.

"A lot of autopsy photos are here. Will we need those?"

Not one juror ever wanted to see an autopsy photograph again.

"Oh look," Bill commented. "The actual .357 is on the list along with the purchase paperwork for both guns. Will we need that?"

"We know who owned the guns," the jurors said.

"The rest of this list has all the furniture, blankets, the reconstructed floor, pillows and other stuff from the scene. We even have access to the boots."

"I don't think we shall need those either," Ken said.

"What about the crime scene analysis flow chart? It was the chart on the wall behind the reconstruction scene."

The jury did not seem very excited to review the documentation of how each family member had been shot.

"We know they were shot and we know how," Ken said as he looked at his watch. "What we need to search for is evidence of premeditation and Michele's role in their deaths. What do you say we start there tomorrow?"

As the day waned into its final minutes, the jurors realized that with the accomplice instruction, it was pointless to define who shot whom on that awful night. Many of the jurors had reached a consensus on the fact that Michele Anderson interchanged as a principal in the murders, the person who fired the gun, as well as being an accomplice, by her participation with McEnroe as he fired his gun. She had been the stage manager of the event and Joseph McEnroe was her other arm of evil.

The problem was relatively simple: Were each of the deaths premeditated or did they come as a result of an argument on that horrific Christmas Eve? Had the killers planned or did they snap?

Any relief the jurors had felt after they made it through the alternate selection had been replaced with a great burden that weighed heavily on their hearts.

Deliberations were not as easy as any of them had predicted.

DELIBERATIONS: DAY 2
March 3, 2016

THE SEMANTICS OF MURDER

"What are our questions and where is our doubt?" Ken asked the jurors. The deliberation door had been closed and chained at 9 AM.

"I know this is off topic but I really want to know about the dang bird and I want to know what happened to the cat they found in the truck," Katie said.

"I think the defense was trying to show she was crazy. Unfortunately, nobody could corroborate Tompkins story about seeing a bird. That's why the defense gave up on it," a juror said.

"I don't understand. How does it show she's crazy?"

"The defense was trying to say that she killed her whole family and she even killed a bird. That's how crazy she was."

"It would take a crazy person to kill six people," somebody commented.

"It's weird. I felt bad for the animals. Remember the dog that the detective fed?" Katie asked.

"It must have been outside when the murders happened," Donna commented. "I would bet they would have shot the dog, too."

"But not the brown cat?" someone asked sarcastically.

Rio raised his hand. "So, tell me if I have this right. McEnroe and Anderson went to Wayne and Judy's house at about 2:30 on Christmas Eve. Anderson got in a fight with her dad and shot him."

"Well, shot at him," a juror corrected. "She missed him."

"Then," Rio continued, "McEnroe ran out of the craft room with Judy. Somehow, Anderson's gun was jammed in her sweatshirt. So, McEnroe shot at Wayne and killed him in the dining room."

"I bet Judy ran to help her husband and then McEnroe chased her."

"Yes. And then McEnroe shot her twice in the kitchen. Then, they hid the bodies and waited for the rest of the family to get there."

"That's premeditation," someone offered.

"So, she shot Scott in the face. She was probably standing by the front of the living room. Where was Joseph, though?" Rio asked.

"He was on the couch between Scott and Erica before Anderson fired at him," Tiffany offered.

"So, according to her," a juror said, "she fired on Scott when he tried to attack her."

"Who's to say that he didn't come after her when he realized his parents were not in the bathroom? You have to wonder if he could have found out they had been murdered."

"We need to stick to what the evidence tells us," Ken countered. "Remember that our personal feelings cannot impact our decision. We will never know what really happened between Scott and Michele. What we know is that he was shot twice and was found on his back on the living room floor. Anderson admitted more than once that she shot him and the ballistics support it."

"Okay," Rio accepted. "Scott is on his back on the floor."

"That's when Erica tried to call 911," Katie said.

"She probably shot at Erica a couple times and Erica was trapped. That's when McEnroe shoots the kids?"

"She said her gun was out of bullets so I would guess she reloaded then, like Scott O'Toole told us," Lisa volunteered.

Ken reined the conversation back in to the task at hand: the jury instructions.

"These are the questions we have to answer: Is it our determination that the defendant, Michele Kristen Anderson, is guilty of murder in the first-degree in the death of Wayne Anderson?"

"Yes," the jurors answered as many nodded their heads.

"Was the defendant Michele Kristen Anderson armed with a firearm at the time of the commission of the crime as charged in Count One?"

Again, the jurors agreed in unison that Anderson was armed when Wayne was murdered.

"Has the State proven the existence of the following aggravating circumstances beyond a reasonable doubt: There was more than one person murdered and the murders were part of a common scheme or plan or the result of the single act of one person?"

Again, the jurors agreed.

Ken repeated the question in the counts regarding Judy, Scott and Erica. It was not until he came to the question of Olivia that the jury hit a roadblock.

"I don't think it was premeditated," Rio said. "I think the kids were an accident. I agree she premeditated the deaths of the adults especially with her and McEnroe coming into the house with loaded guns. I just don't think she planned on killing the kids."

"Remember," Katie said, "the two of them got into the truck carrying a box of bullets. That's certainly premeditation for all of them."

Ken pulled out the evidence list as they had done the day before. Unfortunately, the transcript of the confession had not been allowed back to the jury room. Even if they had the CD, it was no good without a medium to play it on.

The jurors agreed that they needed to hear that confession. It took them fifteen minutes to construct the first question of the day for the court.

"The jury would like to receive State Exhibit #73 in order to listen for answers for specific questions," Ken wrote on an official Jury Inquiry form. Everyone approved the language of the question and Ken texted Kenya.

"While we're waiting," Ken offered, "let's go over the definition of premeditation and the difference between first and second-degree murder."

He called on Lisa, the writer, to read the definition aloud for the jury from their jury instructions.

"Premeditated means 'thought over' beforehand," she read aloud. "When a person, after any deliberation, forms an intent to take human life, the killing may follow immediately after the formation of the settled purpose and it will still be premeditated. Premeditation must involve more than a moment in time. The law requires some time, however long or short, in which a design to kill is deliberately formed."

"What is considered a 'moment in time'?" someone asked.

"Could each squeeze of the trigger be considered more than a moment in time?"

"What is the length of a moment? Is it a second, a minute or a few minutes? I don't understand," Rio commented.

Lisa read the next definition. "A person acts with intent or intentionally when acting with the objective or purpose to accomplish a result which constitute a crime. Do you want me to keep reading?"

"Yes," Ken answered. "It will refresh us as to where we're at."

"To convict the defendant of the crime of murder in the first-degree, as charged in Count One, each of the following elements of the crime must be proved beyond a reasonable doubt," the juror read aloud.

"One: That on or about December 24, 2007, the defendant acted with intent to cause the death of Wayne Anderson. Two: That the intent to cause the death was premeditated. Three: That Wayne Anderson died as a result of the defendant's acts and, four: that the acts occurred in the State of Washington. If you find from the evidence that each of these elements have been proved beyond a reasonable doubt, then it will be your duty to return a verdict of guilty as to Count One.

"On the other hand," the juror continued, "if, after weighing all of the evidence, you have a reasonable doubt as to any of these elements, then it will be your duty to return a verdict of not guilty as to Count One."

A series of discussions were started on the semantics of first-degree murder and it seemed like all of the jurors, including Katie, were unified in their belief of the first-degree counts in the deaths of the adults. The premeditation to kill Wayne and Judy was evidenced in Michele and Joseph's drive up the driveway and walking up the steps. Their premeditation was clear in the clean-up of the crime scene in preparation for Scott and Erica's holiday visit. But, when it came to Olivia and Nathan, it was back to two jurors who questioned whether Olivia and Nathan's deaths were premeditated.

"It looks like they were collateral damage," Greg said. "I don't think anyone can prove they went to the house to kill the children."

Kenya tapped on the door. Ken opened it and the jurors learned that the court had approved the request for the confession. They learned that in most circumstances, they would have had to re-hear the confession from the jury box. The court had made an exception. With that, Kenya provided a laptop for their perusal.

All did not go as smoothly as the jury would have liked. They could not get the password to allow them on the computer. Their next problem was that they could not get the speaker on the laptop to work. After a time, it was clear they would need someone's help getting it to work. It was ironic given that so many jurors were IT professionals in their regular jobs.

One juror suggested that they receive the same transcript of the confession that they had read in the jury box. It was listed as Exhibit #74.

The jurors went through the process of filling out another Jury Inquiry form for the court.

Ken read it aloud.

"The jury requests the transcript, State Exhibit #74, in order to minimize or focus on specific parts in order to make confidential determinations regarding closing statements."

Again, he texted Kenya and the jurors were pleasantly surprised when a transcript was given to them an hour later. They also received their laptop back and the speaker was in working order.

The rest of the morning was spent listening to Michele Anderson's confession to Detective Tompkins. It was not until Anderson changed her story in the confession tape that the jurors stopped the CD every minute or so to replay a segment.

They listened intently as they leaned forward on the deliberation table. They heard Detective Tompkins as he spoke with Michele while she was in the back of a police car at the murder scene in Carnation on December 26, 2007.

"Okay, um, as you know, ah, Joe's been talking to some detectives down on the roadway there," the Detective said to her, motioning outside the vehicle they were in. One could hear the faint hum of a helicopter as it circled overhead. It was muffled and rhythmic. "Okay. Is there any reason why he would have a different version of the events than you? What is that reason?"

Michele pushed her hair back and casually said, "We talked about covering stuff up."

"Covering what?"

"We, okay, we went back and forth whether or not we were gonna confess or cover it up, and he's covering it up if he's not saying the same thing as me," Michele responded.

"Well, I asked you before about if you guys had an alibi in place; what was the alibi?" the Detective asked.

"Getting married, but we also wanted to," she pointed out. "So is that still an alibi?"

The detective cleared his throat. "Well, did you have a discussion about what you were going to tell the police?"

"I said we were just going to say that, and not say anything else, and besides, I wasn't really okay with it," she explained. "We went back and forth. But I can't live with myself."

"No," the Detective said flatly.

"So, I decided to just spill it all because I can't live with myself."

"That goes to show, um, that goes to show what kind of person you are."

"I guilt-tripped him into covering everything up and the lying," she admitted, defeat in her voice. "And then I felt bad about it and decided that, no; I need to just come clean. It is my fault that he is covering it up."

"I understand," the detective said comfortingly.

"Because he did not want to do any of this or cover it up at all. It was me."

"I understand."

"I take full responsibility," she said.

"And I appreciate that," Tompkins responded. "One of the differences in your stories is, that Joe is saying you went up there with the intent of killing your parents. Did you guys discuss that at all? Where would he be coming from, getting that kind of information?"

"I said that I was upset with my parents and my brother and that if the problems didn't get resolved, I, my intent was definitely to kill them," she explained.

"Them being who?"

"Everybody," Michele responded firmly.

"So at the time you guys go up," the Detective began.

"When we went up there."

"That's the information he had," he said in reference to her accomplice.

"Yeah. But he tried to talk me out of it," she admitted.

"Well, what did he say?" the Detective queried.

"It was my fault."

"What did he say to try and talk you out of it?"

"He said to just walk away from these people," Michele answered.

The jurors were not surprised when Ken hit the pause button on the CD.

"She's a liar," Greg said. "I do not trust any of it and that's our prerogative according to our jury instructions."

Ken pulled out a set of jury instructions and began reading the appropriate section aloud.

"You, meaning us, are the sole judges of the credibility of each witness. You are also the sole judges of the value or weight to be given of the testimony of each witness. In considering a witness's testimony, you may consider these things."

He walked to the dry erase board and began using a marker.

"The opportunity of the witness to observe or know the things he or she testifies about. Second: the ability of the witness to observe accurately. Third: Any personal interest that the witness might have in the outcome or the issues. Fourth: any bias or prejudice that the witness may have shown. Fifth: The reasonableness of the witness's statements in the context of all the other evidence and, Fifth: any other factors that affect your evaluation or belief of a witness or your evaluation of his or her testimony," Ken wrote.

"It also says further down," Greg pointed out, "that we may disregard any remark, statement or argument that is not supported by evidence. Clearly, she lied multiple times in the confession and I choose to disregard all of it. My decision must come from elsewhere. And, she does not specifically say that she intended to kill the children. That's where my issue is. I'm not trying to be heartless here. The law says we have to apply the law to what the evidence tells us."

"Alright," Ken said. "I want all of us to be comfortable with our decision. Let's look at the definition of second-degree murder again. Who wants to read it from our jury instructions?"

"A person commits the crime of murder in the second-degree when, with intent to cause the death of another person but without premeditation, he or she causes the death of such person or of a third person," Lisa read.

"So it's the same thing as first-degree murder without the

premeditation," a juror commented.

"What's the difference between intent and premeditation?" a juror asked as she repeated the concern from the day prior.

"Premeditation takes about five minutes," Rio said.

The room exploded into an array of crosstalk and a resurgence of emotions. There were jurors that were adamant that all six murders fell into the category of 'murder one'. There were other jurors who remained quiet and pensive.

"Let's go back to the confession," Ken said.

Lisa hit the play button.

"Did you also shoot Scott's wife and kids?" Tompkins asked the defendant.

"They were running to the phone and I freaked out," Michele answered.

"Okay. How many times did you shoot them?"

"One to each kid," she said as she cried.

Lisa stopped the recording when Greg raised his hand.

"See what I mean? She didn't shoot the kids. McEnroe did. Her lies make everything invalid."

"You have to remember the accomplice instruction," a juror reminded him. "She did not have to shoot them to be responsible."

Ken nodded his head. "Go ahead and continue with the tape."

The room was silent as the jurors listened. They asked Lisa to stop and replay another segment.

"Where was Joe?" Detective Peters asked.

"He was standing to my left, and I, I was just supposed to shoot everybody. He was just there just in case the gun jammed," Michele responded.

"Had you guys talked about that?"

"I told him I wanted to confront my family and was afraid they would attack me because they're abusive and I wanted him to protect me. I guilt tripped him into it."

"This is after your parents were dead or before?" Tompkins asked.

"Before and after that," Michele responded.

"Did anybody try to call 911?"

"Erica," Anderson responded flatly.

"Why did she do that? What alerted her to call 911?"

"Because Scott had bullet wounds in him."

"My God," one of the jurors commented.

"What was the time frame between shooting Scott and the other three people?" Peters asked on the recording.

"I don't know. It all happened at once."

"But was it like a couple of seconds or a couple minutes or what? She obviously had time to call," Tompkins prodded.

"She lunged over the couch even though she, she had been shot twice. I don't know how she did that," Anderson commented matter-of-factly.

"So, she actually called 911 and she had been shot."

"Yeah."

"So, who shot Scott four times?"

"I shot Scott and Erica," Anderson admitted.

"And what about Joe?"

There was a pause as Anderson thought about it.

"He shot the kids."

A short time later in the interview, Peters asked her for more detail on Scott.

"Okay. So you shot him in the throat and where else?"

"And his torso," Anderson responded.

"In his stomach after he was dead," a juror vocalized.

Ken raised his hand to quiet the commentary as the interview continued.

"Okay," Peters responded. "And who fired the other shots into Scott?"

"I shot four into Scott with the revolver and two into Erica. I ran out of bullets," Anderson explained. Her pace picked up. "That's why he shot the kids because I ran out of bullets. He got it unstuck by then. If it was unstuck before, he would not have shot anyone. I would have used the Nine on everybody if it hadn't jammed! It was in that split second, when we were trying, when I ran out of bullets, and he's trying to unjam the gun that she called the cops."

"She was reloading the gun when Erica called the police. That's what I think," a juror said after Lisa stopped the player.

"That's up for debate," another juror argued. "I don't know that we will ever have a complete picture of those events."

"That's why we were hired as jury," Ken commented. "It's our job to figure out, based on our common sense, what likely happened. Let's hear some more," Ken said.

Five minutes later in the confession, Tompkins asked Michele what the kids were doing before they were shot.

"They were clinging to their mom screaming," Anderson responded. "Sorry."

"The one kid is pretty young," Tompkins commented in regard to Nathan. "I mean, do you think he…?

Anderson interrupted him. "I just thought if they saw their parents were dead, they would be scarred for life."

"Were you worried they would be able to identify you?"

"I didn't want them to be scarred for life. I didn't think about that," she said.

"Awful," a juror commented after the CD stopped.

The jurors took a break. Some used the restroom while others got a cup of coffee or a beverage from the refrigerator. They were not as talkative amongst each as other as normal.

Their search in the confession for signs of premeditation continued after the break. A number of jurors flipped through their notes while the confession continued.

"Why," Detective Peters asked, "if you were going to go up there and scare them and threaten them, why did you each have a gun?"

"They were going to attack me and I thought if I fired my gun, it would jam or something," Anderson answered.

"Did you have thoughts of killing them?"

"That week."

"Okay. How far back in the week?"

"I don't know," Anderson said.

"Was it a couple days, or a month prior? How long have you been thinking about killing Scott or his family?"

"I don't know."

"More than a week?" Tompkins asked.

"Two weeks," Anderson responded firmly.

Lisa pressed the stop button on the player.

"It doesn't prove she actually planned to shoot the kids," Greg said.

"They knew all four were coming and they went in the house with loaded guns. She knew they were going to shoot the kids," a juror vehemently argued.

For most of the jurors, the one hundred and twelve page confession was enough to convince them to do what they needed to do.

"But you can't trust her confession," Greg pointed out again. "Since she lied in the beginning, how can you trust a word she says after that? How do you know what the truth is and what is not? I don't think there's enough evidence there to convict her beyond second-degree in the deaths of the children."

"Our job is to figure out the truth," a juror said. "The truth is that she admitted she went up there to kill everybody. Everybody includes the children."

"You're trying to push me into a decision," Greg responded, somewhat accusatory. "With all respect to the victims, I look at it this way. Picture the moment in time after Wayne and Judy had been dragged to the shed. Then, picture the living room. Scott has been shot in the face and is lying on the floor. Didn't Ross Gardner state that Joseph McEnroe was the one who fired the bullets into Olivia,

Nathan and Erica? Anderson was there but she did not fire the gun into the kids. Her boyfriend did. That makes her responsible for the final three deaths in the second-degree."

A lot of jurors jumped into the conversation as they defended their position. None of the jurors wanted to force another juror into a corner.

The two dissenting jurors, Greg and Rio, agreed by the end of the day that they were still on the fence. They were members of a jury and wanted to do the right thing. Most of all, they all wanted to be able to sleep at night the rest of their lives knowing they had made the right decision.

The two children had become the most important aspect of the trial. They represented the senselessness of the murders and were the most innocent of all.

It would cross a number of juror's thoughts that there was a possibility that they would not agree on all aspects of the case. Some worried that they would not be able to agree and that would have been the greatest disservice of all to the victims and their survivors.

DELIBERATIONS: DAY 3
March 4, 2016

A MOMENT IN TIME

It was the first time that the jury was called in for duty on a Friday and all were present at 9:00 AM. One could be sure that many did not want to return on Monday. The overwhelming majority of them were ready to commit their decision to the verdict forms.

"Did anyone have thoughts they would like to share before we get started?" Ken inquired.

Bill raised his hand. "I kept thinking about a 'moment in time' and what it is in regards to the evidence that we've heard. I think we may have missed something at the end of her confession that we need to hear again."

"We can listen to anything you would like."

"I suggest that we start the tape where it corresponds to page 105 of the transcript," Bill said.

Lisa put the CD in the player and found Bill's referenced starting point.

"I should have just walked away from it," Anderson said to the detectives in the Mobile Crime Scene Unit RV. She was still in the company of both Tompkins and Peters.

"Well, we'll cover that in a second," Tompkins responded. "Joe told the other detectives that he had apologized before shooting. Do you recall that?"

"Um hum, yes."

"What did you say or do?"

"Because I wanted them to stop hurting us. I didn't want to have to do this, and we were really sorry for it; we felt really bad," Anderson answered.

"What did you say?" Peters asked. "Did you make any comments to anyone?"

"We all apologized, both of us, when we shot everybody. Even though my father was attacking me, I was sorry."

"Tell me what you…"

"This is excessive," Anderson interrupted. "I should have just walked away. It's not worth it."

"Michele, what did you say to your dad?"

"I said this is not fair that I did so much for this family and everybody abused me and attacked me so much. All I wanted was my money back so I could just leave," Anderson deflected.

"At what point did you pull out the gun?"

"I said, look, I'm sorry and I walked into the kitchen and unwrapped it. I came back and I shot them."

"So, you unwrapped it in the kitchen out of your..."

"No. I had a sweatshirt wrapped around my arm."

"Right," Peters said.

"And the gun was strapped, not strapped, tucked into the sweatshirt and I was just holding it."

"Then you walked into the kitchen?"

"Yeah," she recalled. "I took it out of the sweatshirt and then I just shot them because I was fed up. It's wrong and I take full responsibility."

"We already heard this," Greg commented. "We know what she did with Wayne and Judy."

"Give it a minute," Bill defended.

The CD continued.

"Did you say any words to anybody else?" Peters asked. "Did you apologize to anyone else?"

"I apologized to everybody because I didn't want it to turn out like that but I knew it would," Anderson replied. "Do you understand? I mean, I went up there knowing I would probably shoot these people, but I didn't want to."

"Well, what did you say or do to show these people you were sorry?"

"I just said sorry before shooting them. It's horrible. I'm a bad person."

"Did you hear Joe do similar?"

"What did you hear?"

"He said I'm sorry," Michele answered quietly.

"Who did you hear him say he was sorry to?" Peters prodded.

"Erica and the kids. We both shot Erica. He shot the kids, not me."

"Okay," Tompkins said. "What were the, how were the kids reacting?"

"Nathan looked like he knew," Michele stated.

"What does that mean?"

"Like, like he knew that, that he was gonna die and was accepting it. It was weird."

"That's such crap," a juror interjected.

"How did that make you feel?" Tompkins asked.

"Awful."

"Did you do anything to prevent it?"

"No," Anderson answered softly.

Lisa stopped the recording when Bill raised his hand.

"There's a couple of things," Bill began. "Let's put aside how horrible it was that Anderson apologized to the victims before they were shot. Consider that her feigned apology was before they were killed and, in that, she knew what she was going to do before she did it. Saying that she was sorry took more than a moment in time."

"What of the kids, though?" Greg asked.

"She was in an accomplice role. That means when Joe said he was sorry before he killed the kids, she had time to prevent it. She said in her confession that she encouraged him to shoot them. That took more than a second, don't you think?" he asked the room rhetorically.

"What are your thoughts, Ken?" a juror inquired.

"I don't want to influence those who are still in doubt," Ken stated calmly. "I suggest that we move forward."

"Can we ask the Court what a 'moment in time' means?" Rio asked.

"We could."

Ken pulled an inquiry form from the verdict file and encouraged all the jurors to help him construct the questions.

"The jury requests clarification in premeditation. Specifically a definition of terms: 'Moment in time', and the term, 'Follows immediately'; additionally, an illustrative example of second-degree murder. Also, please define, 'Plan' as it relates to the aggravating circumstance," Ken read aloud when they were done.

All of them agreed to the wording.

Ken sent a text to Kenya who tapped on the door only moments later. He submitted the questions.

"This would have been a lot easier if she had taken the stand," a juror said after the door closed.

"We are not allowed to make a judgment on whether or not she testified," Ken advised.

"I know but it would have been a lot easier."

One of the jurors got a cup of coffee and then looked at the bookshelf with the stationery supplies. He picked up a comic book and some crayons from the basket and sat back down at the table.

"I just figured out what the comic books are for. For those of us who have made our minds, it keeps our hands busy."

Some of the jurors followed his lead.

There was a tap on the jury room door, which Ken quickly answered. Kenya handed him a sheet of paper, the same paper they had filled out an hour before asking for specifics regarding what a "moment in time" was.

"Please reread your instructions," Ken read to the jury after Kenya had placed the chain on the door.

Some of the jurors chuckled when Ken read the response. It was not entirely unexpected to most of them.

"Does anyone have any suggestions?" Ken asked the table.

"I think the ones who are still on the fence need to reread the confession," Katie suggested.

"That's a good thought," Ken affirmed.

Donna spoke up. "What about the 911 call?"

"Are you referring to the Linda Thiele phone call, the post lady who discovered the bodies?" Ken asked.

"No, the call from Erica on December 24," Katie said. "I think our question of premeditation is defined by that call."

The jurors quickly looked through exhibit list and identified the exhibit. However, once they searched through the boxes of evidence stacked throughout the room, it did not take them long to realize that they did not have a copy of the call. In that, they proceeded to build the next question for the court.

When it was complete, Ken read it out loud for the jurors to approve it. "The jury now requests State Exhibit #7 to hear duration of call and to answer other questions."

They whole-heartedly approved it, at which time; Ken submitted it to Kenya.

The jurors waited out the next half hour by rereading aloud the definitions that they had been given in their jury instructions.

Greg and Rio busied themselves as they reread the confession as Katie had suggested.

The jury heard the call to 911 when they returned after lunch.

A table of twelve listened intently when Lisa pressed the play button. It was a short call from Christmas Eve of 2007. The call had been placed at 5:13 PM. The ghosts of Erica, Olivia and Nathan seemed to surface in the room.

"911, please state your emergency," the operators said.

Each of the jurors leaned forward in an attempt to catch every sound.

It may have been gunshots or the sounds of a bad connection just as the 911 call connected.

"No, no, not the kids," Erica's voice begged from the past.

There were other voices in the background. Was it the kids they were listening to? Also, there seemed to be the sound of a male voice? Would that have been McEnroe?

The senselessness screamed at the jurors.

As much as they did not want to, they listened to the tape collectively again. There were tears in many of the jurors' eyes as they strained to listen to the pleas.

One of the jurors mentioned that they should time the tape from when the operator picked up the call to when it was disconnected. They played it again, wrists raised and eyes focused on the stopwatches in their iPhones.

The tape was replayed over and over again. It took a while to get past the horror of it all. It was difficult to set the emotion aside. The jury had become fact finders in the matter and the facts whispered into their souls.

For every time the call played, each juror became a little bit more desensitized.

The call to 911 was eleven seconds in length.

A day prior, Rio had mentioned that premeditation was five minutes in length. Another juror had said that premeditation was determined in the testimony of Mary Victoria Anderson when she stated that Michele Anderson wanted to kill her parents. Still, another juror said premeditation was not decided by the loaded weapons the killers carried up the steps on that night but it was earmarked by the case of bullets put on the floor of the truck.

None of those arguments had convinced all the jurors.

"What are your thoughts, Ken?" someone asked.

Ken scratched his head. "I'm with Greg and Rio as far as the problem with the confession."

A number of jurors groaned.

416

"Just hear me out," he said with a raise of his hand. "I am not a lawyer. I was asked to be part of this jury because of my common sense. I think all of us can agree on that."

"Absolutely," Tiffany commented.

"Our task was simply to match the law to the evidence. We choose the evidence that is the most reliable. When Greg said one couldn't trust her confession, he is absolutely right. I see things as very black and white. In my real life, I specialize in computer technology. If we input a code that is incorrect, the system breaks down," Ken explained. "We cannot say part of the code is good and part is bad. The whole formula has to be discarded. To that, her confession is secondary."

"Go on," someone said.

"I do not think I ever understood what a smoking gun was until now. Erica was the smoking gun."

"How's that?"

"Erica's phone establishes the timeline in this event. Her action tells me that Scott was incapacitated by then. The ballistics evidence, DNA evidence and blood spatter evidence tells us exactly where she was when she made the phone call. It also tells us exactly where the killers were. It also told us that Erica was in a defensive mode. The whole case rests on her phone call."

"So we don't need the confession to make judgments on facts," Donna commented.

"Correct," Ken said. "Erica's phone call establishes our parameters of the difference between premeditation and intent. In effect, it told us that this decision was made beyond just a moment in time."

"How so?"

"Michele Anderson had eleven seconds to change her mind. She had eleven seconds to stop Joseph from firing his weapon. She had eleven seconds to premeditate the deaths of Erica, Olivia and Nathan."

"Which means Joseph McEnroe shared those same seconds to make a decision."

"Although we were not privy to know much about him, it shows the magnitude of the importance of Erica's call," Ken said. "I wish we knew more about him but that is not our task. We must look at the facts and Erica establishes everything we need to know. If she had not made the call, we would be having a very different discussion."

"Rio?" Ken inquired.

He looked at the jurors around him. "I don't know why it took me so long. Thank you for being patient with me. I don't need to know any more. I've made a decision."

"Greg?"

"I've made my decision," he said. "Katie was right when she said I had to look at the entirety of the confession. The tidbits of truth in there line up with the 911 call."

"Shall we take a vote on it?" Ken asked.

The jurors nodded their heads eagerly.

Ken walked to the white board and picked up one piece of paper at a time after the pile was completed. One by one, he marked the 'guilty' column as he read each slip aloud. Everyone in the jury room held their breath. Had they finally come to the end of the road?

There was a unanimous sigh of relief when they learned they had reached a verdict. It took them almost forty-five minutes to ensure each form was signed correctly. Ken texted Kenya and they took the time to exhale and await the court response.

To some juries, this period could be the longest and most uncomfortable slice of time one could realize in a jury room. But, to this jury, it was the immense sense of relief that enveloped them that made the time pass easier on them.

"I feel bad that we focused so much on those kids," a juror commented. "I think each victim was important."

"The kids are what defined her evil and jealous nature."

"What was she jealous of? She was living rent-free. Her parents took care of everything."

"She never grew up. She couldn't accept that her brother was getting on with his own life," Donna commented.

"It's horrible."

"I feel bad for Pamela, Erica's mother," a juror said. "She lost her whole family in one night."

"Can you imagine how Mary Anderson must have felt when she learned her whole family was dead?"

"They would have killed her."

Everyone agreed.

It had been a long road into a valley of the evil that was Michele Anderson. The jurors were tired and, yet, comforted that the journey was almost complete.

The verdict did not yield a sense of victory for the twelve members of the jury. It only magnified the great sadness they held in their hearts for a family of six lost on a Christmas Eve a long time ago.

DAY 28
March 4, 2016

SOLILOQUY OF A JURY

Michele Anderson, flanked by eight guards, was soon led into the courtroom. The female guard unclasped Anderson's pink handcuffs while the two other guards patiently monitored her progress. Anderson never once raised her eyes. She was wore a black blouse and black baggy pants. There were no tears or looks of concern on her face. She barely greeted the attorneys who were seated next to her.

"About midpoint this afternoon, we got word the jury has reached a verdict," Judge Ramsdell informed the court. "So, unless there's a reason for delay, I intend to call them out and hear what they have to tell us. Are there any issues from the State?"

Scott O'Toole stood up. He wore gray pants and a blue suit coat paired with a soft blue shirt and a blue and red colored tie. He smiled at the judge briefly.

"No issues from the State, your Honor."

"Miss O'Connor?" the judge queried.

Colleen stood up. She wore a long black dress with a mauve colored blouse.

"None, your Honor."

Judge Ramsdell smiled courteously and then looked toward the bailiff.

"Kenya? Why don't you go ahead and invite the jurors in," he directed.

I imagined that the verdict watch period for the family of the Andersons must have seemed like an eternity. I also expected the deep worry and consternation they felt was intensified by a jury who was not able to reach a decision in the penalty phase of Joseph McEnroe, the defendant's accomplice. I would like to have told Pamela and Tony Mantle not to worry, but it would have done little good. They would bide the moments that felt like hours along with the rest of us.

The gallery was packed and I considered myself lucky to have found a seat. Reporters and cameramen from The Seattle Times, KOMO-TV and KIRO-TV were present both in the gallery and in the hallway outside the courtroom. A large camera peered from the corner; its sight avoided the jury box and focused on the judge's bench.

The two alternate jurors: Juror #7 and Juror #8, sat quietly together in the second to last row of the gallery, recent strangers to the jury box.

The jurors marched out to a courtroom that stood in silence. Their faces were resolute and devoid of emotion. They confidently took their seats.

Juror #11, the Presiding Juror, spoke for the jury when the judge acknowledged their verdict. He wore a pressed checkered oxford and had neatly combed hair. He handed the Jury Verdict forms to Kenya, who then brought them to the judge.

The court waited silently as he casually flipped through each page. He paused to ensure each page was completed correctly.

"I'm going to ask the court clerk to read the verdicts, please," the judge said as he handed the forms to Suza.

The Clerk took the forms, adjusted the glasses on her nose read aloud as she faced the courtroom.

"Regarding Verdict Form A: We, the jury, find the defendant, Michele Kristin Anderson, guilty of the crime of murder in the first-degree as charged in Count 1. Verdict Form B: Not utilized," she said as she turned another page of the verdict forms.

I heard someone whisper 'Wayne Anderson' from the row in front of me.

"Regarding Verdict Form C: We, the jury, find the defendant, Michele Kristin Anderson, guilty of the crime of murder in the first-degree as charged in Count 1. Verdict Form D: Not utilized," she said.

"Judy Anderson," a voice said quietly.

The court clerk read each of the verdict forms and when she completed each, I heard the names of Scott, Erica, Olivia and Nathan. The jury had found Michele Anderson guilty of first-degree murder in the death of each victim. Despite the question in the morning regarding 'a moment in time', they had managed to disregard any of the crimes as second-degree.

I saw Pamela Mantle squeeze her husband's hand each time a verdict was read.

The court clerk licked the tip of her finger and turned to the thirteenth page of verdict forms.

"We, the jury, returned a special verdict by answering the question: Was the defendant, Michele Kristin Anderson, armed with a firearm at the time of the commission of the murder in Count One? Answer: Yes."

She continued with each firearm count for each of the five additional victims.

Suza turned another page.

"Special Verdict: Aggravating Circumstance. We, the jury, having found the defendant guilty of murder in the first-degree make the following answers to the questions submitted by the Court. Question: Has the State proven the existence of the following aggravating circumstances beyond a reasonable doubt?'

I looked at the jury and saw that few of them looked toward the defendant who shielded her eyes from the looks of anyone.

"There was more than one person murdered," the clerk continued, "and the murders were part of a common scheme or plan or the result of a single act of one person. Answer: Yes."

"Question: Has the state proven the existence of the following aggravating circumstance beyond a reasonable doubt as to Count Four?"

Counts Four, Five and Six referenced the names of Erica, Olivia and Nathan in that.

"The defendant committed the murder to conceal the commission of a crime or to protect or conceal the identity of any person committing a crime," Suza stated from the form. She looked up when she read the next line.

"Answer: Yes."

The defendant showed no reaction when the aggravating circumstances for Olivia and Nathan were read.

Judge Ramsdell nodded his head after the court clerk took her seat.

"Ladies and gentlemen," he said toward the jurors, "what we need to do next is what we call, 'polling the jury'. We will be asking you two separate questions. The first question, as to each one of you regarding your verdicts, is whether these were your own individual verdicts."

I saw some of the jurors nodding their head as if they understood.

"The second question will be slightly different. That question will be whether or not this is your understanding of the jury's verdict as a whole. Okay?"

Judge Ramsdell's eyes scanned the jury box.

"It looks like everyone understands that protocol. So, I'll ask the court clerk to go over each one of those verdicts with you."

Suza picked up her packet and read each count and after each count, she looked for a display of hands.

For each guilty verdict, the judge inserted his words after the court clerk paused.

"Let the record reflect that all jurors answered in the affirmative," he said after he counted the twelve raised hands.

Michele Anderson kept her head down and her hands cupped her eyebrows while the judge polled the rest of the jury.

The jurors would not look at her. They did not care about her reactions anymore. Instead, they hoped the family and those who knew the victims would get some resolution in the face of the horrific murders and their decision.

The sobering fact at the conclusion of any murder trial was that most jurors realized that there could be no good ending. Their verdict did not bring the victims back and it did little to abate the pain that surrounded the crime. It was the best that twelve random citizens could do in the matter of the State of Washington vs. Anderson.

"Ladies and gentlemen, that concludes the polling of the jury. The verdicts appear to be in order and have been filed by the court," the judge said.

He moved some papers aside on his desk and focused on the jurors.

"What that means for you all is that this concludes your services as jurors on this particular matter. As I told you early on in the process," he said in reference to jury selection the prior December, "case law had previously precluded us from answering the question as to whether or not this was a death penalty case."

I suspected there was more than one juror who wondered why this case had not been a death penalty case.

"It is not a death penalty case which means there is no penalty phase for you to sift through which, indeed, means that your service on this particular matter is concluded," he informed them. "Now, what this means is that you're absolved from all those restrictions that I have placed on you for five or six weeks now."

Although the judge had referenced the length of the trial, he did not factor in that their admonishment not to speak with anyone about the case had, in actuality, begun the day they left the courthouse on the first day of jury selection, December 11, 2015. Their term of silence had been three months long. Nobody would quibble over the details because all of the jurors were relieved their duty was finally at an end.

"You're free to do any research you want to about anything related to this case," Judge Ramsdell continued. "You are free to read any articles you might find online about the case. You're free to talk to anybody you wish. And, you're free not to," he emphasized, "talk to anybody about the case. The reason I stress that is because in a few moments, I'm going to excuse you to the jury room."

I imagine the relief for the family was immeasurable, as the jury had sung their soliloquy of guilty verdicts. It must have felt like a grand slam homerun for the prosecution team.

"I'm going to ask you to stick around just for a couple of minutes so I can come back and thank you personally for your service," the judge said. "Once we conclude that process, you don't have to talk to anybody about the case, deliberations or anything. With that being said, I know the attorneys would love to chat with you afterwards if you're willing to stick around for a little while."

I suspected every juror would stay. By the end of the trial, the jury felt a kinship with the judge and, for the winning side, a kinship with the prosecutors. They would certainly ask the defense team why Michele Anderson never spoke with her own attorneys. Sometimes, a trial is not about what a jury hears but about what they did not hear. It would be an eclectic meeting.

The judge leaned forward toward the jurors and pushed some papers aside. The end was near.

"I am sure you have questions that may have come up at some point in time. Often, jurors find it to be a good opportunity to sort of debrief what you've been going through in this process. If you have the time and inclination, I would certainly encourage you to stick around and chat," he finished.

"I want to thank you for your willingness to serve on this case and the patience that you exercised throughout the process," the judge said.

I was going to miss these jurors. We had never exchanged a word but I felt a kinship that only a few would understand later.

"Again, thank you so much for your service. We really do appreciate it. I think you should each be proud of your willingness to step up and do this rather hard task. Thank you very much, folks," the judge closed.

The court stood and I thought of the juror who had been dismissed a number of weeks back. We had stood as a salute to his service and finally, we stood in a salute to this jury of twelve.

I watched the jurors as they marched out of the jury box, finally not afraid to catch their eyes. Although I did not see tears in their eyes, I knew the tears were in their hearts. They had come together as a community for a short time in their lives. It was not their choice that Wayne, Judith, Scott, Erica, Olivia and Nathan Anderson should be thrust into their lives. The journey to discover whom the victims were and how they died had been the impetus for many an impromptu show of emotion. The jurors' hearts had been broken when they looked at the pictures of Olivia and Nathan.

Forevermore, the victim's names would be a part of the jurors' prayers and tattooed on their hearts. The victim's names would never completely leave their thoughts. Each juror's recompense, albeit miniscule, would be in the belief that they did the right thing. Although they could finally rest, there would be many a night of sleeping fitfully, as memories resurged in their dreams.

It was a great sacrifice for a juror to walk the path of justice. All jurors would say that it was nothing compared to what the victim's family must have gone through. They would carry the images of each family member in their minds and keep it in a safe place. When they thought of the Anderson family, they would remember each name with care. It was salve for the scar of the images of death left by the trial.

It would take time and there would be some jurors who would carry on with the good relationships they had built on their journey to justice. If one looked carefully, they would realize that the bond was a manifestation of the spirit of six.

A few weeks after the verdict and shortly before the defendant's sentencing was scheduled, Michele Anderson filed an appeal with King County Courthouse. It was an interesting document marked with careful and neat penmanship. Under the nature of the motion she noted that she wanted to leave the jail based on her "Personal Reconnaissance to hire an attorney, retrieve funds and obtain new evidence".

I wondered what happened to her attorneys, David and Colleen.

Most interesting to me was when she checked the box next to her name as, 'Pro Se'.

I discovered 'pro se' to mean that one was representing him or herself in *lieu* of attorneys in Court.

Some might wonder who assisted the convicted killer in the filing of the appeal.

Many of the jurors would come back for the sentencing even though they were not required to. They would want to hear the song of their soliloquy to Michele Kristen Anderson. They would see the fruits of their labor and the realization of the best justice they could find.

The jury had set the table and it would soon be time for Michele Anderson to sit down to her own banquet of consequences. There would be a great feast of felonies in the deaths of an innocent six.

The sentence of Anderson would not be for another six weeks. In the meantime, I wrote Joseph McEnroe and requested an interview.

I did not expect to get a response.

DAY 29
April 21, 2016

JUSTICE FOR SIX

Spirits were high as people filed into the gallery after the six-week period between the verdict and the sentencing. The hallway was filled with media personnel and cameramen. Nobody sat in the front row as the church pews filled. Judge Ramsdell had designated those seats for the memory of the six victims at the sentencing of Joseph McEnroe. No one, as well, had ever occupied those seats throughout the duration of the Michele Anderson trial.

Jurors were not obligated to return to the sentencing. Despite that, jurors from both the Joseph McEnroe case and the Michele Anderson case found seats in the gallery. The family filled the second and third rows quickly. Smiles were shared and the greetings were personal with hugs, kisses, and pecks on the cheek.

Kenya appeared to gauge the number of people anticipated for the gallery as she counted those in the hallway to the empty seats left open, which quickly diminished by the moment.

"I need all those from the media to go to the jury box. We will need seats for the family," she told us.

Roughly a third of the people got up and relocated to the adjacent jury box. Kenya caught my eye. With no words exchanged, I knew it was okay to stay where I was. I was honored and humbled.

Kenya looked over the gallery a few moments later and the only seats left open were in the front row.

"All former jurors who are here, can you move to the front?" she beckoned.

It was good to have seen so many come back for the final chapter in the search for justice in the Carnation murders.

Five minutes before the beginning of proceedings, Michele Anderson was led in. Her face was down as she survived the gauntlet of media outside the entrance to the courtroom. I watched as the female guard removed the pink handcuffs. The defendant wore a peach-colored jail issued inmate jumpsuit.

The family and those who knew the victims watched quietly. Each of them wore a button of a photograph of Erica, Olivia and Nathan. It was a picture of the last days of their last vacation at the beach in Seaside, Oregon.

"Alright, thank you," Judge Ramsdell said to the defense team once they agreed to move forward with the sentencing phase.

"So, Mr. O'Toole, I don't know how you want to proceed; if you have comments from individuals who want to speak or whether you would like to present your recommendation. Go right ahead, Sir."

Scott stood up and straightened his red tie, which was complimented with a white shirt and crisp charcoal black suit.

"I thought I would like to make the State's recommendation and then to give an opportunity for those who would like to speak to come forth and speak. I think there will only be three or four speakers in front of you today."

The attorney proceeded to walk a file folder up to the judge's bench. He laid the folder down.

"One issue that does occur to me today, is, that the court may be aware that there was some paperwork filed on behalf of Miss Anderson. I don't know if they were filed by Miss Anderson on Friday of last week or by somebody acting on her behalf or direction but the papers referred to Miss Anderson as 'Pro Se attorney'. One paper filed was for an appeal and one was for personal 'reconnaissance', which I assume to mean personal 'recognizance'. I don't know if that's an issue we need to address today, whether Miss Anderson is making a request to go pro se."

O'Toole glanced toward the gallery and then looked to the judge. "You've not received a motion. I've not received a motion but I want to make sure it's out there on the record and if there's an objection being represented by counsel at this point, whether we should hear it or not, I wanted to let the court know."

Judge Ramsdell looked up, crossed his fingers and rested his chin lightly on the crown of his thumbs.

"I saw some of those materials that you're referring to. I got the impression that what she was attempting to do was to file an appeal pro se. But, I don't know exactly what the intention was. Miss

O'Connor?" he asked. "Can you clarify any of that for me?"

Colleen arose while her knuckles rested on the defense table. She wore a black dress with a black and white paisley top.

"My understanding is that she prematurely filed the appeal. We have the proper paperwork. As far as the other, Mr. O'Toole, maybe we could have a meeting post-sentencing, where we can address the issue," the attorney offered.

"All right, then that's the way we'll handle it. Thank you very much, Miss O'Connor," the judge said. "So, Mr. O'Toole, I think we're ready to proceed."

"Thank you, your Honor," Scott O'Toole acknowledged. He took a moment to straighten the podium and the microphone.

"As the court is well aware, on March 4, 2016, the defendant was convicted of six counts of aggravated murder in the first-degree in the names of Wayne, Judy, Scott, Erica, Olivia and Nathan Anderson. In addition on each count, Michele Anderson received a firearm enhancement requiring a minimum of six months incarceration for each offense. The State would request of this Court to sentence the defendant on each of the six counts to a sentence of life in prison without the possibility of early release or parole and, in addition, the sentencing enhancement of six months to five years on each count."

The defendant's hand covered her eyes while the attorney asked that a restitution hearing be discussed later in the afternoon, separately.

"We also ask, finally, that the defendant have no contact with her family for the rest of her life, whether it be direct or indirect with the victim's family for so long as the defendant shall live," Scott stated. "That would conclude the State's recommendation. If the Court were so inclined, we would like to invite those who would like to address the court."

The courtroom was silent as Scott O'Toole directed Lynn Gombiski, Kimberly Moody, Mary Victoria Anderson and Pamela Mantle to the front, near the podium. He turned it so that it faced both the judge and the defense table.

"This is Lynn Gombiski, and like the folks who follow, she has a statement prepared for the court," Scott introduced.

"Thank you," Ramsdell acknowledged.

Lynn held a bottle of water in one hand and leaned slightly toward the microphone. She wore a peach-colored blouse with a patterned coat.

"I'm here on behalf of the citizens of Carnation. It is a beautiful town named after a beautiful flower. There's lots of life in Carnation. Wonderful people work there."

Lynn paused and focused her attention toward the defendant.

"Your mother was one of those wonderful people. She delivered mail to many, many people and they enjoyed having her so much when she delivered the mail. She also gave you life and the best that you could get in your life. Your father was a great coach for little children. And, your brother drove my son to and from football quite often. My son adored your brother and his wife. What wonderful people they were. We all loved them and our community loved them. You put a dark spot on our community."

The defendant quickly looked up and then looked back down.

"Hopefully, after today," Lynn continued, "we'll all be able to clear it up, move on and live happily. Thank you."

"Thank you very much, Ma'am," Judge Ramsdell said.

Kimberly Moody took her turn at the microphone. She had long dark hair. She wore an aqua blue colored blouse with a brown coat. A crucifix hung from a necklace on her chest. She took a deep breath before she spoke.

"Judy was my coworker for ten years and my dear friend. You took that away from us, Michele. It didn't need to happen. I've been there eighteen years as a window clerk. A day has not gone by where one of our customers would come in and say how much they missed her and how much she meant to them."

Kim took a breath.

"She knew all their kids names. She knew which of her customer's kids were going to college next. It was very saddening over the past eight years as we waited for justice. Judy was such a special person. So many of her customers have shared their many memories of her. She truly cared about people. She would be retired now and she would be bringing us her Zucchini bread and cookies every week. It didn't need to happen. None of these lives should have been cut short. There's never, ever an excuse for murder."

The defendant took a tissue from Colleen O'Connor and dabbed at her eyes and nose.

"I'm glad the death penalty was taken off the table because I really feel that life in prison is going to be a lot harsher and you do deserve to be punished. You took something away from us that was very special. I miss her and the whole community misses her.

"Over the past eight years, it's been kind of like living in a fog and when the trial was over I realized that I don't know how, or don't know why, but I forgive you," she told Anderson.

Kimberly paused for a moment as she kept her emotion at bay.

"You may not deserve to be forgiven but you are. I personally felt so much more peace for forgiving you and I'm sorry your mom's not going to be there to mail you Care packages. I know she would have. She was that special of a person. Thank you," Kimberly finished.

She folded her speech carefully and looked at the defendant one last time. She stepped back to allow the next speaker to come forward.

The courtroom was quiet as a church when the adopted daughter of Wayne, Mary Anderson, returned to the microphone.

No one could forget the simple twist of fate that had prevented her appearance at the family gathering on Christmas Eve of 2007. A simple common cold by her son had likely saved her life. One could only imagine the survivor's guilt she must have suffered.

"Ohhh, Michele," she began with a trembled voice. "I want you to know that we loved you so much. You know the truth and you destroyed me. And look what you have done to your life. Do you care what you did to our family?"

Michele pushed some tissues in her face. Her eyes could not hold the gaze of her stepsister.

"Your brother loved you so much. You'll have a lot of time to think about that. I loved you so much. I suggest, that one day, you learn about our Lord Jesus Christ because we all go. I don't know where you're going to go but I know where I'm going to go. And I'll be with them so you think about it, okay?"

It looked like Michele Anderson cried, but one could never tell with convicted killers.

"Just know that they loved you," Mary continued. "Please? Thank you."

Scott O'Toole directed Pamela Mantle, Erica Anderson's mother, to the microphone.

Her face was stern. She wore a white blouse and loose fitted blue sweater with her glasses propped above her hairline. She took a resolved and deep breath before she spoke. In her hands, she had a folded prepared speech.

"There are times I thought this day would never come. There was a lot of what I would consider nonsense that went on just to get a trial set."

Pamela glanced at her notes and continued.

"My daughter, Erica, was fearless. Erica was my oldest child and she was my friend. She was a life-long learner. When she went to college, she studied commercial baking. She was interested in the world and the people around her. She was selfless and put other people first and that's pretty much how she got in this terrible tragedy.

"This tragedy happened on Christmas Eve because Wayne wanted the grandkids with him. Erica and Scott were the kind of people that respected Wayne and Judy's opinion. I know that Erica had taken a lot of extra time off to prepare for that Christmas Eve in 2007.

"When Erica was small, I taught her how to call 911 if there was ever a big problem and the police and firefighters would come help her. When you shot her," she said as she looked at the defendant, "she called 911 not only to save herself but to save her babies. Erica knew you would shoot the kids. She begged you not to do it and you did it anyway because that's how you roll."

Michele Anderson would not look at Pamela.

"I don't think you're big and tough, Michele. I think you're a bully and a coward with what you did to my daughter, Scott, Nathan and Olivia. Nathan was barely a toddler. I feel like you pretty much destroyed any respect I ever had for you. I think you behaved like a coward and so did Joseph McEnroe, conspiring to kill your family and I can't tell you how disappointed I am.

"I hope you know that when you go to Purdy Prison, it's not going to be fun. When you take a look in the mirror, take a look at what you did, all the lives that have been touched by this. And, just think: Was it really necessary?

"Erica never deserved what you did to her. Ever! She tried to be your friend. She tried to teach you how to drive a stick. You got flustered, whined and she still tried to be your friend."

She turned a page on her notes and looked back at Michele.

"I'm broken hearted. Every day I miss those six people. Our lives will never be the same. People say we're going to forget about it. Well, you don't. Not as a mother, and, I'm sure Mary Victoria feels that way. It's just too bad. You had the opportunity at any moment to pick up your junk, get it out of your house, put it in the back of that black pick-up truck, and get the hell out of Dodge. You didn't. You decided to be a brat and make everybody pay. Not only did you make your family pay, you made three communities pay: the community of Black Diamond, the community of Carnation and the community of Snohomish.

"I don't think I could have gotten to this place had it not been for all those people who came forward and said, 'we're going to help you'. That's all I have to say. Thank you," Pamela finished.

She briskly folded her speech and sat down.

The prosecutor turned the podium toward the judge.

"I would like to echo Pamela Mantle's comment. There can be

no sadder statement than Erica Anderson screaming into the phone, 'Not the kids!' I think that's the statement that will haunt everybody who has been touched by this."

He straightened his tie and grasped the sides of the podium.

"I know it has affected Detective Tompkins and the attorneys on both sides. It's affected those who have watched the trial. It has affected members of the press who have been kind enough to report on this case in a very fair manner. But," he said, raising a finger in the air, 'Not the kids', is unforgivable. Thank you."

"Thank you, Mr. O'Toole," Judge Ramsdell said.

He studiously marked a form and straightened some papers.

"Miss O'Connor or Mr. Sorenson?" the judge inquired.

"Nothing, your Honor," O'Connor responded.

"Miss Anderson? Do you have any statements before I apply the sentence?"

"No," she answered.

"It is what it is. It's six counts of aggravated murder and there's not much we can add," Ramsdell commented. "Thank you."

"Are we allowed to speak on behalf of the defendant?" Miss {redacted} asked from the back row of the courtroom.

Many in the gallery turned around, surprised.

"And, uh, in what capacity?" Judge Ramsdell hesitantly queried.

"Just to address the court," she stated as she rose to her feet. She held an iPad in one hand. Microphone wires hung down from her ears.

"Well, and the victims and the fact that I am a witness to the fact that she has been an honorable defendant while in custody. That she's not broken any rules in the eight years and four months that she's been there. She has suffered the same abuse that I have suffered when I was there wrongfully with her and I do believe that justice has not prevailed."

I was not sure if this was a victim impact statement or if it was some sort of allocution. It was unheard of for someone to speak from the gallery.

"I do believe that she is remorseful and the choice for her not to speak is just protecting her appellate process but she's not the monster the media has created. That's not who she is and many, many people and the jury does not get all the facts," Miss {redacted} explained.

The former jurors in attendance would think of Michele Anderson's confession when she exclaimed, 'I'm a monster.'

"Actually," she continued, "Miss Mantle's pain and suffering has been elongated and that no one understands Michele and mental illness has been misunderstood here."

Judge Ramsdell did not look happy, yet, held a firm composure.

"Okay, um, that wasn't the question and I haven't heard the answer. As far as I'm concerned..."

"As a friend," Miss {redacted} interrupted, "of the defendant."

"Thank you," Ramsdell responded. "You had the opportunity to make a statement. Alright?"

The judge moved some papers on his desk and then put a packet in front of him. He adjusted his glasses and read aloud from a script he had prepared ahead of time.

"A witness in Mr. McEnroe's trial commented that the

relationship between Michele Anderson and Joseph McEnroe was a marriage made in hell. I don't think truer words could be said. Without the synergistic effect of the relationship of both individuals, they would likely have remained in obscurity their entire lives. They would have gone unnoticed and unknown and the world would have been a better place as a result."

The judge stopped and looked over the gallery momentarily and went back to his statement.

"Unfortunately, fate did not convene and these two people with personality disorders joined forces in this monumental tragedy and the lives of many will never be the same as a result of that."

He turned a page.

"At Mr. McEnroe's sentencing, this Court set aside a portion of this courtroom where placards and white Carnations were placed and the Carnations symbolically represented the six victims in this case: Wayne, Judy, Scott, Erica, Olivia and Nathan Anderson. At that sentencing, I stressed how these six individuals, were not forgotten by the Court or the Jury. It may not seem that way to outsiders as we focus on the procedures in the trial process.

"But I can assure you that nothing could be further from the truth. Even though we did not know them before their tragic deaths, we all know them now and I doubt that any of us will ever forget them.

"Although I did not know them in life, I think I can safely say that I know what they would want me to focus on at this point. I don't think they would want me to waste this precious opportunity in addressing Miss Anderson."

The defendant had her hands in her lap and stared downward.

"The sentence that I must impose on her is essentially mandated by statute. And they all probably suggest that I have spent enough time talking to her. Instead, I think they would like me to speak with the secondary victims in this case who have suffered so much hardship and grief as a result of Miss Anderson's actions," he explained.

The judge mentioned by name the multiple secondary victims such as surviving family, friends, witnesses, police, and first-responders; even of Linda Thiele, who had first discovered the victims.

"It would also include the jurors, who in fulfilling their civic duty, were thrust into the limelight and exposed to gruesome images and testimony that will forever be a part of their new reality," he explained.

He further recognized the multiple members of court staff who had executed the process daily.

"Nothing will bring these six victims back but your efforts and commitments honor their memory.

"I was astounded that Pamela and Tony Mantle managed to attend the trial religiously and relive the horrifying testimony of that horrible occasion. The fortitude it took to listen to that 911 call in which Erica pleads to save the kids is beyond my comprehension. Yet, you both managed to muster the courage and composure to attend these painful proceedings in order to see for yourself justice was done for your loved ones. For that respect of love for the victims, I am sure they would want me to say a special thank you for them."

Quietly, members of the family let their tears flow.

"Fortunately, this lengthy chapter of your waking nightmare is almost over. I sincerely hope that when you leave here today, you will never have occasion to visit this courthouse again for reasons related to these murders. I also hope that the healing that has been delayed by this process can now begin in earnest and that happier times will prevail."

He looked up from his paper toward the gallery.

Somehow, before anyone knew it, the judge moved into the sentence of Michele Anderson. It was curious that he did not look at her once as he rendered his sentence, as if she was not worth his time.

"As for the sentencing of Miss Anderson, the result is pretty much pre-ordained," he said.

"Pursuant to your convictions, the law mandates that I impose six consecutive sentences of life in prison without the possibility of early release or parole plus a sentencing enhancement of sixty months on each count as well. Restitution will be set at a separate hearing."

The court went through the process of stripping Michele Anderson of her rights, rights she had probably taken for granted before the killing of her family.

She was fingerprinted for the record as a multi-convicted felon.

Colleen O'Connor slid a sheet of paper in front of Anderson as the convict wiped her fingertips with tissue. The attorney whispered in the convicted murderess' ear and directed her to affix her signature at the bottom of the form.

Anderson signed the document, which forfeited her rights to ever own a firearm again.

David Sorenson slid another form in front of Anderson for her autograph.

The convict dutifully signed away her right to vote.

"Counsel? Anything further?" the judge asked.

The attorneys in both sides of the case shook their heads. None of them had any more words to say.

"All right, that concludes this matter to the family and friends of the Andersons. Good luck to all of you and I hope you are able to begin the healing part of the process at this point in time and that your nightmare is over with. Good luck to you all. Thank you," Judge Ramsdell said as he stood.

"Please rise," Kenya ordered the court for the last time.

When the court stood at Kenya's command, we stood as a salute to Judge Jeffrey Ramsdell. He had been the navigator of two trials made from the most horrific of circumstance. He had helped the court row the boat through the quagmires and pitfalls that are part of this intricate thing we call justice.

The jury felt great respect for him because he showed great respect for them. Court always started on time, which was cognizant of the jurors' sacrifice. In the rare time he that he had to adjust the schedule; he communicated and apologized.

Judge Ramsdell showed us that the court is not made up of laws as much as it is made up of living and breathing people. His rooms were filled with horror and he had captained the best justice one could find in the worst of circumstances. He represented all that was good in truth and justice.

As the courtroom doors closed and the trials for the six Carnation murders began its slide toward the annals of history, I thought of Wayne, Judy, Scott, Erica, Olivia and little Nathan Anderson and how they would be part of our hearts forever. One day we would meet in that place that Mary Victoria Anderson spoke of.

As fate would have it, I found myself in the company of some of the former jurors from both McEnroe and Anderson as we decided where to have lunch at the conclusion of the sentence. It was ironic that the establishment was named, O'Donnell's, which reminded us of O'Connor and O'Toole. The server quickly put together a table of twelve and soon the seats were filled.

It was not long after we ordered some Irish fare when the server set up another table adjacent to us. Coincidentally, it was set for Pamela and Tony Mantle's family and friends.

For the next two hours we shared lunch, stories and spoke of friendships that were built in the face of tragedy. The blanket of justice had begun spreading its warmth amongst all of us. For those few moments, all was as right with the world as it could get.

"I'm sorry for your loss," I told Tony at one point.

"Thank you," he said. "It's been one hell of a journey."

"Let me ask you something. During the trial, I thought you had turned around a couple of times and looked at me. Had I done something?"

Tony laughed. "I wasn't looking at you. I was looking at the crazy lady behind you. We did not need to hear her speeches."

"I know what you mean," Leah volunteered. "We didn't need to hear it in the jury room either. The opinions should be left for marches or taken to the local congressmen. The court is a place for the victims, families and justice."

"Amen," Pamela said.

"So, you were a juror on the other killer's trial?" Katie asked.

"Yes," Leah responded.

"Did you find him guilty? Sorry that I don't know anything about him. I had never heard of the Carnation murders until this trial."

"We found him guilty."

"Somebody said you had a hung jury." Donna commented.

"We did," Leah answered. "We agreed until we got to the penalty phase."

"How is that different than the guilt phase?" Tiffany asked.

Leah thought about it for a moment.

"The guilt phase is about the how and the who of the crime while the penalty phase is more about the why of it. What were those things that we might consider mitigating factors? It was not until then that we saw the true colors of our jurors. Be grateful that the State only asked you to decide guilt. The death penalty part of it is more difficult than one might think."

"How so?" Donna asked.

"There was so much more at stake. The defendant in our case took the stand. Our job was to find every reason we could to prevent his getting the ultimate sentence. When McEnroe got on the stand, everything changed for a lot of us."

"In what way?"

"Those who were anti-death penalty fell in love with him. And then, there were those like myself," Leah explained, "that learned what true evil was. It was a painful place to go. I respect each one of you, those who were on the Anderson jury, immensely. You completed an extremely difficult task. But, like I said, be happy that you did not have to decide the next phase. It is a journey no one should have to take."

"Did the experience teach you anything about the law?" Donna asked.

Leah did not hesitate. "I learned that Erica was the hero. I also think the death penalty should be abolished."

A long time ago, when I began this journey into the path of justice, I said that there could be no good ending in a murder trial, only lessons. It was a difficult proposition to face in the matter of the Carnation murders. The best I could find were in the words of Kimberly Moody to the convicted killer:

"It didn't need to happen. None of these lives should have been cut short. There's never, EVER, an excuse for murder."

Justice for six.

BEYOND THE PALE

I was full of apprehension as I drove from Seattle to Walla Walla, Washington. I went through the Cascades and into the rolling hills of central Washington. I turned south and headed through Yakima after going through valleys and valleys of vineyards that spread like random checkerboard squares

My first letter to Joseph McEnroe was sent only days before the Michele Anderson sentencing. Had I sent the letter after sentencing, I never would have sent the letter at all. Once I had spent lunch with the family and former jurors, I came to the realization that the killer's voice was no longer important or material. His fate had been decided the moment he squeezed the trigger of a .357 Magnum into

Wayne Anderson.

A week after the sentencing, I received my first reply from McEnroe.

He wrote, "I have to ask why you want to interview me. Why? What do you hope to accomplish with this project? This was a horrendous tragic event and, while I can't speak of her trial, mine was pretty much my conception of hell. I really regret that people had to endure that. I'm not trying to be judgmental. I just want to understand the motivation here. What do you hope to accomplish?"

It was an entirely unexpected response. Between the lines and under the mask of words, I thought I detected remorse. Maybe it's the fact that, as a former juror and as a witness to two subsequent and unrelated trials, I was wholly unfamiliar with the human trait that death penalty juries struggle to find. DeVault, Arias and Anderson had shown no remorse. That lack of remorse was akin to salt in the wound to the families of the victims.

Subsequently, I submitted my information to the prison for a background and security check and, after four letters, was given permission to visit Inmate #384102. I received a list of rules after I had sent McEnroe a self-addressed stamped envelope. It was against the rules.

The rules, curiously, stated that khaki pants were not allowed. I assumed the guards wore khaki pants and the prison wanted no confusion.

I took a left on State Route 12 and the further I drove inland, the hotter it seemed to get. The landscape changed from picturesque to an isolated wasteland. Another ten miles up the road, there would be a maximum-security prison.

I did not know what I expected to learn. Simply, I hoped a

truthful interview would provide the conclusion to my book on the Anderson trial. Somehow, I had to reach an understanding of his part in the murders.

I expected to see the face of evil.

It was not a task I took lightly. I did not want to give the killer a platform and I certainly was determined not to show any sign of empathy for the deed he committed. Part of me wanted to call Pamela Mantle, Erica's mother, to give her an opportunity to say something to him should she desire. I decided against it because I thought it might open a wound. I don't believe there would be anything she would want to say to him and that would be more than understandable.

The highway finally took me into Walla Walla, a pretty town with a history that dates back to the 1800's. It was a town built around wine and built around a prison. The shadow of the penitentiary stretched along the northwestern part of the city of thirty thousand. Even from the freeway exit, I could see the razor wire wrapped around the perimeter as it reflected the sun.

I checked into my motel, walked the dog and got myself mentally prepared for the visit the next day. I would not be afforded the use of anything but my conversation and memory with the prisoner. The prison rules prohibited a notepad and pen.

I was nervous because I had never been to a prison, except outside the gates of Perryville. I had never experienced the environment I was about to enter barring what I had seen from reruns of Shawshank Redemption.

Frankly, it was one of the scariest things I would ever do for a book.

The next morning, I arrived at the prison at the appointed time for visitors for the Baker block, where McEnroe was housed. Razor wire encompassed the circumference of the fence while prison booths were at every entrance. The air was thick and hot in the burning sunshine of summer. The shadows from the security towers provided little respite from the heat and enhanced my insecurities. Although I could not see the guards behind the tinted glass, I knew I was being watched by men and women who held guns.

I checked in with thirty dollars in cash, my identification and one car key. Guards sat behind a desk. Each one had a television monitor in from of them. I handed the female guard my identification as she processed me. I looked behind me and saw a machine that converted cash into a prison chip card.

"What's that for?" I asked the guard.

"If you would like to have lunch, you need a card to eat. No cash is allowed while visiting the inmates," she explained.

I pictured a cafeteria where I could buy him lunch. Since I would not pay for an interview, I figured it was the least I could do for his time, that which he had plenty of at his disposal. I put all my cash in the machine despite the sign that told me there would be no refunds.

There were about fifteen or twenty people who waited in the lobby to go through the process. Each was issued a locker key and each was searched individually in a separate room. Female guards checked females while male guards did the same with the men. They all wore dark blue latex gloves as they completed their duties.

I walked into the adjourning room with the male guard. I was worried about the latex gloves and the intricacy of the search. Fortunately, although it was personal, it was not intimate.

We were moved to a waiting room. I used the restroom and

soon learned that it had been a mistake. As soon as I left the restroom, I was subjected to another complete search. The guard even checked to see if the soles of my shoes turned. The process made the airport and the TSA seem like kindergarten.

Once I returned to my seat, I saw an older Hispanic lady seated across from me. I smiled at her.

"Your first time here?" she asked.

"Is it that obvious?"

She laughed and nodded her head.

"How long have you been coming here?" I asked.

She thought about it while she looked toward the ceiling.

"My goodness. Ten years? No, no, twelve years now," she corrected.

"Are you visiting your husband?" I asked.

"My son," she answered. I saw tears well up in her eyes. "They don't understand that life is not about themselves. When they do these horrible things, they don't think about what it does to the family."

"I'm sorry," I responded softly.

"Everything is 'me; me; me'. Then," she continued, "they find themselves here. I am in prison with him every day. It is his crime but my sentence. They don't understand until it's too late. I live with that every single day."

I would like to have patted her shoulder or something to show my condolences but I was afraid to break another rule. I looked around while people chatted quietly among themselves. Two windows gave light to the waiting room. Although I could see the blue sky beyond, I could not ignore the shiny razor wire that seemed to mar the beauty of the day.

A poster was on a wall. It had a hotline phone number and stated that prison rape was a crime.

Suddenly, two metal doors closed on one end of the waiting room and two other doors opened. The clang of metal bolts seemed to echo off the white painted walls. We followed two guards as they led us down a corridor. They ordered us to stop while two guards secured the iron doors behind us. The guards in front of us opened the doors and led us to another segment. The process repeated itself another three or four times before we found ourselves at the visiting room.

The air was still and stagnant. The windows we had passed could not be opened.

If one did not know any better, the large room could just as well have been the kindergarten room in grade school. There was a padded mat positioned in the center of the room for the children of prisoners. Along the wall, there was a bookshelf with coloring books and games. In another area, a box of Playskool toys awaited the next child.

Again, we were searched and each of us was designated a table. Each table had four chairs, and some tables had a checkerboard painted in the center. All of the chairs in the room were squarely matched to the points of a compass at each table.

The tables had two laminated pages of instructions taped to the top. The offender was to remain seated at all times. They could only sit in the chair facing east. Their hands were to be visible and on top of the table.

While I waited, I saw the restrooms along the north wall of the room. One set was for men, one for women and one for inmates. I thought it interesting that they were no longer known as men or women. All those who used the restroom were subject to search.

Along the opposing wall, near where I had taken my seat; a row of vending machines stood like sentries. The rules affixed to my table stated the offender was not allowed to use them and a thick red line ran along the floor parallel to the machines. The prisoner was never allowed to cross that line.

Everyone looked toward the door marked, 'Shakedown', as the set of metal prison doors released a small parade of offenders into the room. I waved toward McEnroe when he came in.

He took his seat without looking at me at first. He had dark brown eyes and looked at a forty-five degree angle toward the floor. When our eyes did meet, it was only for moments. He had very white skin after being imprisoned in one way or another since late 2007. He was shaved and his wavy long hair almost reached his shoulders. He wore a faded and worn white t-shirt, khaki pants and a khaki belt, a uniform similar to all the other offenders seated with their corresponding visitors.

The khaki pants rule came to mind and I realized it was quite opposite of what I had expected. All the guards wore blue while the inmates wore khaki's. I certainly would not have wanted to be confused for an inmate had I worn khaki's.

"Thank you for agreeing to visit," I told him.

"I wish it were under better circumstances," he said softly.

"Can I get you a soda?"

"A Diet Coke," he responded. His shoulder twitched.

I used the unmarked debit card for the machine. I ordered a

regular Coke and received a Coke Zero instead.

The side of the can read, "All I do is win."

He took a sip of his soda and looked at me briefly before he turned his eyes downward.

"What I did was, well, beyond the pale. I know that and live with it. But, I want you to tell Pamela that I am so sorry. She probably does not want to hear that. How is she?"

"As well as can be expected, I suppose," I said. "Her last eight years have been this event. So, I expect it hasn't been very easy for her."

McEnroe shook his head slowly.

"I have caused a lot of pain."

I could not disagree. I still struggled with the collateral damage his act caused.

"So, tell me what your daily life is like? What do you do all day?"

His head twitched. It was as if he was throwing his hair back.

"Well, I get up at six or so. I go get my meds and then wait until it's time for breakfast. After that, I walk the yard. It's not a big area. I take laps and then go back to my cell. I'll usually read until lunch and then the afternoon is pretty much the same thing. Walk the yard, read and then eat dinner."

"Do you have any cellmates?" I asked.

"They tell me that for what I've done, they keep me separated from the general population. I live alone in a cell up where the death row guys are."

"Have you ever seen any fights or anything?"

"One or two," he answered. "They keep us pretty contained so I haven't seen much."

"What was it like going through the death penalty?" I asked.

Since I did not have a notepad, my questions probably seemed random and without order.

"It was one of the worst things I have ever been through. It was awful," he said. "I didn't like how Scott O'Toole made my mother look. She was a good person. She did not have boyfriends coming in and out. She worked two jobs her whole life to take care of me, my brother and two sisters."

"Scott was just doing his job," I defended. I liked the senior deputy prosecutor and nothing was going to change that.

"I know," McEnroe said. "I'm sorry."

"Where are your brothers and sisters now?" I asked.

"They're all out of state, mostly California," he said quietly.

"Have they ever visited?"

"Oh, no," he chuckled for a moment. "I've never had a visitor. After what I did, I am surprised that you even visited. It's okay. I deserve to be here."

"Did you think about the death penalty on that Christmas Eve?" I asked.

I remembered lessons from school that the death penalty was a deterrent and it seemed an incredibly good question.

"Never even crossed my mind," he responded casually.

"What did cross your mind?" I asked.

He ruminated over it for a moment.

I looked around the room and was aware of the guards as they watched us. Every table was filled with a prisoner and their visitors. Some prisoners only had one visitor and it was clear that those visitors were their wives. Apparently, it was okay for the prisoner to hold hands, as there were no reactions from the guards. I also noticed that every prisoner had tattoos and they were not the fancy tattoos that a person could get from a neon sign store. The green markings looked primitive on their biceps.

McEnroe did not have any tattoos.

"I used to play C-O-D religiously. I thought it would be like that," he said finally.

"C-O-D?"

"Call of Duty, that game. For some reason, I thought it would all be like that. Even when the gun was firing, it was like I was outside myself, playing a video game."

"It was like a video game?"

"For a time it was," he said slowly. "Then, the reality of it hits you and it was not like a video game."

"Do you think you should have gotten the death penalty?"

"I do," he responded without forethought. "What I did was, well, you know. It does not get any worse than that. So, now I live my life grateful for every moment I have. I try to do good now. I want to make up for what I took away from this earth. I feel like I should make this world better. I even donate my hair to cancer patients now. I know I cannot ever even begin to make up for it."

"Are you content serving life without parole? Does it bother you that you will never leave here?"

"Every day is the same thing," he responded. "I don't have a right to complain about it. I took six people away from this earth. They were six good, good people."

I couldn't help but look at his fingers while he looked downward. The skin of his hands was a pale white. His fingers seemed long and the skin looked soft. He did not have the hands that one who worked outside had. It seemed they were the hands of an artist, delicate in structure.

At the very same time, I tried to wrap my head around the idea that those very same fingers held and grasped a .357.

"So," I began slowly, "how did you think they were good people and then find yourself shooting them?"

"I ask myself that question every day," he said. "It was the perfect storm. Her personality and my personality just fell together. She was bossy and I was depressed. I had never had a real girlfriend before. I thought you took care of them. I thought you did what they said."

"I don't understand."

His head ticked backwards as he looked at me. Then he looked down and away again.

"I don't, either. See, she had a dominant personality. She ordered people around and if you didn't do what she said, she would go crazy. It was easier for me to just listen to her. That doesn't take away from my responsibility in this horrid thing. I hope you understand that."

I nodded my head but did not understand.

"She had been saying this crazy shit for years. I really didn't hang at the main house with her family much. I didn't know, but that what she was telling was probably lies. That's the thing about depression. There's a black spot and you don't think things through," he said ruefully.

"That doesn't explain why you did not walk away."

"You have to understand what Shell was like. She was narcissistic and everything revolved around her. When she was pissed, you better watch out. I was in a tiny trailer with her. She would get consumed with hate and you were either with her or you weren't. If you weren't, the hell was not worth what she put me through."

"If you had to do it all over again, what would you do?"

"I never would have left California or Colorado," he said with a sarcastic chuckle. "Not that I had it great there. I spend countless numbers of hours going through the rooms of hell in my head. In one of those rooms, I imagine the million different ways that I could have left; ways that I could somehow have changed the situation and prevented what happened. At every corner, I had the opportunity to leave and I didn't take it."

"Did you guys do any drugs or alcohol?" I asked as it sounded like a possible influence.

"Shell didn't believe in drugs or alcohol."

"How did you meet her?" I asked.

"I met her online. By mistake," he said pensively. "I thought it was another Michelle who was writing me back. It turns out that I had not met this Michele. It was all a mistake."

"Do you still love her?"

McEnroe pulled his hair back and thought about it before he spoke.

"I never want to see her again. She is in my nightmares and my nightmares have not stopped to this day. She scares the living crap out of me. You don't understand how crazy she is. Once you get sucked in, you can't get out. Yeah, there's a part of me that still loves her. Excuse me," he said.

He raised his hand to get a guard's attention.

A male guard acknowledged him with a wave of the hand. He nodded his head toward me and walked to the front of the room. Two guards watched while another guard searched him. Their task done, he went behind the closed door of the 'Inmates' restroom. The process was reversed when he exited and he came back to the table and sat down.

It had given me time to formulate the questions that had bothered me throughout the trial and had remained unanswered.

"Did you guys have a bird in the trailer?"

He shook his head negatively.

"There were two cats and a dog that I didn't know that well. We had a brown cat with us the night we threw away the guns. That was a bad idea bringing the cat in the truck. The cat kept freaking out. It sucked," he said.

"What about a bird, like a Parakeet or something?"

"As far as a bird? Nah, we didn't have a bird. We did leave the door open a lot so anything could have gotten in there."

"How about the flat tire? The one in Kelso, was it really flat?"

"Yeah, it was flat. It was at the worst time, too. We were really thinking about going to get married and nothing was coming together. The guy that changed it, I do remember him. We were really paranoid at this point in time. He made us leave from where we were at."

"Why didn't you ever get a driver's license?" I asked. He had been in his late twenties the night of the murders and it was always struck me as odd that he lacked one.

"I never got around to it," he said. "You know, I just didn't need one. I used the bus and walked a lot. I love to walk. When I was living in Colorado, I once walked from Boulder to Denver."

"Isn't that a good thirty miles?"

"Yeah," he said. "It took me about twelve or fourteen hours. It was through some mountains so it took some time. Anyway, I met Michele and she had a truck. So, I just never got to it."

"What did you think when you got back to the residence and all the cop cars were there?"

"The cop cars were strange but what was really unnerving was the helicopter," he said. "I never expected it. Shell kept saying we were going to pretend that we did not know anything about what happened. Immediately, I knew that was not going to work. It was like this slowly dawning realization that we had really fucked up."

"Well, you did," I commented.

"I did. Michele knew what she was doing. I should have known. It became like C.O.D.; as if I was watching myself do the kills. No, I knew what I was doing. If only..."

"If only what?"

"I am not making an excuse. However, I did not start taking medication for my depression until I got here. If I had been on medication then, I know this would not have happened. There's no way I would have listened to her. I hate the thought of her and I hate myself for what I did. That night will roll around in my head forever. You may think these four walls are scary but what is really scary, is what I live with every moment of the day. Nothing will make up for what I have done," he said as his voice trailed off.

I took the pause as an opportunity to buy us lunch from the debit card I had purchased. I walked over to the machines and inspected the selection. I looked behind me and was surprised to see Joseph there.

"Inmate 3-8-4-1-0-2!" a guard from across the room barked.

McEnroe turned around.

"Return to your seat and place your hands on top of the table," the guard commanded.

"I'm sorry," McEnroe said as he hurriedly returned to his chair.

The lady I had spent a few moments with earlier guided me.

"You have to select the sandwich, microwave it and put the condiments on it for the inmate."

"Thank you," I said.

I asked McEnroe if he had a preference for lunch.

"No onions or peppers."

I went to the machine, studied its unclear instructions, inserted my debit card and selected his sandwich. I thought I got a cheeseburger and got a Philly Cheesesteak instead. He refused the offer and I found a burger instead. I cooked it in the microwave and put some ketchup on it. Both sandwiches looked like a slab of old canned Spam between two wooden boards.

He ate his sandwich hungrily.

My appetite was compromised by the guarded ambiance in the air.

"Who turned off the oven and unplugged the Christmas lights?" I asked.

He cocked his head and thought a moment.

"I turned off the oven. I wasn't going to at first. I was going to let the house burn down. As far as the Christmas lights, I don't think anyone ever plugged them in. They were not on when we got there. It was light outside, though."

"There was a spot in Michele's confession where she said that you two should just leave. Why didn't you do that?"

"I had a moment of sanity," he said. "That goes through my head all the time. We could have just left. I got so sucked into her craziness that I could not see my way past it. Now I know I could have left and it's what we should have done. They didn't deserve to die. I deserved to die."

Although I did not want to ask the next question, I did anyway.

"Why didn't you run? Why didn't you commit suicide?"

"I almost committed suicide after I fired the last shot. I did. I raised the gun to my chin and I could not do it. I wish I had, though."

"Why didn't you try to run?"

"You can't run from what's inside your head. The thoughts roll around in the four corners of your mind and you cannot escape that," he stated. "As much as I tried to get my mind off of it, I couldn't. I remember watching a Simpson's movie, one of our Christmas presents, and the characters kept reminding me of the family. Then, I would try to play video games and the same thing would happen. You cannot run from images like that."

"Why did you quit your job?"

"I liked that job, too," he said. "I was working for Target. I would stock things and clean things. It was a good job. One night I came home and Shell told me to quit. So, I did."

"Do you work in the license plate factory here?"

"No," he said. "That's for the regular inmates. I'm an assistant janitor. I like it. Everywhere I go, I get the opportunity to make things cleaner, to make things a little better."

He wiped his lips and put his crumpled napkin on his plate. I saw he was finished, picked up his plate and brought it to the trash. As I walked by the vending machine, I bought a couple of candy bars. When I sat down, I gave him a Hershey bar.

McEnroe carefully unwrapped the candy, placed it on the table in front of him and broke it apart into little measured pieces. He picked up a piece and put in in his mouth.

"It's surprising the things you miss," he commented. "I have not had a chocolate bar in eight years."

I declined to comment.

"What was so important that the murders had to have happened that particular night?" I asked.

The fact that it happened on a Christmas Eve always concerned me. It should be that one segment of the year where people have thoughts of peace on earth as opposed to staring down the barrel of a .357.

"It didn't have to happen that night," he said. "A few nights before, I had gotten pissed that she kept bringing it up. I finally told her to either do it or move on. I guess she decided that was the best time to do it. I really did not take it seriously until we were in the house with Wayne and Judy. Once it was rolling, I couldn't stop it. It was surreal."

I changed direction.

"I am sure your trial was like Michele's. What did you think when you saw the crime scene reconstruction?"

His face changed. "It was awful. I could not look at it. I saw that night all over again?"

"Did Ross Gardner get it right?"

"He got the first part right but not the second," he admitted. "He made it seem like it happened really slowly. It didn't. It happened fast. But, does it really matter, though? It's not going to bring them back and it won't change what I did. I wish I could show more emotion but I can only manage that in my cell by myself."

Another subject crossed my mind that I was afraid to broach.

"Mary was supposed to be there that Christmas Eve. Would you have shot her and her son, too?"

"We never would have shot her. Never," he repeated adamantly.

"Then why would you shoot Olivia and Nathan?"

"I was sucked into Shell's anger. I wish I had never done it and they should not have been a part of it. I think I thought in that split second that I would kill myself in the seconds afterwards. There was no difference between anger and love with her. She could flip from one side to the next in the blink of an eye," he tried to explain.

"What did she have against Erica?"

"She hated Erica for taking away Scott. She loved Scott and then hated him at the turn of a dime. But she really, really hated Erica. It was all so stupid."

"It was," I answered. "How could you shoot the kids?"

"Although you won't believe this, I really do love children," he said quietly.

The interview had been a kaleidoscope of ironies.

I thought that the evidence at the crime scene was not congruent with what he had just said.

"I can't talk about that night anymore," he responded.

A guard called out to the room about inmates who were with visitors and who would not be attending the mess hall. Joseph raised his hand and a short time later, a guard walked up and handed him a Tupperware container and a glass of water. I watched silently as he took the lid off and used a plastic Spork to stir the brown stew-looking substance. He removed a bag from the container and poured a white powder into the water and stirred the powdered milk. It looked like he was used to it.

Late in the afternoon, the guards abruptly ended the visitation at the designated time. The offenders stood as they watched the visitors exit to an enclosed area. I saw Joseph McEnroe for the last time through the glass.

He nodded his head toward me and I gave a small wave. I had been his only visitor and it would not surprise if I learned that I was his last.

No one had told me that the byproduct of remorse was that it would make a killer seem human. Had it not been for one day, so many lives would be incredibly different.

Or, so I thought.

I could not get the images of six out of my mind and I could not keep the tears from flowing down my cheeks. I did not want to be sad for him and I did not want to have empathy for him but I did, save for a short time. He would serve his penalty.

There would come a time when I sent Leah, the Presiding Juror of McEnroe, the account of my experience with him. Shortly after that, she wrote me a letter.

"I am writing this from my gut after reading this book and after what some days seem like yesterday, sometimes a hallucination, or years ago.

You were looking for the 'something' that I was when I first saw Joseph McEnroe. You expected to see a monster and a huge tattoo laden man that spat out words and looked like he hated everyone.

McEnroe is that monster hiding under a mask. People tend to believe that he's quiet, shy and unassuming. Because of that mask, people drop their guard and that is what allows him to manipulate them.

Do not be disillusioned by him.

He was the mastermind and driving force for that horrendous action. He planned the night on Christmas Eve. He bought a fake present as a prop. He found the right companion in Michele Anderson, who had the thoughts but not the guts.

He shot two innocent children that did not have to die. What more of a monster is there? He looks okay so it is hard to reconcile.

That is the problem the jury faced.

He is the monster we should all fear! He has no, I repeat, no remorse other than getting caught. He does not care for the Mantles, his family, his mom or even Michele. He only cares about himself who is looking for his fame and fortune and seeing who else he can f**k over.

How can I say that? I looked at him for four days a week for almost five months. He has dead eyes. He told you lie after lie to feed that need of a predator.

When you mentioned that he was behind you while you got him lunch, I was scared for you. You do not know how close you came to being attacked. He had nothing to lose should he have plunged a shank into you. Had you seen his journals, heard his confession or seen his testimony, you would understand my fear for your safety.

As far as Mr. O'Toole and the treatment of his mother, Scott was kind and respectful towards this woman who was under the scrutiny of family and strangers. She was tired, uneducated and wore a clean but ratty housecoat. She told us how she loved her son. She was the bravest woman I had ever seen and my heart broke for her.

Joseph McEnroe wrote several things about her in his journal about his mother, to contrast what he told you. He wrote such things as, 'I hate her', 'that bitch called again' and 'I hate that c**t!'.

The amount of untruths in his short get-together with you is staggering.

The only thing that I can say is that I am sorry to everyone that he is not on death row or that he did not take his own life. He does not deserve Hershey bars, lunch or even your compassion.

He deserves to wake up every morning to think: Is this the day that I die? At least he might have a small inkling of what those six family members felt in their final minutes.

Instead, he gets to get up every morning, breathe the air, read and relive how spectacular he thinks he was. He waits for his next unsuspecting victim to be caught and toyed with until he gets bored.

McEnroe manipulated you just as he had everyone else. If you are looking for the truth of the Carnation murders, your answers lie with him. He is not who you think he is.

With much respect and love,

Leah."

I folded Leah's letter carefully and set it down.

Even former jurors do not like to be lied to. I thought of the jurors in the deliberation room who had discarded any of Anderson's confession as evidence. Her lies had made the confession invalid. The jury had to find truth in other ways.

Ultimately, the jury found the truth in Erica's heroic reach for the telephone.

I thought the interview with the killer would provide closure for the book. Instead, it yielded the birth of another.

The book is closed on Michele Anderson. She will spend the rest of her days in Purdy Prison. There will be less than one percent of a chance that her sentence will be overturned. It is a statistical fact.

I had seen the face of evil. I just did not know it.

He had not shed one tear throughout our interview. Tears signal that words, coming from the mouth, also come from the soul.

It was time to learn the truth about Joseph McEnroe and his part in the Carnation murders.

EPILOGUE
July 31, 2016

DEAR ERICA

Although I am writing you, I am thinking of your whole family. I imagine that all of us are together in Seaside, Oregon, your one particular harbor, in the vein of a Jimmy Buffet song. The sea air rolls in off of the Pacific Ocean, cool and salty. The distant waves provide a constant roar, audible in the background and comforting to the soul. The sand is thick under our toes.

I am seated on a blanket next to you. You are preparing little sandwiches on a blanket with a large Seattle Mariners logo. I see a buffet of snacks including Triscuit crackers, cashews and a variety of other treats. An open cooler beckons someone to take another beverage.

Wayne and Scott are just down a little ways, closer to the water.

They are building a sand castle. It's not a regular sand castle. It is an engineering feat with Wayne as he directed Scott.

"You could have been an engineer," Wayne commented.

"I know" Scott answered, as he brought another scoop of wet sand and began pressing it all onto the base of the sand structure. "I didn't have the patience for it. I like construction. It gives me a sense of accomplishment when the job is done."

"Who's watching the kids?" Erica called out to the men being boys.

"I've got them," Judy said. "Nathan is playing with his bucket of sand and Olivia's showing me her new dance moves!"

Indeed, Nathan patted the beach sand with his plastic shovel. The winds blew his blond hair as he played.

Olivia was doing something between dancing and gymnastics. Her energy seemed boundless as she showed off her various maneuvers.

"I am so sorry for what happened to all of you," I said once the opportunity presented itself.

Erica shook her head. She was peeling the crusts of the bread.

"Nathan doesn't like the crust," she commented. "It never should have happened. It was not about money, it was about Michele never accepting responsibility and blaming all her problems on everyone else. I welcomed Michele into our home. I knew she loved Scott. But, I was never the enemy. She needed to grow up and accept responsibility. Do you think Wayne and Judy needed rent money?"

"I doubt it," I responded.

"Let me tell you something," she said as she spread peanut butter on the crust-free pieces of bread. "They did not want her money. They wanted her to get off her butt and do something with her life. It was not even due until January. I don't know why she and Joe denied us our last Christmas."

"I'm sorry," I offered. "Joe said he's sorry."

Erica dipped a knife in a glass jelly jar. She placed dollops of strawberry jelly on the bread as she thought for a moment.

"Joseph's yesterdays will be the same as all of his tomorrows until one day," she pointed out, "at the gates of his after-life, he will learn that he is to continue with his banquet of consequences."

"I expect the same with Michele," I commented.

"We never had an issue with him. I didn't know until that night that he had that kind of anger in him."

"I don't think anyone could have known," I said quietly.

"Did you know that Wayne and Judy changed their address to a Post Office Box not long before this incident happened? There was suspicion that somebody was stealing the mail. Any idea as to whom might do that?" Erica asked somewhat sarcastically.

"I could guess."

"It should not have happened."

I took the opportunity to hand Erica a letter written by her mother, Pamela.

"Aren't you going to read it?"

She tucked it into her pocket. "I'll read it later. I promise."

"Did you see the memorial that your Seaside family and friends made? It's up at the apex of the promenade. If you look north, you can see it just below the flag. There's a plaque for you at the base of a street lamp."

Erica smiled.

"I know. There's another in Black Diamond at the elementary school that Olivia attended. As well, a memorial is in Carnation at the post office, the same post office that Judy worked out of for many years. We appreciate everyone carrying on our memory."

Suddenly, laughter broke out between Wayne and Scott as someone had started a mud fight. Nathan came running over screaming in delight while Olivia chased after him. Judy was laughing.

The castle in the sand, Wayne's creation, was taking shape with intricate spires reaching from the ground, and the shadows getting longer due to the setting sun. Along the base of the castle, Scott had made spirals of steps. The detail was incredible.

Erica called everyone over when the sandwiches were ready.

"Will you do us a favor?" Judy asked me later in the afternoon.

"Anything," I answered wholeheartedly.

"You make sure and tell Mary that we love her and we are a part of her just as she is a part of us. I know this tore her apart and I know she has been asking herself why she lived," Judy said. "God still has plans for her."

My fingers played lightly in the sand. I let the sand fall between my fingers as I thought of a woman who had narrowly missed death and then had to learn how to survive. It was beyond my comprehension what kind of strength that it must have taken.

"The tragedy in all of this is not so much what happened to us but the ripple effect our deaths had on everyone who knew us," Judy said. "I wish we could have told everyone what they meant to us. Whenever they think of us, let them know that it's us talking to their hearts."

"I will," I said.

Erica interjected. "Also, it's easy to forget all those people who had the task of figuring out what happened. We want all the investigators, first-responders, scientists and the host of personnel whose hearts went into trying to make sense from chaos and tragedy, to know we're grateful. Especially Scott O'Toole, Michelle Morales and Detective Tompkins, make sure they know that we know how difficult it was. They carried the sword of justice with resilience, strength and heart. I wish we could take away the type of pain they were subjected to."

"We will remember," I said.

"I really liked that judge," Scott offered. "His heart was in the right place and he did the best he could in both trials. Tell him his efforts to change the imperfections in the system of justice are not in vain. You tell him to keep following his heart. All of us felt the impact of his giving us seats in the courtroom. Thank Kenya, too. She's a good lady."

"Pamela and Tony were there every day," I said.

"We saw them through both trials," Erica said. "You tell my mother and father that I love them and I am so sorry for the pain this has caused."

"But you couldn't have done anything."

"Nobody could have," Erica said. "Michele and I did not see eye to eye. We never did. Her act was selfish and unprovoked. The damage to those around us was nearly unforgivable. I so wish they did not have to go through it."

Wayne and Scott returned to the castle in the sand and continued working on their architectural feat. The waves of the sea were starting to move closer inland. The tide was making its inevitable crawl up the length of the beach.

Erica and Judy made themselves busy as they straightened the blanket, secured the food and disposed rid of the trash.

Just to the south of us, I saw somebody riding a horse parallel to the waves, coming up the length of the promenade. Olivia ran yelling toward the horse, glee in the shrill of her voice. The horse and rider stopped and the rider jumped off. The horse nuzzled its face into the cheek of Olivia. Her small arms reached around the neck of the horse.

Scott picked up Nathan, put him on his shoulders and walked over to the animal. Erica and Judy looked on as they smiled.

"She loves horses and dancing just like I did as a young girl," Erica said bemusedly.

Nathan babbled excitedly. He acted like it was his first time seeing a horse.

"I don't know how to make sense of all of this," I commented.

"Don't try," Erica said. "There's no trying to make sense of something we can longer change. There is a lesson, though. There's never a reason to murder someone, ever. That is about the only real lesson you will find out of this. I don't think it was preventable."

"I wish I could do something in your honor," I said.

Erica thought about for a minute as she began packing up the buffet on the blanket. "You could do one thing for us this Christmas..."

I was glad to have any opportunity to soothe the sadness in my heart. "Anything."

"I want you to place six ornaments on your Christmas tree this year. On each ornament, I want you to put a name for each of us: Wayne, Judy, Scott, Erica, Olivia and Nathan. Place them on your tree. Just before you plug the lights in, say a prayer for all of those that knew us. When you plug the lights in, and you see the glow of happiness, our spirits will be with you for those few moments. You will give us the Christmas we did not get."

I promised Erica I would.

The sun creeped ever so slowly toward the horizon as the Anderson family packed up their things from the beach. Scott and Wayne loaded the truck while Erica and Judy tended to Olivia and Nathan.

Judy was the first to walk up to me. She hugged me and then looked at me.

"Tell Mary that we are her Guardian Angels. Will you do that?" she asked.

I promised that I would.

"Nathan wants to say goodbye, too," Scott said as he directed the young boy toward me.

I picked him up and held him in my arms. I kissed his cheek. It was cool and soft.

"Bye," he said. His blue eyes were full of youth.

"In you go, fella," Scott said to Nathan as he put him in his car seat.

Olivia walked up and twirled like a little ballerina. "Momma says I could be on Broadway one day."

"I bet you could!" I answered as she jumped into my arms. She felt small. Her long and wavy hair was smooth and fine.

"Let's go, Olivia," Erica called from the truck.

"You keep dancing," I said as she scampered off.

Scott shook my hand. His hand was large and enveloped mine in strength.

"Thank you," he said.

I was confused. "For what?"

"Thank you for remembering us, and not the ones who took us from this earth. That's important," he said as he turned and walked back to the truck.

"Don't forget the jurors," Wayne called to me. "You make sure and tell them thank we thank them for their sacrifice. They can never know how much it meant to us," he said as he pulled himself into the driver's seat.

I would watch mutely as each of you jumped into the truck.

Erica rolled down the window on her side. I walked up; my hands were in my pockets. "What are you going to do now?" she asked.

"I'll probably find another trial," I said.

"You're like some rogue juror, aren't you?" she commented with a smile.

"I've never had it put that way," I said. "Maybe."

"You keep doing what you are doing," she said. "Keep searching for the truths. But before you run off to another trial, you need to finish your story on Joe. He is not who you think he is."

"I know," I said.

"And tell our family and friends that we love them and they are a part of us. Every time they think of us, we are there. Will you do that for me?"

"I promise."

Erica smiled and rolled up the window. The family waved as they pulled out onto U.S. 101, headed north. I watched as their taillights faded into the distance.

I turned around and looked at the sea. Flickers of orange and yellow light from the setting sun burned like fire across the top of the ocean and stretched toward the horizon. The waves moved closer in toward the shore, the inevitable tide pressed the sea forward.

The waves licked and touched the base of the magnificent sand castle that Wayne and Scott had built. Little by little, the towers of the castle began their collapse into the sand and into the froth of the waves.

The only picture I had of it was in my mind.

Slowly, the sea consumed the piece of art. Its granules returned to the land but its memory and the thoughts around it would always be crisp and detailed.

I thought of a family of six and wish I had met them.

The world had been a little better place when the Anderson's were in it.

We will never forget you Wayne, Judy, Scott, Erica, Olivia and Nathan.

Godspeed,

Your friend,

Paul

The End of Book 1:
The Carnation Murders

Banquet of Consequences: A Juror's Plight
The Carnation Murders Trial of Michele Anderson – "A Juror's Perspective" Series: Book 3

Also Written By Paul Sanders: "A Juror's Perspective" Series

Brain Damage: A Juror's Tale
The Hammer Killing Trial (2015) - Book 1

Why Not Kill Her: A Juror's Perspective
The Jodi Arias Death Penalty Retrial (2016) - Book 2

Secret Life of a Juror: Voir Dire
The Domestic Violence Query (2017) - Book 3

Beyond the Pale: Rogue Juror
The Death Penalty Trial of Joseph McEnroe (Coming 2020)) - Book 5

Follow Paul Sanders

Twitter: The 13th Juror MD
Facebook: Paul Sanders
Website: The13thjurormd.com

Dear Reader,

if my story moved you, I would be honored if you rated and/or left a review on Amazon. It helps reach more people like you. Thank you so much! Paul Sanders

Made in the USA
Columbia, SC
23 October 2024

44947466R00263